CAPITAL, ACCUMULATION, AND MONEY

AN INTEGRATION OF CAPITAL, GROWTH, AND MONETARY THEORY

CAPITAL, ACCUMULATION, AND MONEY

AN INTEGRATION OF CAPITAL, GROWTH, AND MONETARY THEORY

by

Lester D. Taylor
University of Arizona.

KLUWER ACADEMIC PUBLISHERS
Boston / Dordrecht / London

Distributors for North, Central and South America:
Kluwer Academic Publishers
101 Philip Drive
Assinippi Park
Norwell, Massachusetts 02061 USA
Telephone (781) 871-6600
Fax (781) 871-6528
E-Mail <kluwer@wkap.com>

Distributors for all other countries:
Kluwer Academic Publishers Group
Distribution Centre
Post Office Box 322
3300 AH Dordrecht, THE NETHERLANDS
Telephone 31 78 6392 392
Fax 31 78 6546 474
E-Mail <services@wkap.nl>

 Electronic Services <http://www.wkap.nl>

Library of Congress Cataloging-in-Publication Data

Taylor, Lester D.
  Capital, accumulation, and money : an integration of capital, growth, and monetary theory / by Lester D. Taylor.
      p. cm.
  Includes bibliographical references and index.
  ISBN 0-7923-7781-8 (alk. paper)
    1. Capital. 2. Saving and investment. 3. Money. 4. Economic development.
  5. Macroeconomics. I. Title.

  HB501 .T37255 2000
  332.4--dc21   00-024640

To H.S. Houthakker,
teacher, collaborator, and friend

TABLE OF CONTENTS

LIST OF FIGURES

Preface

This book has been long in the making. About 25 years ago, I began spending a lot of time puzzling over what capital is and what is meant by capital theory. I read and read, but the more I read, the more confused I became. For a number of years, my hope was that the problem lay with me, that capital theory was a consistent whole, with a great deal of relevance to the real world, and that I was simply unable to grasp what it was all about. Eventually, it became evident that to search for a single concept of capital in the canon of economics was a will-o'-the-wisp and that the problem is not a single concept of capital, but a surfeit of concepts. There are physical capital, capital goods, financial capital, working capital, circulating capital, fixed capital, etc. When appearing without an adjective, and depending upon the writer, 'capital' can refer to one, a subset, or all of the concepts at once. Vagueness and ambiguity concerning capital appear in the writings of all of the great capital theorists, whether Smith, Ricardo, Marx, Jevons, Walras, Bohm-Bawerk, Clark, Wicksell, Schumpeter, Fisher, Hayek, Keynes, Hicks, Robinson, Samuelson or Solow. When I finally came to understand this, it also became clear what to do: develop my own concept of capital and then proceed to theorize about it. The concept of *myros* is the result.[1]

Myros (or *fluid capital*, as it will eventually also be called) is the unifying concept of the book. The basic ideas underlying *myros* are introduced in the Prologue in the context of a subsistence, but otherwise idyllic, island economy whose only good is bread that each person mines each day for his/her own use.

---

[1] I have chosen the word *myros* because of its sonority (at least to my ears and mind) and because of its beguiling hint of a tranquil mythical isle in the Aegean. Its inspiration is clearly Greek, but as far as I am aware the word is 'clean'. My friend, Phil Fleming, who is an expert on Classical Greek, tells me that there is no obvious Greek root for the word; however, my friend and colleague, Dick Newcomb, and also my consultant on Latin, says that there is a Latin root, *murus* (walls), from which *myros* might be seen as a transliteration. As I know nothing about Classical Greek and Latin, I rely on these experts' judgement in support of my whim that *myros* is an appropriate word for the purpose I have in mind, which is to employ a word for capital that is not burdened by centuries of verbal and analytical baggage and connotations. Later, as the concept becomes understood, I will replace the word *myros* by a more conventional term, *fluid capital*.

The climate is benign, and inhabitants sleep under the stars. The bread is storable, but it had never occurred to anyone to store any until one day a young man decided that he wanted a roof over his head at night. However, as constructing a 'house' was going to require time that could not be spent in the bread mine, the young man began (by working some extra hours each day in the mine) fashioning a stock of bread that would sustain him during his days of building a 'house'. This stock of bread represents *myros*.

Once the concept of *myros* comes to be understood, it will be seen that a conservation principle emerges which imposes a variety of constraints on the macro behavior of an economy. Indeed, this book, at its most basic level, is simply a working through of a number of implications of these constraints. The constraints make for a straightforward understanding and analysis of such concepts as the real stock of money, the general price level, and real-balance effects. Indeed, one of the principle conclusions of the book is that a real-balance effect in the aggregate cannot exist. New and illuminating insights are also provided into aggregate supply and demand, natural and money rates of interest, the relationship between real and monetary economies, inflation and deflation, and economic growth and development.

The book has a number of recurring themes, three of which warrant mention here. The first of these is that money is endogenous in a monetary economy and is constantly in the process of being created and destructed. As will be noted at several points, a major failing of neoclassical theory is that it does not allow for a meaningful role for money. The concept of *myros* rectifies this. A second theme is that an economy cannot be treated (as is the case in canonical neoclassical theory) as though it were a nineteenth-century physical system. My views regarding the problems in doing this are presented in Appendix 1. Finally, a third theme is an emphasis on fallacies of composition, of which the absence of a real-balance effect in the aggregate is a prime example.

For the most part, the material in the book is presented non-mathematically. This is intentional for two reasons. In the first place, my concern in the book is primarily with the presentation and discussion of concepts and ideas. Only in a few instances are mathematics beyond arithmetic, algebra, and geometry needed to accomplish this. In the second place, to frame the arguments mathematically would compromise, at least at this stage, the view just stated that an economy cannot be analyzed as though it were a conservative energy system.

The book is directed at several audiences. First -- and foremost -- it is intended for my fellow economists. Although the topics of the book are primarily macro, microeconomics is never far from the surface, and is center stage in

Chapters 5, 10, 12, and 13 and Appendix 2. Among other things, I hope to challenge my brethren into considering whether twentieth-century capital and monetary theory may have taken some wrong turns, perhaps even to convince them that this has indeed been the case. If nothing else, I want to show young economists just beginning their research programs that capital theory, which has been largely dormant since the Cambridge Capital Controversy of the 1960s and 1970s, is still a fruitful and exciting area for research.

A second intended audience is students. Graduate students should find the book useful because it presents a comprehensive view of macroeconomics and monetary theory in a way that is almost totally alien to present-day graduate macro courses. If my own department is any guide, current-day graduate macroeconomics is taught largely as an exercise in dynamic programming. Keynes may be referred to, but never read, and the same is true of Friedman, Hicks, Patinkin, and Tobin. And the thought of having students read Schumpeter never arises, even though *The Theory of Economic Development* is as fresh today as when it first appeared (in German) in 1911. And the same is true of the *General Theory*.[2] Undergraduate students can also benefit from the book, although in most circumstances it will be necessary that they have help from a sympathetic teacher. Appendix 4, which greatly expands the material presented in the Prologue, and includes a number of questions and exercises, has been developed expressly with undergraduates in mind. In addition to Appendix 4, the relevant material for these readers will be the Prologue, Chapter 2, the first part of Chapter 3, and parts of Chapters 12 and 13.

A third intended audience is those who are regular readers, say, of *The Wall Street Journal*, *The Economist*, or *Forbes*. Although the reasoning connected with *myros* may, at first blush, seem subtle and arcane, it is less so (at least in my opinion) than the myths which lie behind most conventional uses of the words 'capital' and 'money'. 'Investors' who are interested in financial markets should be able to acquire a better understanding of how financial markets are tied to the real economy, while those interested in macroeconomics and macroeconomic policy should be able to acquire a better understanding of how financial markets intertwine with the real economy. For this group of readers, the Prologue, Chapters 2-7, and 12-13 are relevant.

The book consists of the Prologue, 14 chapters, and four appendices. The Prologue begins with a number of stories describing the emergence from an

---

[2] For a number of years, my goal has been to read the *General Theory* annually. I don't quite succeed in doing this, but I have probably read it 15 times or so. Each reading provides new insights and understanding. It is a truly amazing book.

economic state of nature of a primitive subsistence economy. The intent in these stories is to illustrate in a straightforward and natural way not only the concept of *myros*, but also the emergence of physical capital, money and a monetary system, loans and interest, inflation, and the creation of a variety of assets, including works of art. The Prologue is intended to be accessible to everyone, and is essential to an understanding of the book. Chapter 1 is mostly a personal memoir that lays out my approach to economics, economic theory, and model-building. Chapters 2-9 comprise the analytical core of the book. Formal definitions of *myros* and other key concepts are presented in Chapter 2, while Chapter 3 provides an overview of the macroeconomic framework. Money and interest are discussed in Chapter 4, and production and investment in Chapter 5. Chapters 6 and 7 focus on the general price level and inflation, wealth, and related topics, while Chapter 8 is devoted to traditional questions relating to macroeconomic equilibrium. Finally, Chapter 9 places the concepts of this book in historical perspective with conventional concepts of capital found in the literature.

Chapters 10-13 are mostly applications and examination of implications of the constraints associated with *myros*. Chapter 10 looks at some misperceptions concerning opportunity and sunk costs, while Chapter 11 discusses trade, exchange rates, and questions related to wealth transfers and monetary overhangs. Included in Chapter 11 is a detailed analysis of the wealth transfers associated with the reunification of Germany following the fall of the Berlin Wall in late 1989. Chapters 12 and 13 focus on saving and consumption and economic growth. Finally, Chapter 14 provides a summary and conclusions.

Appendix 1 is an essay detailing my views on the role of theory in economic analysis, including an argument as to why an economy cannot be analyzed as though it were a conservative energy system. This essay should be read in conjunction with Chapter 1. Appendix 2 is an exercise showing why investment functions do not necessarily slope downward, and should be read in conjunction with Chapter 5. Appendix 3 examines the productivity implications of the oil price increases that occurred in the 1970s. This appendix, while intended to be stand-alone, involves the 'transfer' questions treated in Chapter 11, and can be conveniently read in conjunction with that chapter. Finally, Appendix 4, as already noted, is expressly intended as a pedagogical exercise for students.

During the many years that the ideas in this book have been incubating, I have benefitted from discussions with a number of friends, colleagues, and students, not all of whom are economists, and certainly not all of whom are convinced that what I am doing is correct, or even useful. I am especially indebted to my (now) fellow Jackson Hole resident (and regular golf companion),

Bruce Egan, for his encouragement and financial support (while he was at BELLCORE) when I was first developing the ideas on cost, production, and investment presented in Chapters 5 and 10. Discussions on these topics with James Alleman of the University of Colorado in Boulder, Richard Emmerson of INDETC International in San Diego, Jim Griffin of Texas A&M, and Sandy Levin of Southern Illinois University in Edwardsville have been extremely helpful as well. Both Lester Thurow of M.I.T. and Dennis Weisman of Kansas State University have been willing readers of early drafts of the manuscript and sources of encouragement. The same is true of my colleague in Agricultural and Natural Resource Economics at the University of Arizona, Alan Ker, as well as a couple of anonymous reviewers.

The two people who have made the most enduring contributions to the development of my ideas are my colleagues and friends at the University of Arizona, Barbara Sands and Richard Newcomb. Barbara, in her quest to understand the concept of *myros*, has challenged me at virtually every turn, pointing out errors and uncovering thin and specious reasoning. Any clarity that the manuscript may have is in great part due to her. In addition, for a number of years, she has championed the use of the 'primitive economy' in her undergraduate classes, and Appendix 4 (which was once the Prologue) is included at her suggestion.

Interaction with Dick Newcomb has largely taken the form of a floating luncheon seminar that has occurred over the last 15 years, usually at the Arizona Inn (a few blocks east of the University of Arizona Medical School in Tucson). In the pleasant surroundings of the Inn, we have discussed the many subtleties of neoclassical capital theory, particularly as applied to mineral economics. Dick thinks in terms of Hamiltonians, and I admire the grace and good humor with which he has suffered through many attempts to convince me that this is the route that I should take.

Of non-economists, I am especially indebted to Phil Fleming, logician, expert on the history of science and Classical Greek, and my longtime mentor in numismatics and things collectible. Phil, who has no formal economics background, once absorbed the gist of the concept of *myros* in an hour lunch and immediately picked up on the conservation principle that *myros* entails. My confidence in the ideas of this book soared as a result. I am also grateful to students in courses (both graduate and undergraduate) at the University of Arizona and CERGE-EI at Charles University in Prague, The Czech Republic, where I taught during the spring semester of 1996. Jason Shackit and Jean Abraham at the University of Arizona, and Miana Plesca and Georgi Kambourov at CERGE, warrant particular mention in this regard. Finally, on the production side, I am indebted to Patricia Lenoir, who typed the initial draft of the manuscript, and to Wendy Baylor, my neighbor on Heck of a Hill, who has formatted and produced the final copy. I am especially grateful to Wendy for being both a superb technician and an extremely perceptive reader and editor.

If economics is a science, then, over long periods of time, its methods should guard against taking of wrong turns. However, I think that a wrong turn was taken in macroeconomics when the nascent ideas of Keynes of the *General Theory* were absorbed into mainstream economics in the neoclassical synthesis. In my view, the concept of capital that is developed in this book repoints macroeconomics in a more fruitful direction. Is my concept of capital necessarily the 'correct' one? Of course not. Yet, the conservation laws implied by it seem too simple and natural for the idea not to have basic validity. In his defense of the *General Theory*, Keynes stated that he considered his basic ideas to be definitive, but that he could be wrong in the details. I feel the same about the concept of *myros*.

In turning this book over to readers, I must ask a favor, especially from my fellow economists. If the ideas that are elaborated are to have any chance of being understood, it is crucial that they be approached with an open mind. Many of the concepts are non-conventional, and it is important that readers not attempt to interpret or recast them in a conventional frame of reference. To do so will almost certainly lead to confusion and frustration.

Lester D. Taylor

Heck of a Hill
Wilson, Wyoming
October 1999

PROLOGUE

TALES OF MYROS:
EMERGENCE OF A PRIMITIVE ECONOMY FROM AN
ECONOMIC STATE OF NATURE

This is really a book about capital. However, as the word capital is so overused in economics as to be nearly meaningless in any specific sense, I am going to begin by employing a neutral word -- *myros* -- in its place. Later, once the notion is better understood, the word myros will be replaced with more conventional terminology. One of the major purposes of this book is to show that the concept of myros provides a root concept of capital which allows for most existing concepts of capital to be unified and related in a consistent fashion to one another. In addition, it will be seen that such a root concept offers a framework for integrating monetary and capital theory, and for analyzing the functioning of an economy, whether that economy is in a steady state of subsistence or in a process of sustained growth. Specifically, it will be seen that a conservation principle associated with myros emerges which both implies and imposes a variety of constraints on the macro behavior of an economy, constraints which make for straightforward understanding and analysis of such concepts as the real stock of money, real-balance effects, and the general price level. New and illuminating insights are also provided into aggregate supply and demand, natural and money rates of interest, the relationship between real and monetary economies, and economic growth and development.

In introducing the concept of myros, I will begin in this introductory essay with several tales associated with a subsistence (but otherwise idyllic) island society. The only non-leisure activity on the island is time spent each day in a mine gathering that day's subsistence rations of bread. Each individual is responsible for his/her own bread, and the only instruments used in gathering are hands. The climate is sufficiently benign that everyone sleeps comfortably under the stars, and while bread is storable, no one has ever felt a need to gather more than what is required for the current day. Bread is the only good on the island,

and no one has any possessions of any type. In short, the island society is in what can be called an 'economic state of nature'.

I want now to consider several 'escapes' from this primitive state:

1. One young man on the island unfortunately suffers recurrent dreams of being pounced upon by saber-toothed tigers while he sleeps and decides that he would be more comfortable enclosed at night by four walls and a roof (i.e., he would like to have a house). Materials for building a house are readily available, but the young man estimates that 10 days of his time will be required for construction, during which he will not be able to gather his daily rations of bread. However, since bread is storable, he decides to begin spending some extra time each day (thereby reducing the amount of time he has for leisure) gathering bread that will not be consumed on that day. He does this until his store of bread reaches 10 days' consumption, whereupon he stops going to the mine and begins working on his house. Ten days later, the house is finished, as is his store of bread. Accordingly, he must once again spend part of each day in the bread mine, but secure in his house at night, he is no longer bedeviled with dreams of pouncing saber-toothed tigers.

2. Let us now turn our attention to a young woman on the island who loves her leisure so much that she wishes she had more of it. One day it occurs to her that if she had a 'shovel' she could gather her daily ration of bread in half the time that it takes with her hands. She knows that a shovel can be made from materials on the island, but figures that it will take her five days to do so, during which time she will not be able to gather bread. Obviously, the prospect of spending extra hours gathering the bread necessary for sustenance while she is making the shovel is extremely distasteful, but the prospect of the greatly increased leisure that she will be able to enjoy once the shovel is made more than offsets the distaste. She accordingly proceeds to build up the necessary stock of 5 days' consumption of bread, which is then consumed while she makes her shovel. With her shovel, she begins gathering her daily bread in half the time that had previously been required, and of course revels in her now greatly increased leisure time.

3. Another young woman on the island, we can call her Georgia,

while happy with the amount of leisure she has, feels that she would enjoy it more if she had a picture to look at. Hence, she decides to spend some of her leisure in creating one. Once it is finished, one of her friends (named Alfredo) falls in love with the picture, and tells Georgia that he would much like to have one, too. Alfredo, though, is not such a good friend that Georgia is willing to devote any of her leisure time to creating one for him for nothing, but she says that she would be willing to make one for him in exchange for two days of bread. While Alfredo does not have any extra bread on hand, he finds the prospect of having one of Georgia's pictures so desirable that (by spending extra time in the mine) he begins accumulating a stock of 2-days' consumption of bread. Once the stock is completed, he gives it to Georgia in exchange for her promise to create a picture for him, which she immediately proceeds to do.

4. Finally, let us consider Thomas, who at an early age decides that he would like to spend up to 100 days near the end of his life in 'retirement' (i.e., free of having to spend part of each day gathering his daily bread). He accordingly proceeds to accumulate such a stock of bread. Thomas completes his accumulation by age 50. At age 65, he quits going to the mine and begins consuming from his stock.

In these episodes, we have the building of a house, 'investment' in a tool, the creation of art, and the accumulation of a 'rainy day' fund for retirement. In each case, before the desired end can be achieved, there must be accumulation of a stock of bread which allows for life to be sustained during the days that non-bread gathering activities are engaged in.[1] In this primitive society, myros is accordingly represented by unconsumed stocks of bread. Thus:

1. In the first tale, myros comes into existence on the first day that the young man haunted by dreams of saber-toothed tigers gathers more bread than he consumes. On the day that he begins building his house, the stock of myros consists of 10-days' consumption of bread. At the end of the 10th day of construction when the house is finished, the stock of bread has

---

[1] The only exception is the first picture created by Georgia. However, this is an exception only because Georgia chooses to create the picture during her regular leisure time. Had she done it during food-gathering time, she also would have had to build up a store of bread to sustain her while she created her picture.

been reduced to zero and there is accordingly no more myros in existence.

2.   In the second tale, myros comes into existence when the leisure-loving young woman begins accumulating a stock of bread to sustain her while she makes a shovel. Myros consisting of 5-days' consumption of bread is built up and then subsequently invested in construction of the shovel. At the end of the 5-day construction period, a shovel has come into being, but the myros which provided for its construction has disappeared.

3.   In the third tale, Georgia creates her first picture during her leisure time, so no prior accumulation of myros is involved.[2] However, myros does come existence when Georgia requires 2-days' bread from Alfredo in exchange for the picture that he wants her to create for him. The tale is silent as to what Georgia does with the payment. If she should immediately take two days off from gathering bread, then her 2 days of myros will be consumed. However, if she should decide to keep her payment for a 'rainy day', then myros of 2-days' consumption of bread will continue in existence.

4.   In the fourth tale, myros comes into existence as Thomas accumulates a stock of bread for 'retirement'. At age 65, Thomas's stock of myros consists of 100-days' consumption of bread. If he lives 100 days after this, his myros will have been exhausted, and he must resume daily visits to the bread mine. If he dies before his 100-day stock of bread is consumed, then the myros which remains can be passed on to his heirs.

In these stories, it should be obvious that myros comes into existence only when more bread is gathered in a day than is consumed -- i.e., only when there is *saving*. Hence, myros is created only when there is production in excess of consumption. In the stories, myros is used up: (i) in construction of a durable good (a house) which provides consumption services in episode (1), (ii) in investment in produced means of production (a shovel) in episode (2), (iii) in the acquisition of a work of art (a picture) in episode (3), and (iv) in eventual consumption in excess of production (consumption during retirement) in episode (4).

---

[2] Escape from an economic state of nature clearly requires the existence of labor time that is not devoted to subsistence.

The only use of myros that is not illustrated in the stories is the funding of current production. However, this use of myros could easily be accommodated in episode (3) if Georgia were to begin devoting her food-gathering time each day to the creation of pictures which are subsequently acquired by others in exchange for bread. The pictures thus created can be viewed as representing part of current production. The portion of bread received by Georgia which she consumes daily can then be seen as representing myros which funds (or 'finances') current production.

A major failing of current-day economic theory is that it does not allow for a material role for money. The most sophisticated Walrasian general equilibrium models, for example, remain at base models of barter economies, in that there is nothing essential in the models which depends upon the presence of money.[3] I now want to show, again in the context of the primitive island economy, that the concept of myros provides a foundation for understanding how money can emerge in an economy and also for understanding what is meant by a monetary economy.

Assume that a period of time has passed on the island and that a stock of 1000-days' consumption of bread has been built up by the inhabitants. Unfortunately, though, some new residents have put in an appearance on the island, namely, a colony of rats! As the new residents' appetites for mined bread become manifest, so too does the need for some form of secure storage. One young man (whose name is Fargo) seizes upon the idea of building a 'safe', which he then makes available (for a small monthly payment in bread) to his fellow islanders for storing their stocks of bread. Each individual who has bread in Fargo's safe is given a receipt listing the amount of bread that is in storage. By this time as well, quite a number of islanders live in houses, many of whose walls are graced by pictures that have been painted by Georgia. In fact, for some time Georgia's paintings have been in such strong demand that she now devotes all of her working time to the creation of pictures which she subsequently exchanges for bread.

In fact, Georgia's paintings are so popular that existing examples are traded (for bread, of course) in a secondary market, and Georgia responds to this by regularly raising her prices. Although payment for the pictures is always in bread, it soon becomes apparent to those involved that bread removed from Fargo's safe for payment in exchange almost immediately returns to the safe, so that transfer of ownership of the bread could be effected by the simple device of

---

[3] This failing has long been recognized by Clower (1967) and Hahn (1975) and others. See also the recent series of papers by Kiyotaki and Wright (1989,1991,1993).

exchanging storage receipts or through written instructions to Fargo. As a consequence, endorsed storage receipts and 'checks' began circulating as 'means of payment' (i.e., money) in lieu of actual exchange of bread.

Because of the storage fees collected for use of his safe and the popularity of her paintings, Fargo and Georgia become the wealthiest individuals on the island, and each of them has amassed a stock of 100-days' consumption of bread. At various times in the past, both of them have made loans from their stocks to certain of their fellow citizens so that they could build houses without having first to accumulate the necessary stock of bread. The loans had always been repaid on schedule (with interest). However, once storage receipts and 'checks' started to circulate, Fargo noticed that most of the bread in his safe, in fact, never left the premises. Accordingly, it occurred to him that he could begin making 'house loans' from the bread of others in his safe rather than from just his own stock. In doing this, Fargo was aware that he was creating more claims to bread than there was actual bread on deposit. But he was always prudent to limit the creation of excess claims to a small fraction of the total, and there was never an instance of a requested delivery of bread from storage that was not promptly honored.

In this tale:

♦ A continuing pool of myros (bread) has come into existence;

♦ Bread (or its surrogate in the form of storage receipts) has become the universally accepted means of payment -- money as a medium of exchange has emerged;

♦ Four assets have come into being -- bread, paintings, houses, and a safe (although no transactions involving the trading of houses or the safe for bread are mentioned as actually having occurred);

♦ An institution which provides 'safe-deposit boxes', 'checking accounts', 'mortgage loans' (together with 'interest'), and 'bank notes' has come into existence.

♦ An institution for the creation of money has also come into existence.

Let us now take the tale a bit further. Let us suppose over a period of time that Fargo, through his loan activities, has created bread claims totaling 2000 days of consumption, but that only 1000 days of bread in fact exist. In normal circumstances, this would not create any problems, for Fargo is always able to redeem in full any claims that are presented for actual delivery of bread. However, suppose that there is someone who is jealous of Fargo's high standing in the island community and begins to spread a nasty rumor (completely unfounded, of course) that Fargo has begun living 'high on the hog' and is consuming not only his own bread, but the bread of his fellow citizens as well. Panic ensues, and individuals rush with their storage receipts to get their bread from Fargo's safe. There is a 'bank run', and Fargo is of course forced to close his doors. Any existing storage receipts obviously become worthless. In short, the primitive monetary system which had been established collapses.[4]

Consider, now, a somewhat different scenario. Suppose that the rumor is the same, but that, rather than storage claims of 2000 days of bread, there are in fact only 1000. In this situation, Fargo would be able to honor claims as they were presented, and the bank run would almost certainly come to an end well before all 1000 days of bread in the safe were paid out. Life would probably return to normal, and the monetary system would remain intact.

For a final scenario, suppose that one night the colony of rats are able to breach the walls of Fargo's safe and that, by the time this is discovered and the rats dispatched, half of the bread that was in storage is destroyed. Assume, as above, that the number of storage claims in existence is 1000. If news of what happened were to spread, a bank run would almost certainly occur. As there are 1000 claims in existence, but now only 500 days of bread, claims would again become worthless and the primitive monetary system would collapse as in the first scenario.

The point being made in these stories is a simple one, and it involves the fundamental role of the pool of myros. In all three scenarios, there is a rush to 'liquidity' because of a loss of confidence in the island's 'banker'. When it becomes apparent that the number of storage claims in existence exceeds the amount of goods, the claims lose their value and the monetary system collapses. However, the determining factor as to whether the system will in fact collapse is whether the number of storage receipts exceeds the amount of goods (i.e., the number of days of bread consumption) in the pool of myros. The conclusion, therefore, is that the real stock of money in this simple bread economy is determined by the number of days of bread consumption that is represented in the pool of myros. In the first two scenarios, this number is 1000, but in the third

---

[4] This contingency illustrates that, at base, money can be equated with 'confidence'. Money can come into existence *ex vacuo* through trust and can be annihilated by 'anti-confidence'. A money can accordingly fluctuate between being and nothingness.

scenario it was reduced to 500 because of the destruction caused by the rats.[5]

Generalization of this conclusion is straightforward, and will be one of the first tasks to be undertaken in this book. In a real-world economy, the goods produced are many and complex, and the goods side of myros can only be stated as a value (i.e., in monetary terms), specifically as the sum total of all final and intermediate goods in existence evaluated at current market prices. And just as in the simple bread economy, this aggregate value accordingly provides an upper bound on the real stock of money in an economy. Most of what I plan to do in this book simply involves variations on this and related simple themes.

A final tale involves Auric, a cousin of Georgia. One day while on a walk in the hills, Auric crosses a stream and notices some attractive lumps of yellow metal shimmering below the surface of the water. Auric, who shares Georgia's eye for beauty, picks up one of the lumps, likes it, and takes it home with him. A friend sees it and likes it as well, and offers Auric a day's bread for it. Since Auric knows where he can acquire more lumps, he accepts his friend's offer. The word gets around that Auric has beautiful lumps of metal that he will exchange for bread, and he is besieged with islanders asking him to do so. Everyone, it seems, would like to possess at least one of the lumps. Auric is the only one who knows where the lumps come from, and of course he does not tell anyone, as he soon finds that he can obtain his daily bread much easier through exchange for these lumps of metal than by mining it himself. In time, the lumps of metal came to be universally acceptable in exchange, not only for bread, but for houses and paintings as well -- in short, for anything for which payment in bread had previously been expected and required. Exchange rates, which had previously been denominated in terms of bread, now came to be denominated in terms of lumps of the metal.

The metal is gold, of course, and what is described in this tale is the emergence of gold as still another form of money, together with an associated system of exchange rates. What allows gold to begin functioning as universal purchasing power is that, like bread, it is storable and universally desired. However, 'desired' in this case is because of perceived beauty rather than its being necessary for life.

---

[5] In the third scenario, suppose that all of holders of storage claims understand what has happened and that holders of claims implicitly and simultaneously agree to share the loss proportionately so that no one presents any claims for redemption. It would be understood that the value of each claim has been halved, i.e., that each claim is now only for a half-day's bread. In this case, while the nominal stock of money remains at 1000, the real stock is only 500. The necessary devaluation of the stock of money would have occurred without a collapse of the monetary system. The likelihood of such a scenario occurring in real life is, of course, remote.

CHAPTER 1

PREMISES AND AN OVERVIEW

As this book is rather sweeping in purview, it is appropriate to begin with a brief discussion of the premises which motivate and guide the analyses, together with an overview of the discussion to follow. The overarching concept in the book is that of myros (or what I will eventually rename as fluid capital). Myros is viewed as a fund (or equivalently a surplus), which comes into existence through saving out of current production and is extinguished through consumption, current production, and investment. Myros funds investment, current production, and consumption in excess of current income. Additionally, myros enables assets to acquire value, provides for both the existence and value of money, and is coextensive with the economic wealth of an economy. Myros is fundamental to the understanding of the macroeconomics of an economy, and what few macroeconomic laws that can be identified exist as consequences of the conservation laws which myros imposes. Indeed, most of the analysis of the book can be viewed as a working through of the implications of these conservation laws.

Most of the subject matter of economics, in my view, can be cast in terms of events that have their setting in mythical primitive economies of the type described in the Prologue. Consumption decisions are made, savings come into being, investments occur, values are created, exchange takes place, interest emerges, and money comes into existence in a variety of forms. In principle, these events are no different in their implications than their counterparts in a modern economy, so the device of reasoning from mythical primitive economies will be resorted to frequently.[1]

---

[1] An implication of this paragraph is that there is no difference in principle between the laws governing development in a low-income economy and development in a high-income economy. Institutional settings can differ, but the conservation laws imposed by the pool of myros are invariant. Growth and development will be the focus of Chapters 12 and 13.

My approach to economics is neither classical, neoclassical, nor Keynesian. Equilibria play important roles in my framework, but more as 'attractors' toward which activities and processes are drawn, as opposed to positions of actual attainment. Time is of fundamental importance in the framework, but the concern, for the most part, is with real time, rather than mechanical (or logical) time. My macroeconomic framework is more Keynes and classical, as opposed to Keynesian, and includes virtually no neoclassical elements at all. Yet my theory of value is thoroughly subjective, and therefore neoclassical.

My vision of how an economy evolves and develops is pretty much in line with the events described in the Prologue. There are three things that have to occur in sequence in order for an economy to grow:

1. A pool of myros has to come into existence through saving.

2. The savings in this pool has to fund investment in produced means of production, thereby increasing the economy's capacity to produce.

3. The increased capacity to produce must actually be utilized.

Income is generated through the process of production and is viewed in this book as representing generalized 'claim tickets' to the social product which is created.[2] In a monetary economy, income is paid and received in the form of money. Money, itself, is viewed in this book as a *social invention* which allows specific claims on the pool of myros to be transformed into general claims. There are many ways that money can come into existence, but the standard way, in a monetary economy, is through a banking system, which creates universally transferrable deposits for the purpose of financing current production and the initial finance of investment in newly produced means of production. The bulk of the money stock, accordingly, is in a continual state of creation and destruction.

The pool of myros is increased by saving, both business and personal, and is depleted by funding for investment and current production (or what is usually referred to as working capital), and the excess of consumption over current income. There are two sides to the pool of myros, a 'goods' side and a 'claims' side. The 'goods' side of the pool represents the goods that have been produced but not yet consumed, used as input into current production, or invested in newly

---

[2] The term is from Schumpeter (1934).

produced means of production. The 'claims' side of the pool of myros, on the other hand, represents the stock of generalized claims on goods that has come into existence as a result of current and past saving.

A major deficiency of modern monetary theory is that much of the time it is silent as to how money actually comes into existence. For the most part, the stock of money is treated as exogenous, and the standard litany as to its genesis is of the form: "Assume that the quantity of money is doubled." Probably the best known -- and certainly the most mechanical! -- metaphor for accomplishing this is Milton Friedman's helicopter which flies about the countryside scattering money. The view in this book is that the stock of money is endogenous in most circumstances and that it comes into existence through the joint efforts of two parties: banks that create universally transferrable deposits and businesses that demand these deposits in order to fund current production or provide for initial funding of new investment.

While it might seem otherwise, the foregoing does not ignore the fact that a significant part of the money stock in a modern economy is undated in the form of demand deposits and fiat money. The question which has to be asked, however, is how did these undated stocks of money come into existence in the first place. The answer, as we shall find, is that the processes of creation were for the most part once again endogenous. Moreover, one must also not conclude from this that, with the money stock being endogenous, monetary policy is sterile and ineffective. While the monetary authority cannot control directly the amount of money in existence, it can have strong indirect influence though effecting the terms upon which money is created and extinguished. As a consequence, there is a definite role for active monetary policy, but in ways that depart from conventional practice.

We shall find that the conservation laws imposed by the pool of myros provide an upper bound to the real value of the stock of money, as well as an upper bound to the real value of the aggregate stock of real and financial assets. Moreover, we shall also find that the concept of myros provides a convenient vehicle for defining aggregate demand and aggregate supply and, by extension, the related phenomena of inflation and deflation, together with a reinterpretation of the venerable quantity equation of exchange.

The standard macroeconomic question since the time of Keynes's *General Theory* is whether a competitive market economy can come to rest in a position that is at less than full employment. Keynes's answer was clearly in the affirmative, while the now canonical neoclassical answer is equally clearly in the negative. Although my own view is that such equilibrium-type questions are of limited relevance and interest, the conclusion in this book is nevertheless that an economy can be in equilibrium at less than full employment, and largely for the reasons advanced by Keynes.

In my opinion, the canonical neoclassical model as formulated by Samuelson, Patinkin, and others suffers from two fatal defects as a framework for analyzing practical macroeconomic questions. These two defects are (1) a seriously flawed concept of capital and (2) a paradigm which continues to mimic nineteenth-century energy mechanics. Since the problems inherent in (2) are discussed at length in Appendix 1, suffice it here to say that the basic problem involves violation of a stringent set of time invariances.[3]

The problems with the concept of capital that is used in neoclassical theorizing are both numerous and multifaceted, and in general are what this book is about. Not the least of the problems is that capital is not a single concept in the canon of economics, but a surfeit of concepts. The concept of myros developed in this book provides, in my opinion, an appropriate unifying definition of capital to which all other concepts of capital can be related in a consistent fashion. Unlike with the conventional neoclassical view of capital, myros is not interpreted as a substance, but rather as a fund which in general can only be measured as a value (i.e., in money terms).[4] Among other things, this means that it is not meaningful, in my opinion, to view capital as a separate factor of production whose price is the rate of interest.

In the framework of this book, there are two distinct concepts of the rate of interest, one associated with myros and the other associated with money. The myros rate of interest represents the price which equilibrates supply and demand in the market for myros, while the money rate of interest represents the price which equilibrates supply and demand in the money market. While these two interest rates are clearly akin to the natural and market rates of interest of Wicksell and the liquidity preference theory of interest of Keynes, there are, as we shall see, some important conceptual differences.

I imagine that I am like most economists in seeing that the purpose of

---

[3] See Mirowski (1989, Chapters 5 and 6).

[4] That capital is a substance is uncritically accepted by the present generation of neoclassically trained economists was brought home to me a few years ago by a bright young New Zealand economist, interested in macroeconomics and monetary theory, who was visiting Tucson for a few days. At one point, I asked him how he defined capital. His response was: "Oh, capital! That is the K that appears in the aggregate production function!" Nothing, in my view, better illustrates the poverty of current-day capital theory.

economic theorizing is to construct a framework for embodying economic relationships that are invariant with respect to time and place. Unfortunately, there are few economic relationships which, in my opinion, can aspire to the status of 'law'. Engel's Law regarding expenditure on food and the Law of Pareto regarding the upper tail of the distribution of income would seem to qualify, as would also a Law of Demand in some form or another. However, as the parameters in these 'laws' vary with both time and place, it is clear that there are no relationships in economics which are on par with the great universal constants in the physical sciences. In my view, the closest thing in economics to universal laws is represented in the constraints that are imposed by the pool of myros. These 'conservation laws', as will be seen, impose constraints at each point in real time on the aggregate behavior of an economy's agents. And this is true, moreover, no matter how the economy is organized politically or institutionally.

For the most part, my micro-behavior views are fairly conventional, although not entirely. As far as consumer (or household) behavior is concerned, the framework of this book does not depend in any material way on specific structures of preferences, whether individuals optimize or satisfise, or just what. It is assumed that individuals work, receive income, consume, save, react to risk and uncertainty, and are subject to inertia and other real-time dynamical effects, but in general it is not critical just how these activities and processes are postulated to come about.[5]

On the production side, the analyses in this book are based upon the following inescapable facts regarding the real world:

1. Current production is produced from current productive capacity;

2. Current productive capacity is a legacy from yesterday and is a consequence of past investment decisions;

3. Investment today can only affect productive capacity in the future.

Since the future is unknown, investment decisions are necessarily driven by

---

[5] Probably my most unconventional views concerning demand theory are that consumption behavior should be approached in terms of the structure and functioning of the brain and that consumption decisions are derivative from decisions to maintain acceptable levels of psychological and physiological well-being. For elaboration, see Taylor (1987, 1988, 1992).

expectations, which will almost always turn out to be wrong. As a consequence, a firm's present capacity to produce will almost certainly not be optimal for serving today's demand. What the firm can do, however, is to make optimal use of its current capacity and to optimize, on the basis of expectations of future demands, alterations in this capacity to take effect in the future. Moreover, the future in this context is not an infinite horizon, as is customarily assumed in the literature on investment theory, but a finite horizon that is determined by the firm's normal construction period -- i.e., the amount of time that the firm considers optimal for making new capacity operational in an orderly fashion. In making today's investment decisions, the firm accordingly needs only to consider demands to the end of its normal construction period. Capacity decisions for serving demands beyond this period can be put off until tomorrow.[6]

---

[6] Throughout this book, 'today', 'yesterday', and 'tomorrow' will be used frequently. 'Today' refers to the current period, or simply the present; 'yesterday' refers to the past, usually the indefinite past, but occasionally (depending upon context) to the most recent past period; 'tomorrow' refers to the future, usually the indefinite future, unless the context specifies otherwise.

CHAPTER 2

MYROS AND OTHER
CONCEPTS AND DEFINITIONS

The purpose of this chapter is to establish the concepts and definitions that will be used in the sequel. One of the problems with economics is that much of its vocabulary consists of everyday words such as income, capital, and money that have fairly time-honored technical meanings, but meanings that frequently vary from economist to economist and from one generation of economists to another. As was noted in Chapter 1, capital is a notable example, as there are about as many concepts of capital as there are economists who have thought and written about it.

Cost offers another example. Indeed, consider the following statements regarding cost, all of which can be readily found in the literature:[1]

A. Costs are subjective.

B. Costs are objective.

C. Costs determine choice.

D. Choice determines costs.

E. Prices must be set so as to recover costs.

Of these statements, B and E would seem to contradict A, while D would seem to gainsay C. But, before concluding that this is the case, consider the following:

---

[1] The following discussion is taken from Taylor (1991, pp. 465-6).

A telephone company is debating whether to spend $100 million in acquiring a commercial finance company, or to spend the same amount to replace an aging wire center in a revitalized and growing downtown area. The latter project is finally decided upon when the vice president pushing it threatens to resign if the project is not approved. Upon completion, the new wire center is allowed by the state Public Utility Commission to be put into the rate base at its full value and the telephone company is authorized to set rates that will recover the investment of $100 million over a period of 20 years.

In choosing which project to pursue, the telephone company is guided by the *opportunity costs* of the two alternatives. In the event, it is decided that the risk of losing the vice president in question is too high a price to pay not to replace the aging wire center. This opportunity cost, which is *subjective*, determines the choice of project, and accordingly illustrates statements A and C.[2] The decision to replace the wire center sets in motion a stream of construction expenditures of $100 million. These expenditures are *objective* and are caused by the decision to replace the wire center. They accordingly illustrate statements B and D. Finally, in view of the social contract between the telephone company and the Public Utility Commission, a portion of the $100 million investment is to be depreciated each year according to agreed-upon accounting rules and this depreciation then becomes costs to be recovered through an appropriate set of rates. These costs illustrate statement E.

The point of this story is not that cost is a confusing and confused concept, but that one word -- cost -- is being asked to do too much. There are, as the tale exemplifies, a number of different concepts of cost, and to refer to all of them indiscriminately as 'cost' without proper qualification is to lead to confusion. The same is true for the word 'capital'. The various concepts of capital -- physical capital, financial capital, working capital, etc. -- are all useful in context, but a single word, capital, cannot cover all contingencies of its use without proper qualification. What is needed is a root concept of capital which is both unifying and encompassing. And as was noted in the Prologue and Chapter 1, I believe that the concept of myros provides such an instrument.

MYROS

The concept of myros will be approached in several different ways. To begin with, it is most useful to see myros as representing a pool of accumulated

---

[2] Buchanan (1969) provides a detailed discussion of the nature of costs and choice. See also Buchanan and Thirlby (1981).

savings. This pool comes into existence through saving and is reduced through investment in produced means of production, the funding of current production, and consumption in excess of current income. The pool of myros has two sides -- a goods side, which consists of stocks of unconsumed consumables and finished intermediate goods, and a claims side, which consists of the sum total of unexercised claims to both current and past production.

In a barter economy (with property rights), the two sides of the pool of myros would be trivially the same, for the goods that are not consumed (i.e., that are saved) are actually owned by the individuals involved. The goods themselves are also the 'claim tickets'. In a monetary economy, in contrast, the claim tickets in question initially take the form of money. This is because incomes in a monetary economy are received in money, and saving accordingly occurs through money not being spent. The monies saved can be subsequently exchanged for other forms of assets, both real and financial, so that the values induced on these assets become included in the claims pool on the claims side of the pool of myros.

Of the events described in the Prologue, saving -- and therefore myros -- first emerges when the young man who suffers from bad dreams begins spending some extra time in the mine each day in order to build up a store of bread to sustain him during the 10 days that are needed to build his house. Just before he starts the house, the pool of myros for the economy accordingly consists of 10 days of bread. During the 10 days that the house is being built, the pool of myros is being depleted, and at the end of the 10th day, when the house is completed, the pool is empty. The economy at this point has no myros, as the myros that had existed was consumed during construction of the house.[3]

Myros again emerges when the young woman who loves her leisure starts working extra time in the mine in order to provide sustenance during the five days that she is making her shovel. At the end of the day before she begins work on the shovel, the pool of myros for the economy consists of five days of bread. However, the pool is once again depleted during the five days that she devotes to making the shovel. When it is completed, a shovel exists (as does also the young man's house), but the economy once again has no myros. There can be no further investment in houses, shovels, or whatever until such time as additional myros comes into existence through saving.

---

[3] As noted in the Prologue, implicit in the foregoing is the assumption that latent labor is available in the form of working hours that can exceed the time needed to mine one's daily bread. A subsistence economy that does not have this option is not able to endogenously create myros.

A pool of myros comes into existence a third time in the economy when Alfredo creates a stock of two days' bread in order to acquire Georgia's picture, and then again when Thomas decides to create a retirement fund. From this point on in the story, the pool of myros is never empty, though it ebbs and flows as reserves of bread are increased and then reduced as a result of retirement saving, housing construction, investment in a safe, etc.

Other standard concepts of capital are also evident in the story, namely:

1. Physical (or real) capital, as exemplified by the house, shovel, and safe;

2. Working capital, as exemplified in the bread that is consumed by Georgia while she is producing paintings;

3. Financial capital, as exemplified by the 'warehouse' receipts held by the individuals with bread on deposit in Fargo's safe;

4. Money, as exemplified by circulating 'warehouse' receipts for bread on deposit in Fargo's safe, notes instructing Fargo to transfer bread from one 'account' to another, and finally lumps of gold.[4]

An alternative way of arriving at the concept of myros is to begin with a gross concept of 'capital' -- without an adjective! -- defined as the difference, measured from time immemorial, between the sum total of production and the sum total of consumption. Consumption in this context is to be broadly construed as consumption in the usual sense of the word plus capital used up in production (including wastage and deterioration) and physical capital of the 'white-elephant' type that never produces any output.

'Capital' in this sense is thus a stock (or, equivalently, a surplus). At any one point in time, this stock will consist of two components, a fixed (or sunk) component and a fluid (or liquid) component. The fixed component is represented by the undepreciated portion of produced means of production (of which plant and equipment, as usually interpreted, account for the major share), while the fluid component refers to a pool (or stock) of finished goods and goods in process of production. The fluid component of capital can also equivalently be

---

[4] Obviously, there are other ways that money can come into existence in a primitive economy. For a formal discussion of the conditions that a commodity has to satisfy in order for it to begin functioning as money, see Clower (1967). See also Kiyotaki and Wright (1989).

viewed as being measured by the depreciation reserves of currently existing produced means of production plus the excess of past and current savings over past and current investment.[5]

The fixed (or sunk) component of capital represents what most writers have in mind when they either explicitly or implicitly refer to physical capital. The only important difference is that my definition of fixed capital refers only to the undepreciated portion of the physical stocks of produced means of production. This difference is important to the measurement of fluid capital, but not to the ability of the physical capital to produce output and generate income. A piece of physical equipment can be highly productive even though it is fully depreciated and carried on books at a value of zero.

The fluid component of capital thus represents the fund that is available to be drawn upon to finance and sustain investment in newly produced means of production, to fund the production of consumption goods, and to fund consumption in excess of current income. This fund provides for both finance and subsistence -- finance, because the stock of goods contained in it can be monetized, and subsistence, because the goods themselves are available to be consumed during periods of production. The fluid component of capital clearly corresponds to what most writers would seem to have in mind when they refer to circulating, working, or liquid capital. Ricardo's subsistence fund is clearly related to this concept of capital, as is also the 'wages fund' of other Classical writers. *The fluid component of capital is as what I call myros.* This being the case, myros and fluid capital will henceforth be used interchangeably.

The characteristic of the fluid capital that makes it 'fluid' or 'liquid' is that, it is free to be embodied, through investment, in anything, anywhere. This characteristic is usually referred to as *fungibility*.[6] Fluid capital is perfectly fungible, unlike sunk capital which is at best only partially fungible.[7]

---

[5] Depreciation, as it is used in this paragraph, as well as throughout this book, will be clarified in the next section.

[6] In the neoclassical growth and investment literature of the 1960s and 1970s, the term used was *putty*, as in 'putty-clay' models. The clay, of course, referred to fixed (or physical) capital.

[7] An existing airplane is perfectly fungible between different routes, but the capital that is embodied in the plane can be transformed into an office building (say) only through a recovery of that capital back into the pool of fluid capital through depreciation charges against the revenues generated by the plane.

MYROS RECOVERY CHARGES

A concept which finds heavy use in the discussion to follow is depreciation (or what I will call *myros recovery charges*.) Since my concept of depreciation differs from what is traditionally employed in the literature, it is critical that depreciation as used in this book be understood at the outset. In conventional neoclassical theory in which capital is treated as one of the factor inputs in a production function, depreciation is represented as the 'using-up' (or 'consumption') of capital which occurs during the course of production. That physical capital represented in produced means of production is subject to wear and tear from usage or deterioration with the passage of time, there is no doubt, and to recognize this in determining an economy's capacity to produce is of obvious relevance. However, this is not the concept of depreciation that will be used in this book.

Instead, depreciation in this book is defined in terms of a charge against quasi-rents which returns capital embodied in produced means of production back into the pool of myros[8]. Viewed in this way, depreciation is simply an accounting device for transforming (over some relevant horizon) sunk capital back into fluid capital. Depreciation, as the term will be used in this book, thus represents an instrument for effecting saving, and bears no necessary relationship to physical wear and tear or deterioration.[9] Henceforth, whenever depreciation in the conventional neoclassical sense is at issue, it will be referred as economic depreciation, wear and tear, or some such physical equivalent. Depreciation, as used here, will be referred to as *myros recovery charges*.

To fix the essential ideas, consider the following example. Assume that a firm has just purchased a newly produced machine with an expected useful operating life of 10 years at a cost of $10,000. Assume, however, that in deciding to make the investment the firm used an investment (or 'payback') horizon of five years, rather than the expected 10-year life of the machine. Assume that in the first year of operation that quasi-rents of $4000 are generated by the machine and that the firm's financial managers decide to make a myros recovery charge of $3000 against these quasi-rents. Assume that the $1000 that remains is kept as retained earnings. At the end of the first year, therefore, the firm's books will show a profit of $1000, cash balances of $4000, a myros

---

[8] As used in this book, quasi-rents represents the difference between revenues and the out-of-pocket costs (but only the out-of-pocket costs) of producing those revenues.

[9] The accounting aspects of depreciation will be discussed in detail in Chapter 9.

recovery reserve of $3000, retained earnings of $1000, and an undepreciated balance for the machine of $7000.

Assume that during the next four years quasi-rents continue to be $4000 each year, that myros recovery charges of $3000, $2000, $1000, and $1000 are made, and that all profit is paid out as dividends. At the end of the five years, the firm will show cash balances of $11,000, myros recovery reserves of $10,000, retained earnings of $1000, and a value of zero for the machine. However, since the machine is still 'healthy', it will be expected to continue generating quasi-rents for another five years even though it is now fully depreciated.

While this example may seem an almost trivial exercise in elementary accounting, its essential point is to demonstrate that the myros recovery charges that recover the $10,000 that was initially invested in the machine need bear no necessary relationship to the actual physical life of the machine. Absent tax considerations, the firm is free to take the myros recovery charges in any manner that it chooses (so long as the charge in any year does not exceed that year's quasi-rent). After five years, the $10,000 of fluid capital that was originally embodied in the machine is again fluid capital. No myros remains sunk in the machine even though the machine continues to exist and to generate output and income.

HUMAN AND NONHUMAN CAPITAL

The concept of human capital, and its distinction from physical capital, is central to current economic analysis. As with physical capital, human capital comes into being through investment, hence its creation represents consumption of fluid capital. With physical capital, as we have seen, there are two types of depreciation to be considered: physical depreciation, which represents the physical destruction or deterioration from use or the passage of time, and fiducial depreciation (i.e., myros recovery), which represents the repatriation of the fluid capital expended in the physical capital's original creation.

With human capital, physical depreciation can itself take two forms. The first relates to the deterioration which occurs with lack of use and aging, while the second is the complete destruction which occurs at death. Unlike for physical capital, fiduciary depreciation for human capital seems remote, but the fact that human capital completely destructs at death means that the capacity to produce is permanently reduced unless replacement has occurred through education and training of a younger generation. The expenditures associated with this can be viewed as fiduciary charges against the earnings of the current stock of human capital. Whether this takes the form of prior saving or spending out of current income, the effect is the same: the fluid capital sunk in the sunset generation of human capital is repatriated and reinvested.

While the general principles governing the creation and renewal of human and nonhuman capital are the same, human capital differs from physical capital in its degree of fungibility. Human capital is clearly the more fungible, in that it can entertain different uses much more readily than can physical capital. Even within human capital, fungibility differs in that knowledge- (or intelligence-) based capital has much greater fungibility than skill-based capital. With fungibility, the myros embodied in produced means of production can traverse different uses without the need to be repatriated back into fluid capital and then reinvested. Fungibility, therefore, clearly increases the efficiency of a given stock of produced means of production, and is the reason why intelligence-based human capital, in general, has an advantage over skill-based human capital.

A GLOSSARY OF CONCEPTS AND DEFINITIONS

I now turn to a glossary of concepts and definitions of terms which will be used throughout the book. The listing which follows is logical, rather than alphabetical.

Goods
> A good is anything for which individuals are willing to exchange their labor or fruits of their labor.

Production
> Production is the creation of goods through the combining of labor with natural resources and produced means of production.

Social Dividend
> The social dividend represents the net output (but gross of depreciation) from production for an economy. In most circumstances, the social dividend can be identified with Gross Domestic Product.

Income
> Income is generated by production and represents 'claim tickets' to the social dividend.

Saving

Saving represents that part of the social dividend that is not currently consumed.

Produced Means of Production

Produced means of production are additions to the capacity to produce that are themselves produced. Produced means of production are temporary resources, in contrast to natural resources which are permanent. Produced means of production are durable, but nevertheless will eventually disappear if not maintained or replaced.

Investment

Investment represents the creation of produced means of production. The goods that are needed in the creation of produced means of production are drawn from the pool of fluid capital.

Quasi-Rents

Quasi-rents represent the difference between revenues and the out-of-pocket costs (but only the out-of-pocket costs) of producing those revenues.

Myros Recovery Charges

Myros recovery charges represent charges against quasi-rents that return the capital embodied in produced means of production back into the pool of fluid capital. Alternately, myros recovery charges can be seen as the process whereby physical capital is transformed back into fluid capital.

Sunk Capital

Sunk capital represents that part of the fluid capital embodied in produced means of production that has not yet been transformed (or recovered) back into fluid capital through myros recovery charges against quasi-rents.

Money

Money is a social invention which allows the pool of fluid capital to be transformed into universal purchasing power.

Monetization

Monetization is the process by which the pool of fluid capital is transformed into universal purchasing power through the granting of loans denominated in money. There are many forms that monetization can take, including the creation of bills of exchange, bank notes, checking deposits, etc.

General Price Level

Once a unit of account is established, the general price level is determined by the pool of purchasing power that is established by monetization of assets in conjunction with the stock of goods represented by the goods side of the pool of fluid capital. The general price level is established initially by selecting some good as the numeraire and expressing the prices of all other goods in terms of units of this good. Prices in terms of the numeraire's price may in turn be expressed in terms of the money unit of account.

Natural Rate of Interest

The natural rate of interest is the price which equates the demand for fluid capital with its supply.

Money Rate of Interest

The money rate of interest is the interest rate on money loans, and represents the price for monetizing the pool of fluid capital. In a world of uncertainty and a fractional reserve banking system, the lower bound to the money rate of interest is ultimately determined by the price that has to be paid to get holders of the primary money to give up their immediate claims to it (i.e., liquidity preference).

Assets

Assets represent instruments for transferring purchasing power over time. They come into existence because those with claims on the pool of fluid capital are willing to give up some of their claims in exchange. Assets can take a number of different forms -- money, goods, Old Masters, loans, property rights in produced means of production, etc.

Wealth

Wealth for an individual is represented by the sum of current income plus the value of all assets held. Wealth for an economy as a whole (viewed as a closed system) is given by the sum of current income plus the value (measured in current prices) of all stocks of unconsumed consumables.

CHAPTER 3

THE MACROECONOMIC FRAMEWORK

This chapter focuses on the macroeconomic framework which guides the analyses of the book. We shall begin with an overview that describes how the major components of the framework relate to one another. The constraints (or 'conservation laws') that are imposed by the pool of fluid capital will then be discussed, followed by discussions of the determination of asset values and aggregate demand and aggregate supply. The chapter concludes with a description of the conditions which define macroeconomic equilibrium.

AN OVERVIEW

The essential features of the macroeconomic framework are given in Figure 1. We start with the big box near the right hand side of the figure labeled Capacity to Produce. This box symbolizes the current capacity of the economy to produce goods and services and to generate income. At any point in time, the capacity of an economy to produce is determined by three factors symbolized by oblongs feeding into Capacity to Produce: population, permanent resources, and temporary resources embodied in produced means of production.[1]

Population obviously represents the labor resources that are available to be employed in production.[2] Included in permanent resources are those resources,

---

[1] Cf. Hayek (1941, Chapter 5).

[2] The population resource base is assumed to be measured in terms of hours of 'common' labor, as exemplified (say) in the mythical island economy in the Prologue of 8-hour days spent mining bread. In a modern economy, this might be measured in terms of the skills of a typical high-school graduate. Labor skills beyond the basic skills are treated as human capital and included in produced means of production.

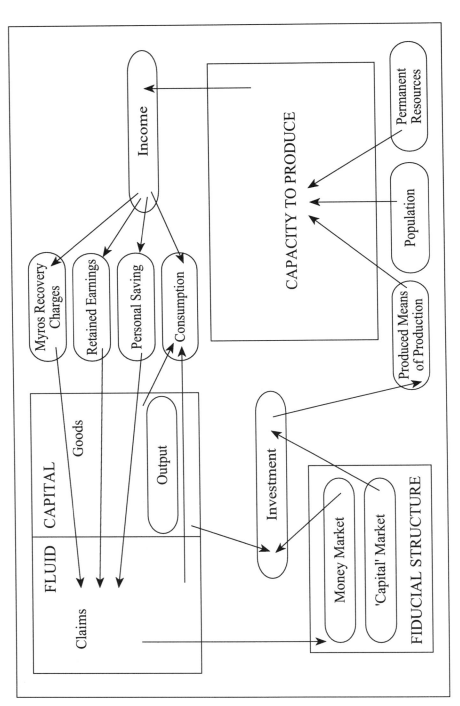

Figure 1

such as land and sunshine, that are not consumed in production and remain permanently intact. Produced means of production, on the other hand, represent resources that, although durable, periodically require replacement if they are not to disappear.[3] Produced means of production are assumed to include both physical plant and equipment (i.e., physical capital) and intangibles such as human capital and technology.

At any point in time, the production capacity of an economy is fixed. The only open decisions regarding this capacity relate to the intensity with which it can be utilized. Actual operation of capacity yields output and generates income, as symbolized by the oblongs labeled Output and Income. The oblong for Income is shown as standing by itself, while that for Output is included in the box labeled Fluid Capital. Output is shown as being wholly contained in Fluid Capital in order to emphasize that the goods and services from current production form the bulk of the goods side of fluid capital; inventories of previously produced goods form the rest. Two things can be done with income: it can be used to purchase consumption goods or it can be saved, as given by the sum of personal saving, retained earnings, and myros recovery charges.

The box in the upper left of the figure symbolizes the pool of fluid capital. This pool is enlarged by saving and reduced by investment in produced means of production, funding of current production, and consumption in excess of income.[4] The box for Fluid Capital is divided in two equal parts, one labeled Goods and the other Claims. This division symbolizes that fluid capital is seen as consisting of two sides, a goods side and a claims side. Saving consists of two components, personal saving and business saving. Personal saving is identified with that part of income which is not consumed (i.e., with the oblong labeled Personal Saving), while business saving is identified with the oblongs labeled Retained Earnings and Myros Recovery Charges.[5]

---

[3] This threefold representation of cooperating determinants of production is the one employed by Hayek in *The Pure Theory of Capital*. While 'original powers of the soil' may have seemed inexhaustible to the Classical economists, present-day land uses clearly suggest otherwise. Even sunshine in many areas can no longer be taken for granted. Accordingly, it is debatable whether permanent resources should even be listed as a separate category.

[4] It might seem that consumption in excess of income should be treated as negative savings and netted into saving. This is not done because the bulk of consumption in excess of income represents the funding of retirement consumption, and how retirement consumption is financed has important macroeconomic implications. These questions will be discussed in Chapter 12.

[5] For present purposes, government saving and investment will be subsumed in business saving and investment.

Investment, which is symbolized by the oblong labeled Investment, converts fluid capital into fixed (or sunk capital) and thus adds to the capacity of the economy to produce and to the potential of the economy to generate income. As with the current production of consumption goods, investment must also be funded from the pool of fluid capital. A common misconception is that investment must be funded by current saving, but this is not necessarily the case. For saving (whether personal or business), defined as the difference between current income and current consumption, is just the current flow into the pool. The pool of fluid capital is itself a stock, and is the result of both current and past saving.[6] So long as the pool is not empty, investment can be funded even if current saving is zero.[7]

The financial system is represented by the box labeled Fiducial Structure. The Fiducial Structure comprises the banking system and a variety of financial intermediaries. This is where money is created and assets and liabilities are generated in exchange for claims on the pool of fluid capital. Money is created by commercial banks in the form of short-term loans.[8] Such loans are made for two purposes: (1) finance of current production and (2) initial finance of investment in newly produced means of production.[9] Expectations are central -- and indeed are the drivers! -- in both cases, short-term expectations in the case of current production and long-term expectations in the case of investment. Owners of current productive capacity form expectations of the output that can be sold during the current period and take these to their bankers. The outcomes of these 'banker conferences' then determine the utilization rate of the existing capacity to produce. If expectations are rosy, and bankers are in agreement, then the utilization rate will be high. The opposite will be the case if short-term expectations are pessimistic.

The money and 'capital' markets are symbolized by the two oblongs in the box for the fiducial structure. The money rate of interest -- i.e., the price at which fluid capital is monetized -- is determined in the money market. Supplies and demands for fluid capital meet in the 'capital' market, as do also the supplies

---

[6] Throughout this book, *saving* (singular) will refer to saving out of current income, while *savings* (plural) will refer to the accumulation of past saving.

[7] In my view, recognition of the possibility of this was one of the most critical insights of Keynes in the *General Theory*.

[8] Money that is created by the discounting at the central bank of IOUs purchased by banks in the commercial paper market will be discussed in Chapter 4.

[9] Money creation for the finance of consumption will be ignored for the moment.

and demands for the various types of assets. The natural rate of interest is determined in this market, together with the structure of asset holdings and prices.

The 'circular flows' connecting the various boxes and oblongs can be summarized briefly as follows. Current production decisions are based upon expectations regarding the revenues that proposed output will generate. On the assumption that these plans are accepted by commercial banks, money from short-term loans is used to buy raw materials and intermediate goods and to pay wages and salaries. Incomes are generated. Wage and salary receivers use some of their income to purchase consumption goods and save the rest.[10] The production period draws to a close, and the goods that have been produced are sold. Production loans are then repaid from the revenues generated from the sale of output, and the process begins anew.

The difference between the revenues which are received from the sale of output and the costs of production represents the quasi-rents from current production.[11] Interest and other fixed obligations have to be paid from these quasi-rents. Myros recovery charges are made against the quasi-rents as well. Whatever remains after all of these 'costs' have been deducted represents the net profit for the production period.[12] This net profit can be paid out to owners as dividends or it can be kept as retained earnings. Business saving for the period will consist of the sum of retained earnings and myros recovery charges. Total saving for the economy will consist of business saving plus net personal saving. The pool of fluid capital is increased or decreased depending upon whether the net addition of goods to the pool is positive or negative. Just as current production requires money to purchase inputs and to pay wages and salaries, the same is true for investment in new capacity to produce. In this case, the money required may be obtained directly from the capital market or alternatively it may

---

[10] It will be noted that consumption is connected to both Goods and Claims in the box labeled Fluid Capital. This reflects the fact that consumption annihilates claims as well as goods.

[11] It is important to emphasize that quasi-rents as defined in this book are gross of any capital charges. The costs which are subtracted from revenues to arrive at quasi-rents represent only the literal out-of-pocket expenditures that are incurred in production. In not including capital 'user costs' as part of production cost, I am of course departing from both Keynes (in the *General Theory*) and conventional usage. As discussed in Chapter 2, capital charges in this book represented accounting charges against quasi-rents, which transforms the fluid capital originally embedded in produced means of production back into fluid capital.

[12] Taxes obviously must also be paid out of the quasi-rents.

be obtained through short-term bank loans which are subsequently refinanced in the capital market.[13]

Since wage and salary earners (and also dividend receivers) receive payment in money, saving initially occurs in the form of money. Savers, both individuals and businesses, have then to decide how to hold their unexercised 'claim tickets' -- whether as money or as some other asset or combination of assets. Sorting all of this out is a primary function of the capital market. Specifically, what goes on in the capital market is equilibration of supply and demand on the claims side of the pool of fluid capital. The price which gets determined in this market is the natural rate of interest. Supply in the capital market is represented by the sum total of all unexercised claim tickets to the social dividend. Demand (i.e., the willingness-to-hold the claims), on the other hand, consists of the demand for these claims on the part of existing holders (i.e, reservation demand), those wishing to invest in new produced means of production, owners of productive capacity wanting to fund current production, and those wishing to consume in excess of their current income.

Supply and demand in the capital market is depicted graphically in Figure 2. Since, at any point in time, the pool of fluid capital is fixed, the supply curve is simply the vertical spike labeled S. The willingness-to-hold curve, in contrast, has the usual downward slope of a demand function, and is represented by the horizontal summation of the four demand categories just listed. D_R represents the reservation demands of existing claim holders who are holding their claims in the form of money. To D_R is then added investment demand D_I, demand for funding current production D_{CP}, and demand on the part of dissavers D_{DS} to obtain the total willingness-to-pay function D. The natural rate of interest is then determined at the point where D intersects with S.

Since all claims on the pool of fluid capital initially take the form of money and since the 'active' demanders for these claims are themselves demanding money, the capital market also, in fact, encompasses the money market.[14] Demanders can acquire the money that they want in either of two ways: (1) by taking out short-term loans from banks or (2) by borrowing existing money from its current owners. In the first case, new money is created, while in the second

---

[13] Cf. Keynes's 'finance' motive for holding money [Keynes (1937b)].

[14] 'Active' demanders refer to those desiring to invest in newly produced means of production, current producers, and those consuming in excess of their income. Reservation demanders, in contrast, represent 'passive' demanders.

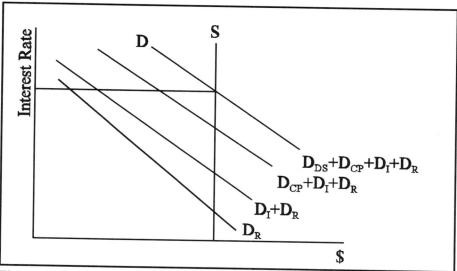

Figure 2

case money being held as an asset (whether by individuals or by financial intermediaries) is transformed into money to be used as a medium of exchange.[15]

CONSTRAINTS (OR 'CONSERVATION LAWS') IMPOSED BY THE POOL OF FLUID CAPITAL

As was noted in Chapter 1, neoclassical general equilibrium theory is plagued by an attempt to fuse two inconsistent theories of value, a classical substance theory for describing the creation of value in production and a vector field theory for describing a general equilibrium in exchange.[16] The result is a combining of two inconsistent conservation principles, one which conserves value in the transformation of inputs into outputs but which alters endowments, and a second which takes endowments as given and conserves the sum of utility

---

[15] In a purely bank-money economy, the holding of money as an asset would seem to create a problem in that it is obviously impossible for all of the loans which created the money in the first place to be repaid. What has to happen in this situation is that a part of the original loans -- specifically, the amount that is being held as an asset -- must be 'rolled over'. For banks to be willing to do this, there must be prospects of an increased stream of revenue (valued in current prices), foreseen by businesses and accepted as valid by banks. Otherwise, banks would not be willing to increase the total amount of loans. *Thus, it follows that, in a purely 'inside-money' economy, an asset demand for money can only be accommodated if the economy is expanding.* This conclusion will be discussed in more detail in Chapter 7.

[16] See Mirowski (1989, Chapters 5 and 6).

and expenditure through exchange. The purpose of the present section is to discuss the conservation principles which inhere in the concept of the pool of fluid capital. These principles, although much less comprehensive than the conservation principles postulated by neoclassical theory, are nevertheless free of inconsistencies.

We begin by making explicit two macroeconomic identities that are used throughout this book. The first of these is that income generated from current production is assumed to be equal to the value of output measured in current prices, while the second (which is actually a consequence of the first) is that saving (i.e., the difference between current income and current consumption) is equal to the value in current prices of that part of current output which is not consumed. The equality of income and the value of current production is a conventional identity in national income accounting and is therefore hardly novel. The equality of saving and the value in current prices of the unconsumed part of current production also corresponds to another well-known identity in macroeconomics, but in a nonstandard form. The identity in question is Keynes's identity (as opposed to his equilibrium equality) between saving and investment. As will be discussed later, however, investment as defined here is not the same as Keynes's definition of investment.

Money has been defined generically as a social invention which allows specific claims on goods to be transformed into general claims through the creation of universal purchasing power. Two points about this definition need emphasis. The first is that money is viewed as a *social invention*, while the second is that money, *qua* money, is defined in terms of *universal purchasing power*, i.e., as a *medium of exchange*. As has been noted, one of the problems with conventional Walrasian general equilibrium theory is that money does not play a useful role. Money can be introduced into the theory, but not in a way that mimics its contribution to economic activity in the real world.[17] This is not the case here, for money emerges naturally as a social invention which allows specific claims in the pool of fluid capital to be transformed into general claims. This occurs through the process of monetization. Effecting this monetization is the primary purpose of a well-functioning banking system.

The conservation principles which motivate this section can now be illustrated through the following propositions involving the pool of fluid capital:

---

[17] See Hahn (1975).

1. The real stock of money is bounded by the pool of fluid capital evaluated in current prices.

2. The pool of fluid capital evaluated in current prices also provides an upper bound to the aggregate value of an economy's assets.

That the pool of fluid capital evaluated in current prices imposes an upper bound on the real stock of money follows almost immediately from the fact that the pool of fluid capital evaluated in current prices imposes an upper bound on the real stock of purchasing power. If a stock of purchasing power is created that is greater than the goods represented in the pool of fluid capital evaluated in current prices, then the general price level must necessarily increase, thereby reducing the real value of the stock of purchasing power that had initially been created. If this stock of purchasing power consists entirely of money created (by whatever means) without reference to the value of the pool of fluid capital in current prices, the real value of this stock of money will be reduced as prices of the goods contained in the pool of fluid capital are bid up. Moreover, it should be evident that this will be true independently of whether the money stock in question consists of bank, commodity, or fiat money or some combination of the three.

That the pool of fluid capital evaluated in current prices also imposes an upper bound to the aggregate value of an economy's assets (or what can be called the aggregate 'wealth' of an economy) is a bit more subtle, for this conclusion follows from the claims side of the pool of fluid capital rather than from the goods side. As has been stated, the claims side of the pool of fluid capital represents the accumulation of unused claim tickets to the social dividend. These unused claim tickets do not manifest any specific property rights to the goods embodied in the pool of fluid capital, but represent instead unutilized income from both the present and past. As we have seen, these unused claims are initially denominated in money (since income is received in money), but will currently be represented in holdings of a variety of financial and real assets (including money held as a store of value).

The question which must be addressed is how do the values of these two classes of assets -- that is, financial and real -- combine to form the aggregate wealth of an economy. Are the two values additive or inclusive? Wealth for an individual can properly be viewed as the current flow of income plus the value of all real and financial assets (including such things as Old Masters and rare stamps and coins). Real and financial assets represent individual wealth because their value can be realized for money through sale. In a closed system, however, the value of real and financial assets cannot be converted to money in the aggregate because of an obvious fallacy of composition. Everyone would be trying to sell at the same time and there would be no buyers. Accordingly, wealth in the aggregate at any point in time is, in essence, measured simply by the pool of fluid capital evaluated in current prices.[18]

A simple example can show that the aggregate value of an economy's assets is inclusive of the values of real assets and financial assets rather than additive. Consider a firm which owns produced means of production and which, in turn, is owned by the holders of its equities. The produced means of production have value, and the equities have value, but the total value of the firm is not the sum of the value of the produced means of production owned by the firm and the value of equities in the firm, for the former will be included in the latter. The total value of an economy's assets, accordingly, must be approached in terms of the total value of the assets that are held by the owners of the unused claim tickets to current and past social dividends. It is evident that the value of these claims in the aggregate cannot be greater than the value in current prices of the stock of fluid capital, which in turn means that the aggregate value of an economy's assets cannot be greater than that amount.[19]

THE DETERMINATION OF ASSET VALUES

Let me now turn to asset values and the way that these are determined. Four types of assets will be considered: equities, bonds, 'Old Masters', and money. In order to keep the discussion manageable, both equities and bonds will be discussed with reference to firms. Firms are viewed as being the direct owners of capacity to produce. Equities represent ownership claims to produced means of production, and their yields or returns consist of residual quasi-rents. Their prices are determined through an interaction of supply and demand. The prices

---

[18] Whether money is a component of aggregate wealth will be dealt with in Chapter 7.

[19] That the total value of tangible wealth is constrained by the value (in current prices) of the stock of fluid capital has important implications for possible excess monetization of the stock of fluid capital. The usual type of commercial loan may be secured by claims to produced means of production, but the claims involved are really claims against current production. So long as the amount of purchasing power that is created does not exceed the current value of the stock of fluid capital, inflation cannot be a problem (except to the extent that expectations may be in error). However, if the value of tangible wealth is monetized as well as the current production that these assets produce, there is great danger that too much purchasing power will be created. The implications of this will be discussed in Chapter 7.

of bonds, on the other hand, represent the current valuations of the stream of payments in the bond contracts.[20]

It is obvious that a good (or an asset) for which there is a fixed quantity in existence must necessarily be held by someone. This means that, at any price, existing holders have to decide, at the price in question, whether they are willing to continue to hold or are willing to sell. The sum of the units that holders are willing to sell represents the 'supply', while the difference between the total quantity in existence and this sum represents *residual* (or *reservation*) demand. Total demand is given by the sum of residual demand and exogenous (or outside) demand. The market-clearing price is then determined at the point where total demand is equal to the fixed quantity in existence.

The details are presented in Figure 3. The fixed quantity of the good (or asset) in existence is given by the vertical spike at S. The 'supply' function from S is given by ss, while the residual demand function, dd, is equal to the horizontal difference between ss and S. The total demand function is given by DD, which represents the sum of residual demand and outside demand, as represented by the horizontal distance between dd and DD. The market-clearing price is accordingly p, for at this price every unit in S is in the hands of a willing holder.

We now turn to the valuation of assets such as Old Masters. For simplicity concerning the basic ideas, assume that, with one exception, all money in an economy is used for transactions only, that titles to the stock of fluid capital are owned by firms, and that the only asset (again with one exception) held as a store of value is equities which are owned by individuals. The one exception is an individual by the name of Rembrandt, who has built up a nest egg of savings that he holds in the form of money. Rembrandt has always been a house painter, but now decides he is going to take some time to create 'fine art' and do his painting on canvas. He finances this leisure activity from his holdings of money to purchase food and other essentials from the economy's pool of fluid capital.

---

[20] Valuation is always a forward-looking process. The current valuation of an asset bears no necessary relationship to the original cost of the asset, nor to the myros recovery charges that may already have been charged against past quasi-rents. The expectations that drive valuations can (and do) change, so that an equity that seemed attractively priced yesterday need not be so today. Also, the myros recovery charged against quasi-rents in general bear little (if any) connection to an asset's current prospects for generating quasi-rents. An asset can continue to generate quasi-rents long past the time that its original construction costs have been returned (via myros recovery charges) to the pool of fluid capital. The asset is still part of the economy's produced means of production, and has a value even though it may be carried on the books of the owning firm at zero.

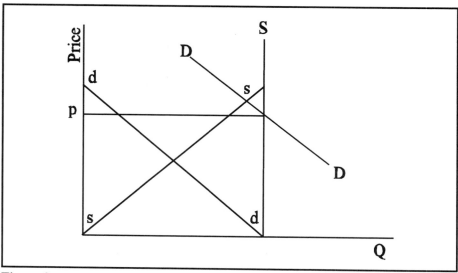

Figure 3

Like Georgia in the Prologue, Rembrandt's motivation at the start is simply to paint for his own enjoyment and to use his paintings to decorate his house. It is not long, however, before his friends and neighbors are badgering him to sell paintings to them for their own homes. Rembrandt finally agrees to sell a painting to a friend at a price that rather surprises him, since it is considerably in excess of what he could have earned had he spent the time it took him to paint the picture in painting houses instead. This gives Rembrandt the idea of turning his home into a studio and devoting all of his time to painting pictures for sale to others. Let it be said that Rembrandt was extremely successful in doing this, as his paintings were in great demand at ever increasing prices.

Enough of Rembrandt himself, what we want to do now is to inquire how the prices of Rembrandt's paintings are determined and how they are able to maintain a value. To begin with, it is clear that the prices for Rembrandt's paintings are arrived at through voluntary exchange between the buyers and Rembrandt. We need not spend much time on the supply price, for this will be determined by the greater of Rembrandt's reservation demand price for his own paintings and the opportunity cost of his time. It is the buyers' willingnesses-to-pay that are of most interest.

On our assumptions, the wealth of buyers consist of their current flow of income plus the value of the equities they own. If we assume that Rembrandt insists on payment in money, then a portion of the current stock of money will be diverted to Rembrandt in payment for his paintings. If the money comes out of current saving, then initially the paintings can be viewed as any other good in the economy. The same is true even if the purchase of the paintings were to be financed out of existing holdings of equities, although in this case it would be necessary to sell some equities to people with money in order to get the money insisted upon by Rembrandt. The immediate effect would therefore be downward pressure on the price of equities, and hence an increase in their yield.

Suppose, now, that Rembrandt dies so that the total number of his paintings in existence is fixed for all time. Because his paintings are objects of desire by many, they are frequently traded at prices which, in general, increase from one year to the next. This fact does not go unnoticed, and Rembrandt's paintings come to be seen as a vehicle for transferring purchasing power over time. In short, they join equities as a second form of asset in the economy. Old Masters provide no direct yield in terms of income (except for flows of consumption enjoyment), but they nevertheless (not necessarily and not in all cases) *can* provide a positive yield over time through price appreciation.

Why is this? What is the basis for Old Masters maintaining a value in the absence of a stream of income? Ultimately, the basis of value for a collectible (i.e., Old Masters viewed generally) is someone with a willingness-to-pay to own the object as an end in itself.[21] For individuals, their willingnesses-to-pay clearly depend upon their individual wealth. For an economy as a whole, however, the valuation of Old Masters depends upon the pool of fluid capital evaluated in current prices. Old Masters, once they become so, can in general increase in value over time only because the capacity of the economy to generate income increases as a result of saving and investment. There is no other reason. Old Masters do not have an intrinsic value that is independent of an economy's pool of fluid capital and its capacity to generate income.[22]

For valuations -- seen simply as calculated present values -- to be translated into actual prices, it is obviously necessary for those doing the valuations to have the wherewithal to translate desires into action. In other words, a willingness-to-pay, based upon calculations of present value, must imply an ability-to-pay in the event that the willingness-to-pay is at least as great as the price of the asset.

---

[21] In Chapter 12, we will analyze such objects as examples of position goods.

[22] Pigou, in his 1943 and 1947 papers on the classical stationary state, included Old Masters with fiat money as giving rise to a wealth (or real-balance) effect in the event of a continuously falling price level. For reasons already noted, there can be no real-balance effect for fiat money (including gold and silver), and neither can there be a real-balance effect for Old Masters. For, as we have just seen, the valuation of Old Masters, as with the valuation of all assets, depends upon the pool of fluid capital valued in current prices. As prices fall, so too will the value of the pool of fluid capital evaluated in current prices. Real-balance effects will be discussed in more detail in Chapter 7.

The ability-to-pay, for any individual, is obviously constrained by the individual's wealth. For an economy overall, however, the aggregate ability-to-pay is constrained by the pool of fluid capital evaluated in current prices.[23]

A modern economy obviously contains a large variety of assets of varying complexity. The principles which govern their valuations, however, are those which have been discussed. Consider, for example, the owner of vineyard who decides that she wants to sell the vineyard 15 years hence, but to own all produce from the property during the intervening 14 years. A contract is drawn up and then sold for a certain amount of money. The terms of the contract state that the contract can always be sold at the option of the current holder, whoever that might be. While this contract is clearly a 'forward' contract, its current value is determined in the same manner as any other current asset.[24]

AGGREGATE DEMAND AND SUPPLY

We now turn to aggregate supply and aggregate demand, which were introduced by Keynes in the *General Theory* and have been important concepts in macroeconomic theory ever since.[25] In the present framework, aggregate demand and aggregate supply are defined as follows:

Aggregate Demand
   Aggregate demand represents the total pool of purchasing power seeking to acquire goods.

Aggregate Supply
   Aggregate supply represents the current stock of goods, valued in current prices, that is available to be acquired.

---

[23] This is yet another way of seeing that the pool of fluid capital valued in current prices imposes an upper bound on the aggregate value of assets in an economy.

[24] The same principles apply to the valuation of all futures and forward contracts, options, warrants, swaps, etc.

[25] Keynes, it will be recalled, defined aggregate supply and aggregate demand in terms of aggregate employment and aggregate expenditure. Aggregate demand, for Keynes, represented the amount of expenditure that producers *expected* to receive from employing a particular amount of labor, while aggregate supply represented the amount of expenditure that producers *had* to receive in order for that amount of labor to in fact be employed. Equilibrium was then assumed to occur at the point where aggregate demand and aggregate supply are equal. In contrast with Keynes, aggregate demand and supply in current-day macroeconomics is usually defined in terms of the level of aggregate real output and the general price level. The general price level did not figure in Keynes's definitions because of his assumption that the price level was unaffected by output changes at less than full employment.

Aggregate demand thus consists of a pool of purchasing power. No price level is implied, except that which is implicit in the price expectations that underlie the short-term loans funding current production. With aggregate supply, however, a price level is explicit. Indeed, as will be discussed in Chapter 6, aggregate supply can be interpreted as implicitly *defining* the current price level.

The pool of current purchasing power represents money that has been created by the banking system in response to demands of owners of produced means of production, and those intending to invest in new capacity. It also includes the money earmarked for consumption out of the current flow of income. Let v denote the period of production, which will be assumed, for simplicity, to be the same for every producer. Loans are then made for the purpose of financing the production of goods which will become available v time periods from the time that the loan is made. Assume also, for simplicity, that inputs (including labor) are purchased continuously.

The goods that are currently available were 'contracted for', and their finance created, v time periods in the past. If income that is not saved is spent on consumption goods instantaneously with its receipt, this means that the pool of purchasing power currently confronting goods will include contributions from all vintages of money creation from v time periods in the past to the present. Under the assumptions that have been made, this pool can be approximated by the amount of money in existence (ignoring money held as an asset) at v/2 time periods in the past.

On the average, accordingly, the expectations that drive the current availability of goods were formed v time periods in the past, whereas the expectations that create the current pool of purchasing power were formed only v/2 time periods in the past. In other words, the expectations that determine aggregate demand are formed v/2 time periods later than the expectations that determine aggregate supply. In view of this, it follows that aggregate demand and aggregate supply at time t can differ for two separate (although not necessarily unrelated) reasons:

1. Faulty forecasts of aggregate demand, v time periods in the future, on the part of producers (and their bankers);

2. Changes in expectations concerning aggregate demand (for v time periods in the future) between v time periods in the past and v/2 time periods in the past.

With regard to 2, a potentially inflationary scenario would be one in which expectations concerning aggregate demand are increasingly optimistic, while a deflationary scenario would be one in which expectations concerning aggregate demand are increasingly pessimistic. If all goods should be bought and sold in spot markets which continuously clear, then the general price level would rise and fall continuously as aggregate demand exceeds or falls short of aggregate supply. Since most markets do not clear continuously, however, aggregate excess demand/excess supply will be accommodated, in substantial part, through changes in inventories or changes in unfilled orders. Prices for these goods will change only when excess demand or excess supply persists.

Detailed discussion of the general price level and inflation will be deferred until Chapter 6.

MACROECONOMIC EQUILIBRIUM

In traditional fashion, it is natural to define a steady-state equilibrium of an economy in terms of equilibrium of aggregate demand and aggregate supply. As will be discussed in detail in later chapters, this concept of equilibrium encompasses the following conditions:

1. Realization of the expectations that drive aggregate supply;

2. Equilibrium in the market for the pool of fluid capital, in which the demand for fluid capital is equal to the supply;

3. A stable general price level.[26]

While this definition of macroeconomic equilibrium is outwardly the same as that of Keynes in the *General Theory*, there are some important differences. Keynes repeatedly made the point that a dollar of investment, operating through the consumption function and the multiplier process, would eventually give rise to a dollar of new saving. For Keynes, the economy is not only in equilibrium when aggregate demand and aggregate supply (on his definitions) are equal, but equivalently (ignoring other leakages and injections) when saving and investment are equal. However, in the present framework, equilibrium does not require that current saving and current investment be equal. In the *Treatise on Money*,

---

[26] It will be shown in Chapter 7 that equilibrium of aggregate demand and aggregate supply and stability of the general price level are equivalent conditions.

Keynes allowed for saving and investment to differ, but this was in disequilibrium. In the present framework, saving and investment can be unequal in equilibrium as well.

An equivalent way of defining macroeconomic equilibrium in the present framework is in terms of the equality of inflows into the pool of fluid capital with outflows. Inflows are represented by the sum of net saving (both personal and business) and myros recovery charges against revenues, while outflows are represented by investment in newly produced means of production and the 'finance' of current production. Conventional analysis focuses on just saving and investment, and thus ignores the inflows into the pool of fluid capital from myros recovery charges and the outflows from the financing of current production. When inflows into the pool of fluid capital equal outflows, there is clearly no necessity for saving and investment to be equal.

The implications of saving being different from investment in steady-state equilibrium will be discussed in Chapter 8.

CHAPTER 4

INTEREST AND MONEY

One of the biggest controversies sparked by the *General Theory* concerned the determination of the rate of interest. Until the *General Theory*, the generally accepted view was that the rate of interest was determined in the capital market, defined in terms of the demand and supply of savings. The demand for savings was represented by the investment demand function, which depicted a negative relationship between investment and the rate of interest, while the supply of savings was represented by the savings function, which described a positive relationship between the interest rate and the amount saved out of income. The market was assumed to clear at the point where supply equals demand, thereby establishing investment, saving, and the market rate of interest.

Keynes objected to this, for he saw the equality of saving and investment being determined by the Principle of Effective Demand. Hence, the rate of interest had to be determined in some other way. This other way for Keynes was by Liquidity Preference.[1] Rather than viewing interest as a reward for not consuming (which is the view that Keynes attributed to the Classical economists), Keynes saw interest as the payment for giving up liquidity (i.e., the giving up of claims to money). For Keynes, accordingly, the interest rate was determined by the demand and supply of money, rather than by the demand and supply of saving.

Following publication of the *General Theory*, the two theories of interest became known as Liquidity Preference and Loanable Funds theories and a heated debate was ignited, with Keynes on one side and Ohlin and Robertson, among others, on the other side.[2] The rate of interest in the Loanable Funds theory was determined at the point where the supply of loanable funds, as given by the sum

---

[1] Keynes (1936, Chapter 13).

[2] See Keynes (1937b, 1937c), Ohlin (1937), and Robertson (1937).

of current saving, dishoarding, and the creation of new money, is equal to the demand, as given by the investment demand for funds.

In my view, there is truth in both theories, not because they are equivalent (as has been argued by some neoclassical theorists),[3] but because conceptually (as discussed in Chapter 3) there are two relevant rates of interest, a *natural* rate and a *money* rate. The Classical economists were correct in saying that the interest rate is determined in the capital market, but the capital market in question should refer to the entire pool of fluid capital, rather than just the inward and outward flows resulting from saving and investment. The natural-rate of interest emerges from the interplay of demand and supply in this market. On the other hand, Keynes was correct in stressing liquidity preference as a primary determinant of the money-rate of interest.

FACTORS MAKING FOR THE EXISTENCE OF INTEREST

Before going into the details of how interest rates are determined, it will be useful to discuss the factors responsible for the existence of interest in the first place.[4] To begin with, it is clear that capital cannot exist in the absence of saving. At some point, these has to be a decision on the part of someone not to consume all of the product that is available. This can be seen as the first act of saving and the creation of the first stock of fluid capital.[5] This stock could be carried over for consumption at a later time or alternatively it could be used to fund the creation of a more productive method of production. If a decision is made to create a more productive method of production, this can be seen as the first decision to invest, the first creation of produced means of production, and (assuming that the new method of production lasts for more than one production period) the creation of the first stock of fixed (or sunk) capital. In such circumstances, it is not unreasonable that the decision to invest is made by the same person as made the decision to save, in which case the saving and investment decisions are one and the same (as per Smith, Ricardo, etc.).

The pool of fluid capital grows through the flow of new saving and the return of 'old' fluid capital through myros recovery charges against current

---

[3] See Hicks (1946, Chapter 12).

[4] There is nothing new in this discussion, for all of the points have been discussed by Fisher and others.

[5] Cf. the young man's decision to build up a stock of 10 days of bread in order to build a house in the Prologue.

production. The increase in the size of this pool represents, in most basic terms, economic growth. What are the incentives for this pool to grow -- i.e., for capital to accumulate? The driving force is the fact that capital (in the form of produced means of production) is productive, in the sense that a given amount of labor working in cooperation with produced means of production and permanent resources will produce a greater output than the same amount of labor working with just the permanent resources. Or as Keynes put it, capital (again in the sense of produced means of production) generates a positive yield over its lifetime.[6]

Investment in produced means of production, however, requires waiting. *Always*, there is an initial period of waiting because produced means of production require time to construct before they can begin to produce.[7] An additional amount of waiting *may* be required because the period of production for any single unit of output may be increased. Since people in general prefer present goods to future goods, those with claims to present goods must be offered a reward if they are to give up these claims in exchange for claims in the future. This would be the case even in the absence of uncertainty. The existence of positive yields from use of produced means of production is what allows this reward to be paid.

Investment in produced means of production, however, is just one of the demands on the pool of fluid capital. There are two other demands: a demand for consumption in excess of current income (i.e., negative saving) and a demand for financing operation of the current capacity to produce (usually referred to as the demand for working capital). In most economies, the demand for working capital represents the largest demand on the pool of fluid capital, and monetizing fluid capital in response to this demand is one of the primary functions of commercial banks.

Time preference means that, *ceteris paribus*, present goods are preferred to future goods. However, since time preference is not constant across individuals, those with lower time preference can be induced to exchange their claims to present goods with those with higher time preference for claims to future goods through payment of suitable rewards.[8] The effect of such exchanges of current for future goods on the pool of fluid capital is either to reduce it (if the present

---

[6] See Keynes (1936, pp. 135-37).

[7] Cf. Cassell (1903).

[8] See Fisher (1930).

goods would otherwise have been saved) or to leave it unchanged (if the present goods would otherwise have been consumed). In either case, it is clear that a desire to exchange future consumption for present consumption represents a demand on the pool of fluid capital.

When there is a pool of fluid capital already in existence because of past saving, there is obviously no necessary connection between current investment and current saving. This point was made forcefully by Keynes in one of his 1937 *Economic Journal* papers defending the *General Theory*, when he states (paraphrased) that investment can be thwarted by a lack of finance, but never by a lack of saving.[9] Keynes's point was that, provided the banking system creates the finance for withdrawing goods from the pool of fluid capital, investment can proceed in the absence of (current) saving.

DETERMINATION OF MONEY AND NATURAL RATES OF INTEREST

Let us now turn to the determination of the natural and money-rates of interest. Consider, to begin with, Figure 4, which is similar to Figure 2 in Chapter 2, and depicts the market for fluid capital. The vertical line labeled K represents the existing stock of fluid capital, including the inflow from myros recovery charges. The curve labeled s represents the inflow from current saving. D_g represents the demand for fluid capital for financing goods-in-progress. The horizontal distance between D_g and D_g+D_c represents the exchange of future consumption goods for present consumption goods, while the horizontal difference between D_g+D_c and $D_g+D_c+D_I$ represents the demand for fluid capital to finance investment in new produced means of production. The curve labeled $D_g+D_c+D_I$ thus represents the aggregate demand for fluid capital. In the absence of current saving, the market-clearing rate of interest would be r^*. However, with saving (as represented by the curve labeled s) in the picture, the market-clearing rate of interest will be r.

In my view, it is compelling to call r determined in this fashion the *natural-rate of interest*, for it represents the price that equates the demand for fluid capital with supply.[10] As the figure is drawn, current saving is seen to add

---

[9] Keynes (1937b).

[10] Readers are reminded once again that this concept of the natural-rate of interest differs from the usual definition of the natural rate, which (per Wicksell) is the rate which equates investment and saving.

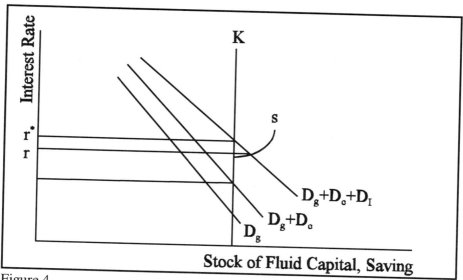

Figure 4

significantly to the stock of fluid capital. For wealthy economies like the U.S., current saving is small relative to K, so that the market-clearing r will be much closer to r^*.

Let us now bring money into the picture. In real life, the goods represented in the stock of fluid capital are not exchanged directly between holders and demanders, but are transferred through the intermediary of money. The value represented by the stock of fluid capital is first monetized, loans are made, and the general purchasing power created is used to purchase the needed amounts from the unconsumed consumables and capital goods that constitute K. Loans are not denominated in units of fluid capital, but in money, and interest accordingly is also reckoned in money.

In approaching the question of how the money-rate of interest fits into the picture, it will be useful to delve into what has always been considered one of the more opaque parts of the *General Theory*, namely, Keynes's discussion of own-rates of interest. Keynes begins his discussion of interest in Chapter 17 by reminding readers that the money-rate of interest ". . . is nothing more than the percentage excess of a sum of money contracted for forward delivery, e.g. a year hence, over what we may call the 'spot' or cash price of the sum thus contracted for forward delivery." [Keynes (1936, p. 222).] Keynes then goes on to say that, for every capital asset, there would appear to be an analogue to the rate of interest on money -- a 'wheat' rate of interest, a 'house' rate of interest, etc. For the 'wheat' rate of interest, there is a definite quantity of wheat to be delivered one year hence which has the same exchange value today as 100 quarters of wheat for 'spot' delivery. If the former quantity is 105 quarters of wheat, the 'wheat' rate of interest can then be said to be 5% per annum. For every durable commodity, there can be said to be a similarly calculated rate of interest calculated in terms of itself. Keynes call these rates of interest, *own-rates*.[11]

Keynes noted that each capital asset, viewed as an instrument (or vehicle) for transferring purchasing power from the present to the future, possesses three different attributes in differing degrees as follows:[12]

1. Some assets produce a yield or net output, which he denoted by q;

2. Most assets, except money, suffer some wastage or involve some carrying cost through the mere passage of time, irrespective of their being used to produce a yield. Keynes denoted this wastage, or cost, by c, and noted that the line between q and c is hard to draw, but that all that matters is the difference between the two, $q - c$;

3. Finally, there is a third factor, which Keynes called the *liquidity premium*, which reflects the potential convenience for security that some assets possess in the power to dispose of them. Keynes denoted this liquidity premium by l.

The total return of an asset, then, will be given by the sum of these three factors, $q - c + l$.

Capital assets possess these three factors in differing degrees. Money has no yield (i.e., $q = 0$), negligible carry cost (i.e., $c \approx 0$), but substantial liquidity premium because money as an asset can be converted into money as medium of exchange instantaneously and without cost. Produced means of production have both yields and carrying costs, but in general little liquidity. An Old Master, on the other hand, has no direct yield (except for psychic enjoyment), often substantial carrying cost (insurance, etc.), and little liquidity. Keynes notes that investment in physical capital assets eventually leads to a reduction in their yields, so that $q - c$ becomes negative. Since the liquidity premium for money dominates the liquidity premium for any other asset, the liquidity premium for

---

[11] Keynes (1936, pp. 223-24).

[12] See Keynes (1936, pp. 225-28).

money establishes a positive floor to the return on assets. This is the reason Keynes gives as to why the money-rate of interest "rules the roost" over all other own-rates of interest, and accordingly establishes its critical importance in determining the general level of economic activity.[13]

As we have seen, for money to exist in any meaningful sense, it is necessary that an economy possess a stock of fluid capital, which means that there has to have been prior saving. There does not have to be a stock of produced means of production for money to exist, but there does have to be a stock of unconsumed consumables. Money, in the circumstances, can be either commodity money or 'trust' money or both. The former can exist because the commodity is widely desired as an end in itself, while the latter can exist as a 'receipt' for goods in the pool of fluid capital.[14] A banking system (broadly construed) greatly facilitates the monetization of the stock of fluid capital. Although the presence of a banking system is not necessary for money to be created, it can be done much more efficiently with one than without. As an economy develops and becomes more and more monetized, the banking system comes to play a larger and larger role in the functioning of the economy. Indeed, a sophisticated financial system itself is an integral part of an economy's produced means of production.

As an economy develops, finance comes to play an increasingly important role in determining the level and pace of economic activity. While the pool of fluid capital (measured at current prices) *always* sets an upper bound on the real stock of money, a wealthy economy has large stocks of both fluid capital and money and other financial assets. As a consequence, the connection between the two stocks becomes vague and ill-defined. Similarly -- and more importantly -- the connection between the money-rate of interest and the natural-rate of interest also becomes ill-defined, and the money-rate of interest achieves immense importance.

The money-rate of interest achieves this importance because, in a monetary economy, goods are purchased and incomes are paid in money. An operator of produced means of production needing goods as inputs does not borrow these goods 'on the come' directly (except through trade credit), but borrows money and purchases the goods with money. Similarly, wages are paid not in goods, but

---

[13] From the foregoing, it should be clear that the money-rate of interest and the natural-rate of interest (as defined here) bear no necessary relationship. Whether the two rates will be equal in equilibrium will be discussed in Chapter 6.

[14] Cf. von Mises's view that any form of money originates as commodity money. See v. Mises (1934, p. 132). For other views as to how money emerges from a barter economy, see Clower (1967) and Kiyotaki and Wright (1989, 1991).

in money, which also has to be borrowed (even if the operator borrows from himself). And even if goods used as inputs are acquired on trade credit, payment is eventually in money, not finished goods. The availability of money, and the price at which it can be obtained, is thus of enormous importance.

At this point, it would seem that the money-rate of interest is a payment for obtaining money, rather than (per Keynes) a payment for giving it up. Keynes, it will be remembered, identified three motives for holding money: transactions, precautionary, and speculative (which he associated with liquidity preference). The demand for money that has been discussed in the preceding paragraph is for transactions. Keynes took the amount of money needed for transactions purposes as being determined by the level of economic activity. Specifically, in the *General Theory*, Keynes assumed the amount of money in existence as exogenous, determined by the monetary authority. The transactions motive has first claim on this stock, and what remains is then available to satisfy the precautionary and speculative motives. Keynes saw the precautionary demand as also being determined by the level of income, so that the residual that remains is what is available to satisfy the speculative (or what I prefer to call the liquidity motive). Since this residual has to be held by someone, Keynes accordingly saw the money-rate of interest as representing the price at which this stock of money was in the hands of willing holders. Since, in Keynes's world, the alternative to holding money was bonds (specifically, consols), the price in question was the interest rate on bonds.[15]

In the *General Theory*, Keynes adopted the view that the monetary authority could control the supply of money, so that the stock of money was taken as given. Also, he assumed that the only alternative to holding money as an asset is bonds. Real assets could also be held, but their yield, for reasons noted earlier, would be no greater in equilibrium than the liquidity premium on money. Thus, for Keynes, the important tradeoff in determining the market rate of interest was the money-rate of return on bonds in relation to the liquidity premium for money.

Keynes's assumption that liquidity preference derives from expectations concerning future movements in the rate of interest has received a great deal of criticism. Tobin in his classic 1958 paper reformulated liquidity preference in

---

[15] In one of his 1937 *Economic Journal* articles [Keynes (1937b)], Keynes added a fourth motive for holding money, the 'finance' motive, which he defined as a holding of money that is built up by businesses in anticipation of financing new investment. In my view, Keynes's discussion of the finance motive is especially insightful, because it deals directly with monetization of the stock of fluid capital (although just for the purpose of financing investment in produced means of production). Except for the Post-Keynesians [See, especially, Davidson (1978)], however, the finance motive has never received much attention. Meltzer (1988), for example, dismisses it as of no importance and avers that Keynes did not accord it much relevance either.

terms of behavior towards risk. Shackle, in *The High Years of Theory,* gives yet another alternative interpretation of liquidity preference which does not involve a 'bootstrap' basis for the interest rate: namely, that a loan of money involves the giving-up of something certain in terms of liquidity in return for something inherently uncertain (repayment at a future date). Interest is the payment for giving up this certainty.[16]

In my view, the assumption that the money supply is exogenous is untenable. The money stock is created through monetization of the stock of fluid capital. Obviously, monetary authorities have influence -- perhaps even a great deal of influence -- through the standard instruments of monetary policy (including moral suasion), but there is much that those desiring claims to money can do to circumvent a particular thrust of monetary policy. For goods can be purchased on IOUs (i.e., through trade credit), banks can create reserves through inducing depositors to shift their deposits from a category with a high reserve requirement to a category with a lower reserve requirement, etc.

The time when liquidity preference would appear to be most operative is when a bank is trying to shift funds into an interest-bearing account. For it is at this point that a holder of money (which for now is assumed not to pay interest) must decide to give up a claim to money for an interest-paying asset which has less liquidity. Inducing holders of money to acquire interest-bearing deposits is one of two ways that the banking system as a whole can, by its own efforts, increase its capacity to lend and therefore to increase the stock of money.[17]

The upshot of all this is that there is little question but that liquidity preference is a factor in determining the money-rate of interest. Whether it is the *only* factor, however, is another matter. For this to be the case, it would be necessary that every point where the interest rate is a factor in balancing the demand for money with its availability be ultimately attributable to liquidity preference. This especially has to be the case at those points where money is actually created, by which I mean the points at which the pool of fluid capital is monetized. The standard way this is done is through business borrowing at commercial banks.[18]

[16] See Shackle (1967, Chapter15). I find this an attractive interpretation of liquidity preference, although this is not to deny that the speculative motive can at times be a strong factor.

[17] The other way, obviously, is for banks to borrow from the central bank.

[18] Historically, money creation through business borrowing embodies what came to be known as the Banking School of Monetary Control (or equivalently as the Real Bills Doctrine). The premise of this school is simple and attractive. Banks are to make loans only for the purpose of financing

The stock of money created by business borrowing is constantly being extinguished and renewed, and its size expands and contracts in response to the production needs of the economy. In the *Economic Journal* article referred to earlier, Keynes (1937b) clearly describes this revolving fund of finance, but his reference was to what he called a fourth motive for holding money, namely, the 'finance' motive. As noted in footnote 15, however, Keynes's focus in the finance motive was not the finance of production of consumption goods, but a build-up of finance for current investment.

If the venerable Banking School's terms of reference are broadened to include Keynes's finance motive, then in my view the Banking School's philosophy (i.e., the Real Bills Doctrine) provides a sound guide to monetary control. Even so, I believe that its ultimate focus on the value of current production is incorrect. Clearly, current production is what has to be financed, but the source for this finance is not the goods being financed, but the pool of fluid capital. The pool of fluid capital being monetized is what enables the unconsumed consumables and intermediate goods that comprise the goods side of the pool to be drawn into current production. Most of the time, money creation on the basis of pending output will not cause any problems (in terms of inflation) because the pool of fluid capital will be sufficient to provision at current prices the current plans to produce. It is clear, however, that too much money can on occasion be created by this process as a result of businesses having too rosy expectations concerning the amount of output that can be sold -- and bankers going along with these expectations -- so that more money is created than there are goods available, at current prices, in the pool of fluid capital.[19] The result will be inflation.[20]

So much for the moment for money as a medium of exchange. What about money as a store of value? A point repeatedly emphasized by Keynes in the *General Theory* is that a decision to save is a decision to postpone consumption from today until some time in the future. In a monetary production economy,

---

current production, with the loans to be paid off by the proceeds from sale of the output, which is to say that the loans are self-liquidating. By restricting money creation to this form, the amount of money is carefully controlled -- in essence, the value of current production providing an upper bound on the amount to be created -- and risk (provided the bankers are adept at their jobs) is minimized (although obviously not eliminated altogether). For a discussion of the origins of the Banking School and the controversies which surrounded it, see Schwartz (1987).

[19] Cf. the discussion by Keynes of borrower's and lender's risk in Chapter 11 (p. 144) of the *General Theory*. See also Minsky (1975).

[20] The foregoing illustrates in yet another way the fact that the real value of the stock of money (viewed in terms of means of exchange) is bounded by the pool of fluid capital valued at current prices.

since income is paid in money, a decision to save is initially a decision to hold money as a store of value. Yet, money is only one of many assets that can be used to transfer purchasing power from the present until some time in the future. Accordingly, once there has been a decision to save, there is a further decision as to what vehicle to use in pursuing the desired transfer of purchasing power. Keynes's point in the *General Theory* was that, *ceteris paribus*, people would prefer to hold money because of money's perfect liquidity. For people to give up this certainty, payment of interest is necessary.[21]

Let me now turn to what might seem an unusual question: In an 'inside-money' world, can money be held as a store of value?[22] What I have in mind with this question is the following. Assume for the moment that all money is bank money created by loans for the purpose of financing current production (both consumption goods and investment). This means, accordingly, that all money is dated, in the sense that the loans that created the money have specific dates of repayment. Assume, now, that some individuals decide to save a part of their income (which is paid to them in money), and in doing so decide to hold the saving in the form of money. If the loans that created the money, have to be repaid, where is the money to come from that is to extinguish the loans (since a part of it is now being held by savers as an asset)? The answer is that a portion of the original loans -- specifically the portion which corresponds to the money being held as an asset -- has to be rolled over, so that the money being held as an asset is not extinguished. Clearly, for banks to be willing to do this, there has to be the prospect of an increased stream of revenue (valued in current prices), foreseen by businesses and accepted as valid by banks. Otherwise, banks would not be willing to increase the total quantity of loans.

In a fractional reserve banking system, the additional loans that are needed to fund the stock of money being held as an asset require new reserves. These new reserves can be provided by the central bank or, alternatively, they can be acquired by inducing individuals holding money as an asset to give up some of their liquidity. In the absence of reserves provided directly by the central bank, it would thus seem that Keynes's liquidity preference is indeed the margin at which the money-rate of interest is determined, even in a world in which there are many other forms and types of assets. This is because the liquidity premium for

[21] Keynes saw bonds as the only alternative asset to money, but this is obviously not the case. An individual's portfolio decision is not just between money and bonds, but between money and a wide range of assets, both financial and real. Economists who have modeled this portfolio decision in a general equilibrium framework include, among others, Tobin (1969) and Friedman (1974).

[22] The standard reference on the distinction between 'inside' and 'outside' money is Gurley and Shaw (1965).

money provides a floor to the asset-rate of return.[23]

On the other hand, suppose that the additional reserves needed to sustain an asset demand for money are provided by the central bank. How is the money-rate of interest determined in this situation and what role, if any, does liquidity preference play? The easiest case to deal with is a change in the reserve ratio. If the reserve ratio is reduced, reserves are released, and banks can make additional loans at the existing money-rate of interest. Reserves for loans do not have to be attracted from existing holders of money as an asset by paying a higher liquidity premium.

What about open-market operations? To analyze these, it will be assumed that the central bank deals only in government debt. This is not a necessary assumption, but it is obviously realistic and can be viewed as abstracting from all risk and uncertainty relating to default. If the central bank wishes to increase the reserves of the banking system, it can do so by purchasing government bonds in the open market. Ultimately, this increases deposits of banks at the central bank, and therefore reserves, thereby laying the basis for additional loans and hence the creation of money. The purchase of bonds in the open market leads to an increase in their price, and hence to a decrease in their yield. The increase in reserves means that additional loans can be made with no upward pressure on the money-rate of interest, because those already holding money as an asset do not have to be bribed by higher payments in order to give up liquidity. While the purchase of bonds will reduce the bond-yield, the yield cannot fall below the pure liquidity premium of the marginal holder of money-as-an-asset. Liquidity preference in this case is active only to the extent that it provides a floor for how far the money-rate of interest can fall.

Finally, there remains borrowing by banks from the central bank. A decision by a bank to borrow from the central bank reflects a conclusion that this is the most economical way to acquire reserves. Use of the rediscount window would thus seem to be the only circumstance in which the central banks can fuel a creation of money at a money-rate of interest that is lower than the pure liquidity premium of money. This would be the case if the rediscount rate were so low that banks could lend at a rate that is below that the banks would have to pay in order to overcome the marginal liquidity preference.

To summarize this discussion on the determination of the natural and money-rates of interest:

---

[23] Consequently, for the point that he was wishing to make, Keynes would seem to have been not only justified, but logically correct, in assuming bonds to be the only alternative asset to money.

1. The natural-rate of interest is seen as representing the price which clears the market for the pool of fluid capital. This is determined by the interaction of the demand for fluid capital (comprised of the demands for investment in produced means of production, finance of current production, and consumption in excess of income), and the supply of fluid capital (comprised of the stock of fluid capital plus the inflow from saving).

2. The money-rate of interest is the own-rate of interest on money, which because of the pure liquidity premium on money (in conjunction with the other characteristics of money) sets a lower bound to all other asset rates of interest.

3. In an 'inside-money' world, money is created through bank loans negotiated for the purpose of financing current production of consumption goods and investment in produced means of production. The interest rate on these loans can be viewed as *the* money-rate of interest. The level of this rate is determined ultimately by the price that banks must pay to holders of money-as-an-asset in order to free up the reserves needed to finance (in a growing economy) an ever expanding pool of loans. This price is determined by marginal liquidity preference. The *money-rate of interest* is thus seen as the price of creating new means of payment (in an inside-money world), but its level in turn is seen as depending upon the pure liquidity premium of money held as an asset.

4. All other returns on assets (viewed as vehicles for transferring purchasing power from the present to some time in the future), both financial and real, are related through portfolio adjustment to the money-rate of interest -- and ultimately to liquidity preference.

A WORLD WITH FIAT MONEY

The discussion to this point has assumed an inside-money world. We now turn to a world in which there is government (or fiat) money as well. The government can create fiat money directly by running the printing press or indirectly by selling bonds to the central bank. Money created in this way is in general perfectly substitutable with bank money, but unlike bank money, it is not dated at the time of creation. Among other things, this means that increases in the demand for money to hold as an asset, which may arise out of current saving, can be accommodated by an accumulation of fiat money without putting any upward pressure on the money-rate of interest.

On the negative side, however, the power of the government to create money directly also means that, unlike for bank-created money, there is a form of money creation that can avoid the discipline imposed by the pool of fluid capital. Since businesses form their plans for production on the basis of current and expected flows of income, a well-functioning banking system will in general not over-monetize the pool of fluid capital. But this is not the case for government, for the government can create money without regard to the pool of fluid capital. If too much money is created, the obvious result will be inflation.

Specifically, let us consider the case in which the creation of fiat money causes expectations of inflation by those holding money as an asset. In this situation, the carrying cost of holding money increases from what is negligible in ordinary circumstances to an amount that is at least as large as the expected inflation. Money, in this situation, will still have a pure liquidity premium, but the overall yield on money is reduced by the expected inflation. What now will happen to the money-rate of interest?

In this situation, it would seem that the own-rate of interest on money would cease to "rule the roost", for the overall return on money will no longer be held up at the pure liquidity premium, but will fall below the liquidity premium because of the now (inflation-induced) positive carrying cost. Indeed, the overall return on money can now be negative. However, because the expected inflation can be factored into the prospective yield on real assets, the return on real assets can continue to be positive. The asset whose own-rate of interest is expected to be highest will become the standard bearer in this situation, and the money-rate of interest will become equal to this own-rate of interest plus the expected inflation.

In an inflationary environment, however, the standard bearer in general will vary from one time period to another. First, one real asset will be the preferred store of value, then another, and so on and so forth. The upshot is that inflation, among other things, robs a monetary economy of a basic certainty and stability by eliminating money as a store of value. Nevertheless, money continues to function as a medium of exchange, and indeed is needed in ever larger quantities. Creation of these ever larger quantities requires an inflation premium to be added to the money-rate of interest in order to keep banks whole in terms of the price level that is expected to prevail at the time that loans are repaid. Since inflation is also factored into the expectations of businesses, the borrowers will in fact be willing to pay the inflation premium.[24] In this way, the money stock, now functioning only as a medium of exchange, always adjusts to a real value that is determined by the stock of fluid capital.[25]

THE CONCEPT OF VELOCITY AND THE DEMAND FOR MONEY

The standard approach to the demand for money is in terms of the demand for real balances -- i.e., the demand for a real stock of money. The usual point of departure is Marshall's cash-balances equation,

(1) $M = ky$,

where M is the stock of transactions balances, y is current income, and k is the reciprocal of velocity.

The usual interpretation of velocity is that it is primarily an institutional datum, determined for the most part by the payment habits of the economy. There is obvious truth in this, especially as regards the average transactions balances that are held by households and businesses related to the payment of wages and salaries. Velocity, however, is both more and less than this; more in that one of its main determinants is not focused on, and less in that (in reciprocal form) it is more a consequence of the demand for money than a determinant. The purpose of this section is to elaborate upon these statements.

As was noted earlier, most discussions treat money as something that is apart from production and the generation of income. In general, the stock of money at any point in time consists of two components, fiat money in the hands of the public and bank money (which we can take to consist of all deposits subject to transfer by check).[26] The amount of fiat money in the hands of the public can indeed be treated as a quantity that exists independently of the current level of economic activity, by which I mean that it has not come into being

---

[24] Cf. Fisher's distinction between the nominal and real rates of interest, in which the nominal rate differs from the real rate by the expected rate of inflation.

[25] The foregoing suggests that the monetarist view that inflation always *follows* the creation of money is not true as a general proposition. Certainly, the monetarist conclusion is valid with respect to the creation of fiat money, but not with respect to the creation of bank money. For with bank money, the money is created in anticipation of inflation, so that it is *expected inflation* which determines how much money will be created. Bank money, once created, can (and usually will) ratify the inflation, but its creation is not the initial cause of the inflation.

[26] Travelers checks and unutilized credit card lines will be ignored.

because of current economic activity. Fiat money, at the time that it comes into existence, is not dated for extinguishing. This is not the case for bank money, however. Bank money *is* dated for extinguishing, in the sense that the loans that create it become due and are expected to be paid off. The amount of bank money in existence at any point in time does not exist independently of the of the level of economic activity, but is part and parcel of the process that determines the level of economic activity; the desire and willingness to produce is what gives rise to the amount of bank money in existence in the first place. The bank money component of the money stock is thus not a stock that is constantly turned over; rather, its quantity is constantly being created and destroyed.

Fiat money in the hands of the public largely serves retail trade, and the same dollar can pass through several hands even in the course of a day. It accordingly makes sense to speak of velocity with respect to fiat money. Velocity with respect to bank money, however, seems to me to be a highly artificial concept. In most cases, the length of a commercial loan will be related to the period of production for the recipient of the loan. Production loans in agriculture, for example, are usually of longer duration than loans in retail and wholesale trades. Relating velocity to just the payment habits of the economy would therefore seem to overlook the contribution of the average period of production, as measured by the average length of a commercial loan. *Ceteris paribus*, more bank money will be created for a longer period of production than for a shorter period of production, which means that velocity will appear to be larger, the shorter the period of production.[27]

Businesses and households are usually depicted as demanding certain stocks of money, and either the monetary authority accommodates these demands or else interest rates adjust to equate the demands with available supply. Businesses demand money because they have to finance current production and investment. Households, on the other hand, demand money because they need to finance current consumption and financial transactions, and also because they want to hold money as an asset. There is an important difference, however, in the way that money is obtained by businesses and in the way that it is obtained by households. Businesses acquire money initially as loans and then again through sales receipts, out of which the loans are repaid. Most of the money acquired by

---

[27] As I review this (in the summer of 1999), 'e-business' on the Internet has emerged as a major force in the way that firms do business with one another. Not only does the Internet allow firms to connect directly with customers, but it also allows them to connect directly with vendors and suppliers on a real-time basis. Purchase orders can be executed more quickly and economically using the Internet, and payment is more rapid. Periods of production are thereby reduced, resulting in a more rapid turnover of business bank loans and a slowing in the rate of growth of the primary money supply. For an extended discussion of these and other effects, see the survey on e-business in *The Economist*, June 26th - July 2nd, 1999.

households, in contrast, is obtained as income. Households in receipt of income face two decisions: (1) how much is to be spent on consumption goods and (2) of the amount saved, how much is to be held as money. The former, in conjunction with the frequency with which income is received, determines household demand for transactions balances, while the latter adds to household demand for money to hold as an asset.

The conclusion at this point is that both business and household demands for transactions balances are in great part passively determined; business demand as a consequence of current decisions to produce and to invest in new capacity, and household demand as a consequence of decisions of how much to consume out of current income. Sequentially, however, the former comes first, for business demand for new bank loans creates most of the transactions balances that are used by both businesses and households. Because of this, it seems to me that the point of departure in analyzing the demand for money should always be the demand for bank loans. Household demand for transactions balances can still be meaningfully related to current income,[28] but in focusing on business demand to begin with one does not lose sight of the origin of the money that is being demanded.[29]

POWER OF THE MONETARY AUTHORITY

As has been noted at several points in these pages, a major failing in monetary theory, in my opinion, is lack of attention to the reasons why money is created. One of the biggest problems, as mentioned in the last section, is the tendency to treat money as a stock that somehow exists independently of the level of economic activity.[30] I want to turn now to the power that the monetary

---

[28] As well as to short-term interest rates *a la* Baumol (1953) and Tobin (1956).

[29] A useful parallel can be drawn between the discussion in this section and Keynes's discussion in Chapter 3 in the *Treatise on Money* of the three predominant types of bank deposits. The three types of deposits in question were referred to by Keynes as income, business, and savings deposits. The first two represent the transactions balances held by households and businesses, while savings deposits represent money held by households as an asset. At the time, Keynes's orientation was still very much in the Cambridge tradition of the Quantity Theory, so that his discussion is largely concerned with the volumes of deposits that are demanded in relation to volumes of transactions, with an eventual focus on the price levels relevant to each of the 'circulations'.

[30] A good part of the post-Keynes fault for this can be attributed to Keynes himself because of his assumption in the *General Theory* that the money supply is controlled by the Monetary Authority. In one of his 1937 papers in the *Economic Journal* defending the *General Theory* [Keynes (1937b)], Keynes clearly displayed understanding of the basic endogeneity of the money stock, but he restricted attention to what he called the 'finance' motive for business holdings of money. He was very explicit in describing the money demand associated with this motive as constituting a revolving fund. He

authority has to affect monetization. In the U.S., the central bank has three entry points: (1) it controls the amount of primary money available to the banking system; (2) it sets the discount rate; (3) it can exercise 'moral suasion'. In a fractional reserve banking system, primary money (which consists of cash held by banks and bank deposits at the central bank) represents the reserves of the system. In the U.S., the market interest rate that the central bank is most able to influence directly is the Federal Funds Rate, which is the rate that banks pay to borrow reserves from one another overnight. When the Federal Funds Rate is lower than the discount rate, this price represents the marginal cost of reserves to the banking system.

Obviously, the central bank can control the level of the discount rate, but it cannot control whether banks actually use the rediscount window (except during times of tightening when it can warn banks against overuse). Through the discount rate and its ability to control the amount of excess reserves in the banking system, the central bank can exert strong influence on *short-term* interest rates, which is to say rates on 60-90 day commercial loans. On longer-term rates, the central bank's influence is much less. Indeed, on very long-term rates, its influence would seem to be confined to whatever effects it might be able to exert on expectations.

As has been discussed, long-term rates are formed in what we ordinarily think of as *the* capital market, for it is in this market that the claims on the pool of fluid capital are exchanged for bonds and equities -- i.e., where liquid claims associated with current and past saving are exchanged for claims against the earnings of the stock of produced means of production. Although, in principle, the central bank might be able to exert some influence on long-term rates by buying or selling long-term government bonds, its policy has never been to do this. And even if it did, it is not clear that it could have much effect, because long-term rates are so sensitive to expectations of inflation, which much of the time are beyond the control of the central bank.

In essence, therefore, what the central bank is able to influence is the terms on which monetization of the pool of fluid capital proceeds. It does this through the volume of reserves that it allows the banking system to have and by setting the price at which banks can augment their reserves by borrowing through the rediscount window. Banks, however, can also increase their reserves by inducing the public to part with money that is being held as an asset. Indeed, during periods of monetary stringency, this may be the only source that banks have for

---

failed, however, to extend this reasoning to the whole of bank-created money.

acquiring reserves. In this situation, accordingly, both money and natural-rates of interest are determined purely by liquidity preference.

THE COMMERCIAL PAPER MARKET

The discussion to this point has implicitly assumed that current production is financed through bank loans. Clearly, this is not entirely the case, for many companies acquire short-term financing in the commercial paper market rather than through bank loans. Major participants on the buyer's side in the commercial paper market include banks, money market funds, and corporations with either a temporary or permanent surplus of money. The funds supplied represent current and past savings. For corporations the savings in question reflect myros recovery charges and retained earnings, while for households they represent decisions to hold assets in the form of near monies. Banks participate in the commercial paper market as both buyers and sellers. As buyers of commercial paper, banks may simply be recycling the savings of their depositors. However, if the paper bought is in turn discounted at the central bank, the result is a creation of new money. On the other hand, as sellers of commercial paper, banks are using this market as a source of reserves.

The commercial paper market can be viewed as the short-term counterpart to the private placement market for investment in produced means of production. As the commercial paper market increases in importance, conventional short-term loans at commercial banks become less important in providing finance for current production. This is undoubtedly a reason why commercial banks in the U.S. have moved strongly in recent years into mortgage lending, consumer loans, and the provision of other forms of financial services.

One also can wonder, however, whether the increasing amount of current production in the U.S. being financed through the commercial paper market is not a reflection of the greatly increased fiat money made available by the large federal deficits during the 1980s and first half of the 1990s. If so, then fiat money is, in effect, substituting for bank money in the monetization of the pool of fluid capital. The fiat money in question is not created directly, but rather indirectly through the purchase of new government debt by commercial banks. The government disburses the funds generated to the public in payment for goods and services. To recipients, money created by the sale of bonds to commercial banks is no different than any other money. What is not spent for consumption will initially be held as money as an asset, and can therefore become available to the commercial paper market. Since the money involved has been created through the sale of bonds, it is not dated in the sense that a short-term bank loan to a business or individual is dated. The only way that it can be extinguished is through a net reduction in government debt, but this cannot happen so long as deficits persist. The money in question has accordingly become *de facto* fiat money, and can provide a permanent source of funds to the commercial paper market.[31]

SOME NOTES ON MONETARY POLICY

An insistent theme throughout this book is that money is endogenous and its creation is part and parcel of the working of a monetary production economy. In most circumstances, money is created for the purpose either of financing current production or the initial finance of investment in produced means of investment. In the United States, most new money created takes the form of demand deposits arising from loans at commercial banks. Since money is destructed by the repayment of old loans, the most important indicator of money creation at a point in time will accordingly be net new borrowing at commercial banks. If to this is added the net increase in credit card debt and the net increase in currency in the hands of the public, then one should have a pretty good fix on the increase (or decrease) in the stock of money for use as a medium of exchange.

The foregoing accords well with measuring the stock of money at a point in time in terms of the traditional M1, defined as the sum of currency in the hands of the public, all deposits subject to transfer by check, and travelers checks. M1 is probably about the nearest that one can get to a measure which, in principle, represents the pool of purchasing power constituting aggregate demand (as aggregate demand has been defined in this book).[32] However, for a number of years, M1 has been de-emphasized by policymakers as the measure of the money stock to be used for policy purposes in favor of the more inclusive measures M2 and M3. The idea seems to be that what is most important to the short-term behavior of an economy is the amount of ready liquidity that is available, and M2 and M3, which includes time and savings accounts and certificates of deposit, are better measures of this liquidity.

---

[31] It becomes *de jure* fiat money at the point when the central bank purchases the bonds in the open market in order to provide the banking system with more reserves.

[32] Even so, it is still almost certainly far from a perfect measure. Aggregate demand, as it has been defined in this book, represents the pool of purchasing power confronting the currently available supply of goods and services, and will consist of money that is earmarked for financing current production and investment in produced means of production plus money earmarked for consumption in excess of income. Because a significant portion of currency in the hands of the public is outside of the country, and many travelers checks are held as precautionary reserves, M1 will in general probably overstate this pool of purchasing power.

In my view, however, the focus on M2 and M3 for policy purposes misreads the reasons why households and businesses hold interest-bearing near monies. In most cases, these deposits and certificates represent the outcomes of portfolio choices that are removed from the initial savings decisions that give rise to the claims that were used to acquire the deposits in the first place. For holders with high liquidity preference, time and savings deposits and certificates of deposits in essence represent risk-free idle balances that earn interest. The balances may be idle for only a short period of time, as with businesses holding temporary excesses of cash, or the balances may be idle for a long period, as with many older households that feel more comfortable holding a significant part of their assets in near cash.

I do not mean to imply by this that policymakers are wrong in paying attention to more inclusive measures of money, only that these should not be the exclusive focus. The events during the summer and early fall of 1998 provide a good example of the potential dangers of a narrow focus on broad monetary aggregates. The Russian devaluation in August 1998, in conjunction with the continuing financial problems in the far east, created so much uncertainty that there was a stampede away from risk in international financial markets. The United States was viewed as a safe haven, and in particular there was a rush into U.S. government securities. Yields on the latter fell, while -- in response to the increased uncertainty -- yields on non-government long-term securities rose. The M2 and M3 aggregates also rose, as many investors reacted to the increased uncertainty by shifting assets from stocks and bonds into thrift accounts and deposits. During that time, if monetary policymakers had just focused on M2 and M3, they probably would have been led to believe that an incipient inflation was at hand. However, this was not the case, as the movement into interest-bearing near monies (as into U.S. Treasuries) was a response to uncertainty, rather than preparation for a consumption binge.

In my view, rather than concentrating on the behavior of the M2 and M3 aggregates, the quantities that monetary policymakers should most focus on are commercial bank loans to business (including commercial paper which is discounted at the central bank), installment credit loans to consumers (including credit card loans), the states of business and consumer confidence, and changes in asset values in relation to the growth in real income and output. The last is particularly important to monitor because if asset values as an aggregate should begin rising faster than the increase in real income and output, this is almost certainly an indication that the banking system is creating too much money. And, as will be emphasized in the next chapter, the contingency especially to be guarded against are loans in which assets are being mortgaged in order to buy other assets.

The states of business and consumer confidence are important because these states reflect the expectations that drive current production and investment in new produced means of production. A growing economy with a stable price level requires a combination of expectations that results in the creation of a 'right' amount of purchasing power, namely, an amount equal to the goods contained in the pool of fluid capital evaluated at current prices. Commercial bank lending is obviously key to the creation of this 'right' amount of purchasing power, hence the importance to policymakers of keeping a close watch over the amounts and types of loans that are being created.

CHAPTER 5

PRODUCTION AND INVESTMENT

The focus in this chapter is on the role of capital in production and the relationship between demand, short-run marginal cost, and investment. The point of departure is the simple truism, noted in Chapter 1, that current demand has to be served from current capacity, which is fixed. Current production decisions, accordingly, involve the choice of how much of current capacity is to be utilized. This depends upon expectations of current demands in relation to current short-run avoidable costs of production. Current investment decisions, in contrast, depend upon demands expected in the future in relation to the expected short-run avoidable costs of operating the capacity which is expected to be available for serving those demands.

In the framework presented in this chapter, there is a short run of a traditional sort. Specifically, the short run is defined in terms of the current production decision period using the plant which is currently in place. In general, there is no problem in identifying this short run with the short run of Marshall. However, there is no Marshallian long run, in which production structures are allowed to adjust optimally to demands. The long run in this chapter is defined in terms of a real-time long run, in which firms, through their current investment decisions, are able to adjust production structures for serving expected future demands.

The long run, accordingly, is seen as consisting of two horizons:

1. A *construction horizon*, which represents the length of time, beginning from scratch, that a firm requires to bring new capacity into production in an *orderly* way, and

2. An *investment horizon*, which represents the length of time, once the capacity is in operation, that the fluid capital expended in its constructed is to be recovered.

CAPITAL AND PRODUCTION

I shall begin with the relationships between capital and production. It is not meaningful in my view to treat capital sunk in produced means of production as an input into production in the same manner as labor. Machines, buildings, etc., obviously have a physical reality, but it makes more sense, in my opinion, to see the stock of produced means of production as combining (or cooperating) with permanent resources and labor to determine the capacity to produce and the potential to generate income. At any given time, this capacity to produce is not a variable, but a constant. What is variable is the output that is to be produced.

The standard neoclassical way of expressing production possibilities is via an aggregate production function,

(1) $Q = f(K, L),$

where K denotes 'capital' inputs and L denotes labor. Assuming appropriate continuities, marginal physical products are obtained through differentiation. In my view, the capacity to produce at any time t is better expressed as

(2) $Q(t) = \Phi[L(t), t],$

where Φ represents the existing structure of production. With this framework, one can speak about the marginal productivity of labor, but not of the marginal productivity of physical capital, since physical capital is embodied in the 'shape' of Φ, and therefore is fixed. Time t is included as an argument in Φ to remind us that the 'shape' of Φ changes through time as a result of investment and retirements.[1]

Let me now turn to the matter of how one might go about defining substitution between capital and labor. During the Cambridge Capital Controversy of the 1960s and 1970s, the standard way of approaching this question was through a comparative static analysis involving the comparison of alternative stationary states. Accordingly, let a steady-state reparameterization of the function in expression (2) be given by

(3) $Q = \Phi(L; \alpha),$

---

[1] It should be noted that the physical capital embodied in Φ is not the fixed capital defined in Chapter 2 (which is net of myros recovery charges against revenue), but rather the produced means of production that are in place at t. The two differ because myros recovery charges usually bear little relationship to loss of ability to produce.

where α denotes a particular stock of produced means of production. If we now differentiate this expression with respect to α, it is tempting to interpret the resulting partial derivative as the marginal product of 'capital', although only in the sense of the added steady-state output that would be forthcoming from the addition of another 'unit' of produced means of production. While this exercise may have some formal validity, it does not, in my view, have any real-world meaning. For it assumes that the embodiment of produced means of production in Φ can be parameterized, and it is not clear, as a practical matter, that it is possible for this to be done.

As has been noted, investment and current output is funded by the pool of fluid capital. Current output accordingly depends every bit as much on the pool of fluid capital as it does on the input of labor, which means that the output function in expression (2) should be written as

(4) $Q(t) = \Phi[L(t), K(t), t]$,

where $K(t)$ is understood to represent the stock of fluid capital.[2]

A key concept in determining the level of current output is short-run marginal cost. 'Short-run' in this context will be defined in terms of some relevant short-term period of production under the assumption that the capacity to produce is fixed. This upper limit to production can be represented as a vertical spike, as Φ^* in Figure 5. Short-run marginal cost will be defined as the *avoidable* cost of producing one more unit of output. The short-run marginal cost curve then describes how marginal cost changes as the *utilization* of Φ varies from 0 to Φ^*. For the usual reasons, one can see this curve as rising with Q, and especially steeply as Q approaches Φ^*.

To be included in short-run costs are only the out-of-pocket expenditures of producing output. Obviously, this will include direct expenditures for labor and materials, including expenditures that do not vary with output once the decision

---

[2] I am not aware that fluid capital has ever previously been viewed as a 'factor' in current production, but it is clearly an important element. Production requires the purchase (and therefore the finance) of material inputs and labor, payments of rent, etc. Some of the classical economists (Ricardo, in particular) viewed capital as providing advances on production, but it is not clear that the fund involved was seen as separate from the stock of produced means of production. In any event, it is clear that production can falter from a lack of 'finance' for goods-in-process. Indeed, one can imagine a circumstance in which so much of the pool of fluid capital goes into the construction of the capacity to produce that not enough remains to finance current production. Plants stand idle, because there's no fluid capital to finance their operation. For an analysis of how taking into account the need to finance current production can cause the investment function to slope upward, see Appendix 2.

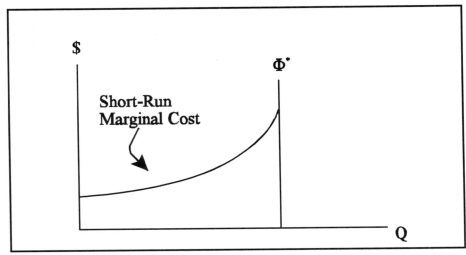

Figure 5

to produce has been made. An engineer 'babysitting' a telephone switch would be an example of the latter. Capital expenditures, as usually understood, are *not* included in short-run marginal cost. No depreciation is included, nor user costs in the sense of Keynes. However, all expenditures necessary for the operation of plant and equipment (such as oil and grease) are to be included.

The short-run marginal cost curve is a key instrument for planning the level of current production, because it provides a floor to the price (or in the present context, the revenue) that *must* be obtained from the sale of output. Prices below the short-run marginal cost curve would leave producers with literal out-of-pocket losses. However, once the position of the short-run marginal cost curve is known, the actual revenues obtained will depend upon demand conditions.

If (as is implicitly assumed to this point) output is sold either in a spot market or by contracts whose durations do not extend beyond the period-of-production, capital charges (i.e., interest and myros recovery charges) and other financial obligations of firms must be charged against the quasi-rents generated by revenues in excess of short-run costs. On the other hand, if output is sold under contracts that extend beyond a single period-of-production, contract prices (and therefore revenues) will include some capital charges. The extreme would be a contract which extends over the full planned life of the underlying produced means of production, in which case the contracted revenues would include *all* of the capital charges. This is the only situation that calls for long-run marginal cost being the floor to price.

Current decisions to produce are thus determined by the relationships between short-run marginal cost and expected demand. The capacity to produce is already in place, and the only question is how much of the capacity is actually to be utilized. Planned production, however, is one thing, while actual execution is something else. This is because production requires 'financing', which draws upon the pool of fluid capital, initially in terms of money (as a means to transfer goods) and then ultimately in terms of goods.

FROM PRODUCTION TO INVESTMENT

Investment converts fluid capital into fixed (or sunk) capital and adds to produced means of production. By adding to produced means of production, investment adds to the capacity to produce and to the potential to generate income. As with current production of consumption goods, investment has to be 'financed' out of the pool of fluid capital. A common misconception is that investment is financed by saving, but this is not necessarily the case. For saving, whether business or personal, is just one of the flows into the pool of fluid capital. A dollar of fluid capital is a dollar of fluid capital no matter how it gets into the pool. And, as we have seen, investment can be financed, so long as the pool is not empty, even if current saving is zero.

Keynes emphasized that, in general, investment is undertaken by different people and for different reasons than those who save. Keynes was not the first to note this, but no one before him (except possibly Marx) attached as much importance to the fact. Individuals save out of current income because they want to transfer income from today to some (usually indefinite) time in the future. Businesses invest in produced means of production because they foresee an opportunity to make a profit. At the time of Adam Smith, these were often (or even usually) the same people, but this ceased being the case a long time ago.

A simplified view of the investment decision is described in Figure 6. Let Φ^* denote the existing capacity to produce current output, and let DD represent the current demand (or willingness-to-pay) to utilize this capacity. The market for capacity is obviously cleared at a price per unit of capacity P_s. P_s thus represents a spot price. The upward-sloping curve that begins at P_0 from Φ^* represents the short-run supply curve of the capital-goods industry -- i.e., the supply curve for newly produced means of production. Any point on s represents the price at which the capital-goods industry is willing to supply (over some relevant period of time) the corresponding amount of new capacity measured from Φ^*. The (new) capital-goods market will clear at a price of P_f, with investment in new capacity of I. Whereas P_s represents the *spot* price of existing capacity, P_f can

Capital, Accumulation, and Money

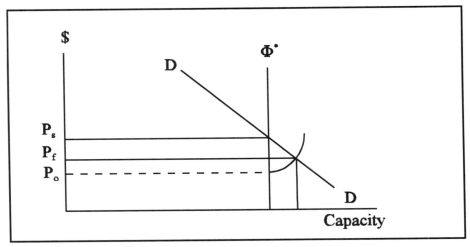

Figure 6

be interpreted as the *forward* price for new capacity.[3] Note that for investment to take place, it is necessary that the spot price be greater than the minimum price that firms in the capital-goods industry have to have in order to begin producing new produced means of production.

Let us now delve behind the investment decision depicted in Figure 6. In approaching this, it is important to keep in mind that the curve DD represents the willingness-to-pay for holding capacity to produce as a function of the unit price of that capacity. It *does not* represent an aggregate demand function, defined as the demand for output from the capacity as a function of the price of output. What really needs to be described is what goes on in the neighborhood of the market-clearing spot price P_s. Consider, accordingly, an investment (as contemplated by some individual or business), where investment in this context is taken to refer to a stream of prospective yields from a particular configuration of produced means of production.[4]

Following Keynes, let $q_1, \ldots, q_n$ denote a stream of prospective yields over an investment horizon of n periods. Specifically, let

(5) $q_i = R_i - C_i,$

where:

---

[3] Davidson (1978) refers to this price as the forward flow-supply price.

[4] Cf. Keynes (1936, p. 136, *passim*).

R_i = the revenues from sale of output in period t

C_i = the cost (defined as the short-run avoidable cost) of producing these revenues.

The willingness-to-pay for this investment (i.e., stream of prospective yields) will
be

$$(6) \quad \xi = \sum_{i=1}^{n} \frac{q_i}{(1+\rho)^i}$$

$$= \sum_{i=1}^{n} \frac{R_i - C_i}{(1+\rho)^i} ,$$

where ρ denotes the discount factor. A necessary condition for the investment to
be undertaken through the purchase of existing capacity is for $\xi > P_s$. This is in
the spot market for produced means of production. If ξ is less than P_s, but greater
than P_f, the investment might be undertaken through the purchase of newly
produced means of production.

The formula for ξ obviously represents the present value of the stream of
prospective yields calculated at a discount rate of ρ. Setting ξ equal to P_s and
solving for ρ gives what Keynes called the marginal efficiency of capital, or
equivalently what Fisher called the internal rate of return. Both Keynes and
Fisher compared the value of ρ to the market rate of interest in deciding whether
the investment would be undertaken. In my view, it is better to specify a value
for ρ and then compare the resulting ξ to the value of P_s, as this represents a
straightforward comparison of willingness-to-pay with the cost of the investment.

Risk and uncertainty (in the sense of Knight and Keynes) can be seen as
entering into the investment decision at four places in the formula for ξ, namely,
in the estimation of R_i and C_i, the choice of a value for n, and in the choice of the
discount rate ρ. If, for example, the investment decision is being made in an
atmosphere of increasing uncertainty:

1. Estimates of R_i will be shaded *downward*;

2. Estimates of C_i will be shaded *upward*;

3. n -- the 'payback period' -- will be *decreased*;

4.   ρ -- the (subjective) rate of discount -- will be *increased*.

The usual approach to dealing with risk and uncertainty is to treat it all as risk and to roll it into a 'risk premium' to be added to the market rate of interest in choosing the value of ρ. This, in my view, does away with much of how uncertainty operates on real-world investment decisions -- payback periods are shortened (not just because more remote yields are made small because of a higher discount factor), and expectations concerning revenues and costs become less sanguine. The consequence, among other things, is a much weaker connection between decisions to invest and the market rate of interest than is usually posited.[5]

In interpreting the foregoing, it is to be emphasized that the investment being considered involves a particular configuration of capacity, whether already existing or purchased new from the capital-goods industry. It may represent the purchase of a 747 to carry passengers, lease of the same, or the purchase of a factory to make tennis rackets. The spot price, it must also be emphasized, is the price which places the existing stock of produced means of production into the hands of willing holders.

Let us now look at the investment decision for an individual firm. For concreteness, assume that the firm is an electric utility and that the production capacity in question is generating capacity. The analysis is based upon assumptions as follows:

1.   Generating stations are not only durable, but they require a considerable amount of time to build. Accordingly let h denote the number of periods that constitutes the firm's capacity-planning horizon, by which is meant the period over which new capacity begun today can be brought on line in an orderly fashion.

2.   The planning horizon h is to be viewed in a normal sense, in that capacity, in event of unanticipated factors, could be put into place more quickly, but at a higher cost.

3.   The firm has an ongoing construction program that reflects past investment decisions. The program is reviewed each period to see whether the capacity needs for within-horizon periods as

---

[5] Cf., the loose relationship between investment and the rate of interest in the surveys of investment decisions in the U.K. undertaken in the late 1930s. See Hall and Hitch (1939).

foreseen yesterday square with these needs as foreseen today. If not, projects can be accelerated or delayed as current circumstances dictate.

4. The motivation of the firm is assumed to be to produce electricity at each point (i.e., period) within the planning horizon at minimum cost, given the plant that is available.

The details of the investment decision, for the end of the planning horizon, are depicted in Figure 7. Two periods are represented in this figure, the current period, labeled 1, and the last period of the planning horizon, labeled h. The curve D_1D_1, represents the current-period demand function for generation capacity, which D_hD_h represents the demand h periods in the future, *as anticipated from the current period.*

The spike at Φ_1, denotes current-period generating capacity, while Φ_h denotes the capacity that is currently planned for the end of the planning horizon. The curve ab represents the short-run marginal cost curve (as defined earlier) of operating the capacity in Φ_1, and cd represents the same with respect to Φ_h (as expected from the current period). In deriving ab, it is assumed that existing capacity is ordered by operating efficiency (as measured by out-of-pocket operating expenses), so that the newest, most efficient plant is represented near the origin, while old inefficient plant is represented near Φ_1. This means that the curve ab will, in general, never fall, and (assuming a mix of plants of different vintages) must be higher at Φ_1 than near the origin. The curve cd bears the same relationship to Φ_h as ab does to Φ_1, but with one important difference: the information is essentially current for the calculation of ab, while it is all based upon expectations for the calculation of cd.

If the ongoing construction program (which reflects past investment decisions) unfolds as planned at the beginning of the current period, the demand D_hD_h that is foreseen for the end of the planning period would have an anticipated short-run marginal cost of P_h per unit of capacity. However, since demand h periods in the future can be served not only by capacity that (as of yesterday) is planned to be in place at that time in the future, but also by capacity the construction of which can be started today, how D_h is to be served is subject to some choice. We will now examine how this choice is determined.

Let the horizontal line labeled β represent the average price per unit of capacity at which new capacity, started in the current period, can be brought on line at the end of the planning horizon. The value of β thus represents not only the operating expenses of production, but *all* capital costs as well. In Figure 7,

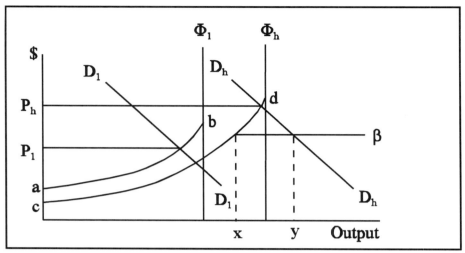

Figure 7

we see that for outputs beyond x, output can be produced most efficiently from new plant to be constructed from scratch. For, to the right of point x, β lies below the short-run marginal cost curve of utilizing the currently planned existing plant. From the figure, we see that the current period could involve plans to initiate up to y - x new units of capacity to come on line h periods in the future.

The point to be kept in mind in assessing this conclusion is that the *total* unit cost of new capacity has to compete with only the *marginal* operating cost of existing capacity. To the left of point x, the short-run marginal cost of operating Φ_h, is less than β, so that output demand less than x will be most efficiently served from (what at the beginning of the current period is planned to be) existing plant. To the right of x, β is less than points on cd, so that demand in excess of x would be most efficiently served by new plant. *This crossover of short-run marginal cost from being less to being greater than the total cost per unit of new capacity is what drives the decision to invest in new plant.*

We will now look into the investment decision at point x in more detail, beginning with the way that β is calculated. With some realism, we can imagine that as the firm's capacity planners note that D_h cuts cd in a steeply rising portion of the curve, they go to a 'catalog' (i.e., book of blueprints) of new-generating plant and begin to cost-out a variety of plant designs, under the assumption that new plant started from scratch today will be up-and-running in the final period of the planning horizon.

For each plant design, the *total cost* of designing and constructing the plant, including all foreseeable getting-started expenses and all interest on loans that are taken out during the period of construction, is calculated. Let g(i) denote all of the construction and construction-related expenditures for a particular plant during period i in the construction horizon. The total (projected) cost of the plant, calculated at the end of the construction period, will accordingly be

(7) $G = \sum_{i=0}^{h} g(i)(1+r)^i$,

where r is an appropriate rate of interest. Let k denote the installed capacity of this plant. The value of β for this plant would then be calculated as

(8) $\beta = \dfrac{G}{k}$.

A β will be calculated for each plant type and design.

I now turn to how the earlier treatment of the investment decision fits into the present analysis. Earlier it was noted that a necessary condition for an investment to be undertaken is that the present value of the prospective stream of yields be greater than the cost of the investment. In the present context, this condition can be represented as

(9) $\sum_{j=1}^{n} \dfrac{R_j - C_j}{(1+\rho)^j} > G$,

where:

R$_j$ = The revenues expected from operating the plant in time h + j

C$_j$ = the (avoidable) cost of producing R$_j$

ρ = an appropriate discount rate.

It is to be noted that the point in time at which evaluations are made is the *end* of the planning horizon, which is h periods into the future. This reflects the assumption that it (normally) takes h periods for new plant started today to be up-and-running. Capital expenditures for the plant accumulate at an interest rate r [see equation (7)]. However, in contrast with capital expenditures, which accumulate interest to the time that the new plant goes into service, the stream of prospective yields from the plant is discounted to that point in time. Note that capital costs are accumulated at a rate r, while prospective yields are discounted at a rate ρ. In general, ρ will be greater -- possibly substantially greater -- than r. The reason for this difference is that r represents the interest costs of *building the new plant*, while ρ represents the rate at which the firm *discounts the future quasi-rents that the plant is expected to generate.*

The calculations just described will be made for each plant type and design that is in the firm's present catalog of blueprints. In the end, the plant that will be selected for construction will be the one which yields the largest excess of ξ over G.

A point to be emphasized is that, in evaluating the stream of prospective yields, the length of the payback horizon n need bear no necessary relationship to the expected productive life of the plant. The only thing that can be said *a priori* is that n will never be greater than the expected productive life. What determines the time that plant is ultimately taken out of service is when its short-run marginal cost of operation is in the most steeply rising part of the short-run marginal cost curve, defined with respect to *current* capacity to produce.

The payback horizon, on the other hand, represents the period over which the firm *wants* and *expects* to recover the capital that was initially invested in the plant. A plant can continue to generate quasi-rents long after the capital that was initially invested in it has been returned (via myros recovery charges against quasi-rents) to the pool of fluid capital. Such plant remains productive, and therefore has *capital value* (defined as the present value of its stream of prospective yields). We must take care, however, not to identify capital value defined in this sense with capital defined either as fixed (or sunk) capital or fluid capital. Finally, it should be noted that the analysis to this point implicitly assumes that the demand at time h which drives current investment decisions is permanent in the sense that it is expected to persist at least as long as the length of the payback horizon.

To this point, I have focused on the investment decision related to the decision to initiate completely new investment projects. What about projects that are already in progress that are consequences of investment decisions made in periods in the recent past? As noted earlier, the firm is assumed, in the current period, to review each ongoing project, specifically to decide whether a project is to continue according to today's inherited schedule, to be moved up, or to be delayed. Each review involves the same considerations as for the decision to initiate the construction of new plant that is to come on line at the end of the planning horizon.

In discussing how construction-work-in-progress (or the ongoing construction program) is changed in response to changes in within planning-horizon expectations, let us begin with the case in which there is a change in demand for the current period in relation to what was expected in the immediately preceding period (i.e., 'yesterday'), a change that is expected to be permanent. In analyzing this situation, it is to be noted, to begin with, that *nothing* can be done regarding the amount of capacity in this (the current) period, for today's demand must be served from whatever capacity is inherited from yesterday. The first capacity that can be affected is the first period after the current one. If demand has increased, the capacity scheduled to be in place at the start of period 3 of the current planning horizon could be accelerated to be in place at the start of period 2. On the other hand, if demand has decreased, the capacity scheduled to be in place at the start of period 2 could be delayed until the start of period 3 (or later).

Each of these actions will have costs as well as benefits. In particular, there will be two types of costs and benefits, namely, changes in quasi-rents and changes in capital costs. The circumstances at the start of period 2 are described in Figure 8. The curve D_2D_2 represents the (now) expected demand for period 2. The vertical line at Φ_2 represents the capacity that was scheduled (according to yesterday's plan) to be in service at the start of period 2, while Φ_3 is the same for period 3. Φ_1 represents the capacity that is available in the current period (i.e., period 1). The curve labeled ab represents the short-run marginal cost of operating Φ_2, and similarly for cd and ef with respect to, Φ_1 and Φ_3. Finally, for reference, yesterday's expected demand for period 2 is given by the curve D_2D_2, so that the figure describes an increase in demand.

We now turn to the calculation of the appropriate benefits and costs that would arise from an alteration in the ongoing construction program. Since we are dealing with an increase in demand, the question is whether capacity scheduled to be in service at the start of period 3 -- Φ_3 -- is shifted to the start of period 2.

In the figure, we see that the short-run marginal cost of serving D_2 from Φ_2 is expected to be P_2, while expected short-run marginal cost of serving D_2 from Φ_3 (if it were moved up) would be P_3.[6] The quasi-rents from using Φ_2 will be given by the area aP_2b, while the quasi-rents from using Φ_3 would be given by the area eP_3g. Let π^2 denote the former and π^3 the latter. Finally, let $\Delta^+\pi$ denote the difference between π^3 and π^2. In general -- and this is important to note -- $\Delta^+\pi$ can be of either sign.

---

[6] Since we are dealing with an increase in demand, we can (at least for the moment) ignore Φ_1.

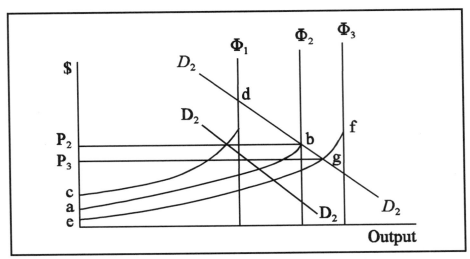

Figure 8

Assuming that it is physically possible to do so, moving up the in-service date of Φ_3 will clearly entail capital expenditures that are in addition to those that are part of the inherited construction program. Denote this increase in capital expenditures that would have to be incurred in the current period by Δ^+G. If the difference between $\Delta^+\pi$ and Δ^+G is positive, the firm will have incentive to move up the in-service date of Φ_3, but not if the difference between $\Delta^+\pi$ and Δ^+G is negative.

Suppose that the difference between $\Delta^+\pi$ and Δ^+G is not positive, so that the in-service date of Φ_3 is not moved up to the start of period 2. The question that must next be asked is whether the in-service date of Φ_4 will be moved up to the start of period 3. A figure similar to the one above can be constructed, but with reference to period 3. The demand curve D_3D_3 will replace D_2D_2, and the reference Φ's will be Φ_2, Φ_3, and Φ_4. The quasi-rents for serving D_3 from first Φ_3 and then Φ_4 will be calculated as before, and the differences between the two compared with the additional capital costs that would be incurred (including interest expense) in moving the in-service date for Φ_4 to the start of period 3. If the difference between $\Delta^+\pi$ and Δ^+G is again negative, the analysis proceeds to period 4 and calculation of the benefits and costs of moving up the in-service date of Φ_5 for serving D_4, and so on for the remaining periods within the planning horizon.

Question: Does a move-up in the in-service date of Φ_2 (say) imply that the in-service date of $\Phi_3, \ldots, \Phi_h$ will also be moved up? This will not necessarily be the case. In Figure 9, the demand curve D_3D_3 represents revised expected

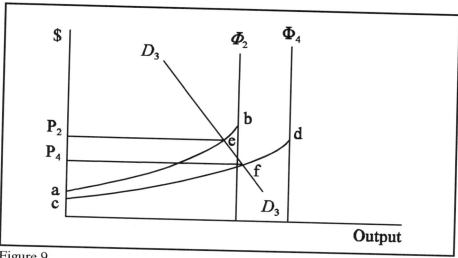

Figure 9

demand in period 3. The vertical line at Φ_2 denotes the now planned capacity for period 2, which was the planned in-service capacity for the start of period 3 (according to yesterday's construction schedule), but now planned to be moved to the start of period 2. Finally, Φ_4 represents the in-service capacity for the start of period 4 according to yesterday's construction schedule. Φ_3 has been moved up, will Φ_4 as well? Whether this will be the case depends (as before) upon whether the difference between the change in quasi-rents and the capital costs (including interest) associated with the move-up is positive.

The quasi-rents corresponding to Φ_2 and Φ_4 will be given by aP_2e and cP_4f. As before, the difference between these two quasi-rents can be of either sign. The capital cost associated with the move-up will be the difference in capital costs (including interest) between what, beginning in the current period, the construction cost would be if Φ_4 were put into service at the start of period 3, and what the construction cost would be if Φ_4 were put into service (according to the inherited plan) at the start of period 4. A similar analysis must be undertaken for each succeeding period in the planning horizon. The analysis for the last period in the horizon is the one depicted in Figure 7 which is the one that began the discussion.

Let me now turn to a decrease in demand in the current period that is expected to be permanent. For a decrease in demand, the concern will be with delays in the ongoing construction program, rather than move-ups. Beginning with period 2 of the current planning horizon, the first question to be asked is whether the (now) expected demand for period 2 should be served by the

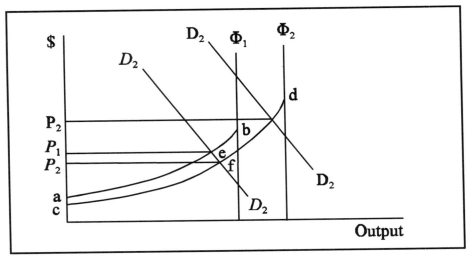

Figure 10

capacity of the current period or whether it should be served by the capacity that was planned (per the inherited plan) to be in-service at the start of period 2 -- i.e., is D_2 to be served by Φ_1, or Φ_2? The situation is described in Figure 10.

D_2D_2 represents the demand in period 2 expected in the inherited plan, while D_2D_2 represents the demand in period 2 that is currently expected. The quasi-rents from using Φ_2 to serve D_2 are represented by cP_2f, while the quasi-rents from using Φ_1, are given by aP_1e. To delay placing the capacity represented by Φ_2 into service from the start of period 2 to the start of period 3 will result in a capital saving. The condition for Φ_2 being delayed is for the sum of the capital saving (including interest) and the difference in quasi-rents to be positive.

If Φ_2 is delayed, the next step is to check whether the delay carries into subsequent periods, that is, whether $\Phi_3, \ldots, \Phi_n$ should be delayed as well. Each period should be analyzed sequentially, using as comparison Φs the Φ that would be inherited by that period in relation to the Φ of one delay removed. To illustrate, suppose that the capacity represented by Φ_2 is delayed through period 3. Then, the comparison for period 4 will be Φ_2 with Φ_3, not Φ_2 with Φ_4. And so on and so forth.

If, rather than in the current period the permanent change in demand is expected to occur in the jth period of the planning horizon, the analysis as just described, for both an increase and a decrease, is to be applied beginning with the period in which the change in demand is expected to occur.

ROLES OF THE MONEY AND NATURAL RATES OF INTEREST

The natural rate of interest, it will be recalled, represents the price that equilibrates demand and supply in the market for fluid capital. On the demand side, an increase in current maximum prospective outputs on the part of individual firms could cause an increase in the streams of future prospective outputs, which in turn could cause an increase in the streams of future prospective quasi-rents. Since it is the latter which drive investment decisions, the result could be an increase in investment and therefore an increase in the natural rate of interest.

However, a different scenario can also be envisioned which operates on the cost side, namely, where (say) a prospective decrease in the real wage rate leads to a lengthening of the period of production -- i.e., to a less mechanized structure of the production process -- and hence to a lessened demand for investment.[7] In this case, the pressure on the natural rate of interest would be downward. Consequently, it follows that the overall impact of a prospective decrease in the real wage rate on the natural rate of interest is ambiguous.

As has been discussed, however, the money rate of interest can intercede between the natural rate of interest and both saving and investment. As we have seen, new investment is financed through the intermediary of money, that is, firms wishing to invest must first acquire an appropriate stock of money. Assuming that the money in question is obtained through bank loans, the cost of this stock of money is the money rate of interest. In the short run, as we have seen, the money rate of interest bears no necessary relationship to the natural rate. A high money rate of interest can clearly forestall investment, even though the natural rate might be sufficiently low to encourage it.[8]

FINANCING OF INVESTMENT: AN ILLUSTRATION

Let me now turn to an example that shows how investment in new capacity might be financed. Assume that the time required for the new capacity to go on line is 6 months. This means that finance will have to be arranged not only for the plant, equipment, and materials to be purchased, but also for the wage payments that will be required in putting the new capacity into place. The sum total of this finance represents the capital, drawn from the pool of fluid capital,

---

[7] The circumstances under which this contingency can arise are described in Appendix 2.

[8] Cf. Keynes discussion of the 'finance' motive for holding money [Keynes (1937b)].

that will be invested in the project.

Suppose that the investment will total $10m, of which $8m is for plant and equipment and $2m for labor. Suppose, further, that $6m is financed internally and $4m externally, $2m through the sale of new equity and $2m through the sale of 10-year bonds. Of the $6m financed internally, assume that $2m is drawn from the firm's demand deposits and that $4m is raised through the sale of government bonds from the firm's portfolio. Of the $4m financed externally, assume that the bonds are purchased by a pension fund, while the $2m of equity is purchased by an individual who paid for the shares through the sale of $2m of equities in another company.

Without further specific assumptions, there is no way of saying how much of the $10m is financed out of current saving, how much out of current myros recovery charges, or how much is simply drawn out of the pool of fluid capital. The only thing that can really be said is that $10m of purchasing power is required by the firm for pursuing the investment, $2m of the firm's own cash and $8m from outside the firm, with the latter consisting of $4m from the firm's sale of government bonds from its own portfolio, $2m from the sale of equity, and $2m from the sale of its own bonds. The firm gives up interest on the government bonds, will have to pay interest on its own bonds, and will expect to pay dividends on the equity.

At one extreme, all of the $10m investment could be drawn from current saving. This would be the case (say) if the $2m from the firm's own cash came out of current retained earnings, if the $4m of government bonds were purchased by an insurance company out of current premium payments, if the $2m of bonds sold to the pension fund were purchased out of inflows into the fund out of current income, and if the individual that purchased the shares of the second company did so out of current income. The other extreme would be all $10m that was raised represented restructuring of asset portfolios, so that the $10m investment would be financed from the already existing pool of fluid capital.[9]

The firm undertakes the $10m investment because fluid capital invested in new produced means of production is expected to be productive -- productive in the sense that, over some specific horizon, use of the produced means of production is expected to generate discounted quasi-rents that are in excess of the $10m cost of the investment. The $10m of fluid capital invested will be recovered through myros recovery charges against the quasi-rents, while the

---

[9] This case also illustrates how investment can occur in the absence of current saving.

opportunity cost of the capital that remains sunk (i.e., embodied) in the produced means of production is accounted for in the rate that was used in discounting the expected quasi-rents.

CHAPTER 6

GENERAL PRICE LEVEL AND INFLATION

I turn now to what I have always thought are among the most difficult topics in economics, the concepts of the general price level and inflation. Inflation is, and always has been, easy to define as a rise in the general price level. But, what is meant by the general price level and what are its determinants? Of the two questions, the first is logically prior, for one has to know what the general price level is before changes in it can be discussed. The real task, accordingly, is to come up with a *definition* of the general price level that is fruitful for further analysis.

DEFINING THE GENERAL PRICE LEVEL

The usual response to the question of what is the general price level is that it is an index number, specifically, a price index. This seems unassailable. Irving Fisher spent many years thinking and writing about how such an index should be defined, and the same was true for Keynes. An important question, however, is whether any index that is devised is simply an artificial construction devoid of meaning beyond the context within which it is defined, or whether an index can be defined that is meaningful in its own right.

Let us begin with the classic equation of exchange, MV = PT, where the terms have their usual meanings. My first question is which of these terms can meaningfully be measured.[1] That M, the stock of money, can be measured there seems little question. For once a definition of money is settled upon, measurement (in principle) is simply a matter of counting. Also, there seems little question but that the *right-hand side* of the equation of exchange is in principle

---

[1] That all of the terms in fact *are* measured in some form or another is not the issue; the question is which of them can be *meaningfully* measured.

measurable, for once the transactions (together with the time period) that are to be measured are specified, the matter is once again one of counting and adding-up. This, however, is with reference to the monetary value of transactions as represented by $\Sigma p_i T_i$, rather than by PT, where $T = \Sigma T_i$ and P represents some price level.

Since M and PT (viewed as $\Sigma p_i T_i$) are in principle measurable, velocity V, can then be measured as

(1) $V = \Sigma p_i T_i / M$.

Note that this makes the equation of exchange an identity. The question now is whether it is meaningful to replace the volume of monetary transactions $\Sigma p_i T_i$ by PT, where P represents an index of the general price level. This question will be returned to in a moment.

The preceding refers to the totality of all transactions (obviously with reference to some specified period of time) in an economy. There is also a standard quantity equation that refers to income (or GDP). In this quantity equation, the right-hand side represents the monetary value of final transactions. The stock of money is still defined as in the total transactions equation, but now velocity has to refer to income (or GDP) transactions. The conventional way of writing the income equation of exchange is as

(2) $MV = \Sigma p_i Q_i$.

where p_i and Q_i represent the prices and quantity of the ith component of final output. Even more conventionally, this is written as

(3) $MV = PQ,$

where P denotes an index of the general price level and Q denotes real output. A common practice is to represent P by the GDP deflator and Q by real GDP.

Ex post, there is no question but what $\Sigma p_i Q_i$ can be represented by PQ, where P and Q are as just defined. The key question, however, is whether the general price level in an *ex ante* sense -- or better still, in a sense that stands apart from its individual constituent prices -- is a meaningful concept. Can we, for example, imagine the general price level as representing, in some abstract sense, the mean level of a series of interconnected 'lakes' that represent the markets in an economy in which individual prices are formed? Or is it better to think of the general price level as the mean level of a single big 'lake' that represents all of the markets in an economy rolled into one?

In the *Purchasing Power of Money*, Fisher likens the Equation of Exchange to a physical balance, with MV on the left side and PT on the right. In Figure 11, the stock of money (M) and the amounts of goods (Q_1, Q_2, Q_3) are interpreted as weights, while velocity (V) and prices (P_1, P_2, P_3) are interpreted as distances that M, Q_1, Q_2, and Q_3 are from the fulcrum of the balance. The Equation of Exchange is depicted in this figure in the form $MV = \Sigma p_i Q_i$. In Figure 12, the Equation of Exchange is depicted in its usual form as $MV = PQ$. M and V are as before, but now P represents an average price that applies to all of the quantities hanging from the same point ($Q = \Sigma Q_i$).

Fisher conducts all of his monetary analysis in terms of the Equation of Exchange. He is a quintessential quantity theorist: V and T are taken as constant (or exogenous), so that P and M must necessarily vary proportionately. For Fisher, however, the causation is clearly from M to P, that is, the general price level is determined by the stock of money.[2] A point that Fisher makes repeatedly is that prices (specifically, goods prices) are determined independently of the general price level, or alternatively the general price level is determined independently of prices:

> We have seen that the price level is not determined by individual prices, but that, on the contrary, any individual price presupposes a price level. We have seen that the complete and only explanation of a price level is to be sought in factors of the equation of exchange and whatever antecedent causes affect this factor. The terms "demand" and "supply", used in reference to particular prices, have no significance whatever in explaining a rise or fall of price *level*. In considering the influence affecting individual prices we say that an increase in supply lowers prices, but an increase in demand raises them. But in considering the influence affecting price *levels* we enter upon an entirely different set of concepts, and must not confuse the proposition that an increase in the *trade* the (Q´s) tends to lower the price *level*, with the proposition that an increase in supply tends to lower an individual price.

---

[2] The Quantity Theorists -- and Fisher, in particular -- are dogmatic in connecting inflation to changes in the stock of money. As we have seen, excess aggregate demand is at root caused by excess monetization, so that there is truth in the dogma. In my view, however, it is better to see the problem in process terms, as the creation of a tide of purchasing power that floods onto the goods side of the pool of fluid capital and drives up market-clearing prices.

A major problem with quantity theorists, with the exception of Wicksell, is that they neither specify a reason why excess monetization occurs, nor do they spell out a mechanism whereby the excess purchasing power that is created eventually leads to inflation. The standard litany of quantity theorists is: "Suppose the quantity of money is doubled." Clearly, the most fanciful *deus ex machina* for bringing this about is Milton Friedman's helicopter that flies about spreading money to one and all.

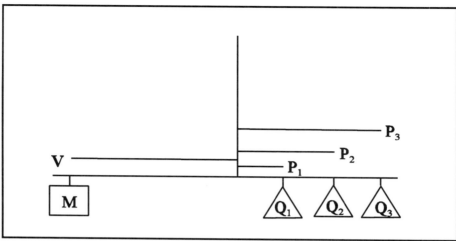

Figure 11

Trade (the Q´s) is not supply -- in fact it is no more to be associated with supply than with demand. The Q´s are the quantities finally sold by those who supply, and bought by those who demand. [Fisher (1911), p.180, italics in original.]

Much of this paragraph strikes me as mystical. Nowhere in Fisher's writings have I been able to find a place where he discusses the determinants of the volume of trade, except to note that this is determined by technology and tastes. In view of the time period that Fisher formulated his ideas and he was writing -- *The Theory of Interest*, his last great book, was published in 1930 -- this is hardly surprising. Fisher almost certainly accepted the view of the time that real activity was determined independently of monetary matters and that equilibrium for real output was always at full employment.

At one point in *The Purchasing Power*, Fisher describes the difference between individual prices and the price level in terms of a wave/water-level analogy. He notes that the shape of individual waves in a body of water are independent of the water level, but that given the level, a high wave (or waves) must necessarily be offset by a low wave (or waves). The water level in this analogy represents the price level, while the height of waves represents individual prices. The tops of waves, measured from the mean water level, represent prices above the mean level of prices (i.e., the general price level), while troughs, again measured from the mean water level, represent prices below the mean level of prices.Fisher's wave/water-level analogy provides a useful point of departure, but I think it can be made even more meaningful by viewing the water in terms

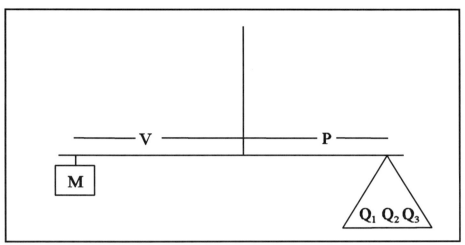

Figure 12

of its total volume rather than its mean level and then taking into account the capacity of the reservoir in which it is held.

As has been emphasized throughout these pages, the stock of money, apart from fiat money, arises through the monetization of the pool of fluid capital. Money is created through the granting of credit (i.e., loans) by banks primarily for the purpose of financing current production. The stock of money, accordingly, is also a pool that is constantly being extinguished and replenished through the paying off of existing loans and the granting of new ones. The *size* of the pool at any point in time is therefore primarily determined by the *interactions of expectations* of firms and banks as to how much ought to be produced out of existing capacity. As production proceeds, income is generated, which represents claims on current output. However, since income is paid in money, these claims at the point that income is paid are represented by money. Income can accordingly be seen as a pool of monetized purchasing power that is juxtaposed against current production (both represented as flows). If all production were destined for current consumption, then the income generated would just be equal (in current prices) to the value of current production. The pool of purchasing power represented by current income could therefore not put upward pressure on the monetary value of current production -- i.e., there could be no upward pressure in this situation on the general price level.[3]

---

[3] I am abstracting, for the moment, from the fact (discussed in Chapter 4) that the expectations which drive the current supply of goods and the expectations which drive the current flow of income are in general separated by one-half of an average production period.

However, there are two other sources of demand for current production that need to be considered, investment and consumption that in the aggregate is greater than current income. Since the pool of fluid capital represents the *maximum* that is available in a closed system to consume or invest, it is simply a matter of arithmetic that the general price level will tend to rise whenever the aggregate of planned consumption and investment purchases, at current prices, is greater than the pool of fluid capital (also evaluated at current prices).

Let us suppose for the moment that this situation actually holds, i.e., that aggregate planned purchases is greater than 'aggregate supply' (as represented by the stock of fluid capital).[4] How will upward pressure on the general price level be manifested?[5] Fisher would appear to say that this somehow happens directly, without the intermediary of individual prices. But this does not make sense. While the excess purchasing power that causes the inflation can arise independently of individual prices, individual prices have to figure in the actual inflation. A preponderance of transactions simply has to occur at higher prices. The way that this will come about is that the excess purchasing power will drive willingnesses-to-pay (i.e., demand) functions to the right, thereby increasing market-clearing prices. If the excess purchasing power funnels into all markets, all prices will increase. If the excess purchasing power funnels into just a few markets, prices in these markets will increase, but prices in the other markets will not go down because there is no diminution in the purchasing power going into them. Indeed, prices in these other markets may actually increase as well because of substitution. The general price level will go up in either case.

The foregoing describes the classical *demand-pull* type of inflation of 'too much money chasing too few goods'.[6] This situation can occur in two ways. The first is through the creation of too much credit by the banking system, while the second is through too much government spending financed by borrowing from the central bank. If the banking system were to make loans only for the purpose of financing current production, then in general the only way that banks could create too much credit would be because expectations are too rosy as a whole.

---

[4] I put aggregate supply in quotation marks in this sentence in order to distinguish aggregate supply as it is being conceived here from the aggregate supply that was defined in Chapter 3. Aggregate supply defined there refers to the flow of output that is currently emerging from production, whereas the aggregate supply defined here refers to the entire stock of goods embodied in the pool of fluid capital. The latter differs from the former by the addition of held-over inventories of finished goods from past production.

[5] I put to the side for now the question of how an excess of purchasing power could come to exist in the first place.

[6] The situation is actually better described as too much purchasing power chasing too few goods.

On the other hand, government purchases financed by borrowing can easily lead to too much aggregate demand. This is clearly most likely to arise when the bonds that finance the expenditure are sold to the central bank, for this is equivalent to running the printing press. It is less likely in the case of bonds sold to the public, for this will usually involve a transfer of existing purchasing power from the public to the government.

As has been noted, income in general is generated in the form of monetized purchasing power. However, we have also noted that, for any given flow of income, the money with which the income is paid has been created prior to its payment. This means, among other things, that the current price level, in an important sense, is already embodied in the flow of current income. Spending out of current income, accordingly, cannot be a contributing source of excess aggregate demand. The source of excess spending has to be in the monetization that takes place prior to the payment of income.

A clear implication of the foregoing is that inflation arises not from the income generated by current production, but from the purchasing power that has been created to finance current production. For this is the pool of purchasing power which pours onto the existing stock of goods and services and either ratifies or changes current prices, and therefore affects the current price level. If this pool of purchasing power (measured as a flow) is greater than the stock of fluid capital valued at current prices, then at least some market-clearing prices must increase, thereby leading to an increase in the current price level (and hence inflation).[7]

The preceding implicitly assumes competitive markets in that any excess purchasing power leads to an increase in the general price level. By the same token, any shortfall in purchasing power will lead to a decrease in (at least some) prices, and therefore to deflation. With competitively determined prices, it is unambiguously clear that inflation (and deflation) is a monetary phenomenon, in that movements in the general price level are tied to 'abnormal' monetization of the stock of fluid capital. I want to turn now to the case in which prices (at least a number of 'key' prices) are not determined competitively, but are administered in some form or another. The question is whether inflation can occur in the

---

[7] As discussed by Von Mises in *The Theory of Money and Credit* -- and in great detail by Schumpeter in *The Theory of Economic Development* -- demand-pull inflation necessarily results in 'forced savings'. This is because the 'extra' purchasing power allows goods to be bid away (through higher prices) from those with lower willingnesses-to-pay. Indeed, Schumpeter saw this process as the essence of development, because it is the (new) purchasing power in the hands of entrepreneurs which allows resources to be transferred from old uses into new uses. Forced saving will be discussed below.

absence of aggregate spending that is in excess of current aggregate supply. As labor accounts for more than 60% of factor payments, let us consider a situation in which labor is hired under a contract that specifies a wage increase that is in excess of productivity gains. Suppose, too, that the firms involved possess some market power in their product markets in the sense that they face demand functions that slope downward. Suppose, also, that there is unemployment.

Figure 13 describes the short-run demand and cost conditions for a typical firm. The firm's short-run capacity to produce is given by the vertical line at K, the short-run marginal cost of operating this capacity is given by the curve ab, and the demand that it expects to face is given by DD. From earlier discussion, we know that the firm would never choose to produce more than q (since an output greater than q could only be sold at a price that is less than short-run marginal cost), but it may choose to produce an amount less than q which could be sold at a price greater than p. The actual amount the firm chooses to produce will depend upon how much market power the firm feels it has. The details of this need not concern us.

Since wages are the major component of short-run cost and since the money wage is assumed to be increasing faster than the rate-of-growth of productivity, the firm knows that its short-run marginal cost curve will be higher next period than in this period. If the firm thinks that its experience is typical of costs and incomes in general, it will also expect next period's demand function to lie to the right of where it is this period. Real demand might be expected to be the same, but money demand would be expected to be higher. In these circumstances, the firm will need a larger loan to finance production for next period than was needed for this period. The firm's bankers will almost certainly go along with the request. The larger pool of purchasing power that is created will allow the higher prices that are expected to actually materialize.

The foregoing describes an inflation that is a cost-push type. The stock of money in this situation is seen to increase *in anticipation* of the inflation. *Actual* inflation is, of course, caused by the larger pool of purchasing power pouring onto the same amount of goods (for the firms and markets in question), but the larger pool was created in the first place by the *anticipation* of higher prices. An increased money stock in this situation is, in effect, a consequence of inflation rather than the cause.

The appropriate framework for analyzing the determination of the general price level, it seems to me, is to balance the existing pool of fluid capital, valued at current prices, against the pool of purchasing power that has been created in anticipation of current production, which is also valued in current prices. If the

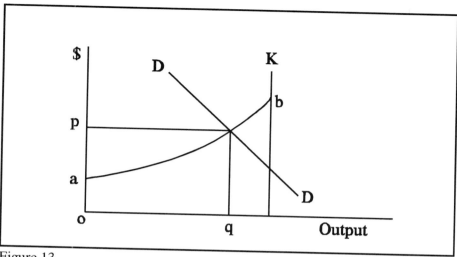

Figure 13

two pools are equal (in volume), there should be no change in the general price level, though there might be changes in individual prices. If the pool of purchasing power is larger than the pool of fluid capital, we should expect prices in general to increase, leading to an increase in the general price level. On the other, if the pool of purchasing power is smaller than the pool of fluid capital, we should expect the general price level to decrease.

In non-competitive circumstances, on the other hand, different results could obtain. If the pool of current purchasing power is larger than the pool of fluid capital, then we should once again expect, for reasons already noted, the general price level to increase. However, if the pool of purchasing power is smaller than the pool of fluid capital, the general price level may not decrease because of failures of administered prices to be reduced. In short, excess aggregate demand will lead to inflation, but a shortfall in aggregate demand need not lead to deflation.

In defining aggregate supply as the pool of fluid capital valued in current prices, an index for the general price level is thereby implicitly defined. The weights in the index correspond to the physical quantities that comprise the goods side of the pool of fluid capital. Since the pool of fluid capital can in principle be valued at each point in time, the index in question is accordingly well-defined in terms of a current quantity-weighted price index. Changes in the general price level can then be defined in terms of changes in this index.[8]

In Figure 14, let the stock of fluid capital valued at current prices be represented by the vertical line at K^*. Define K^* on the vertical axis as well. Let K, defined on the vertical axis, represent the pool of purchasing power that is confronting the goods embodied in the pool of fluid capital. K in this context, can be viewed as *aggregate demand* and K^* can be viewed as *aggregate supply*. Since $K > K^*$ in the figure, aggregate demand is greater than aggregate supply, the general price level must therefore rise in order for constituent markets to clear. The increase in the general price level will accordingly be given by the ratio of K to K^*.

PROBLEMS ARISING FROM EXCESSIVE MONETIZATION OF ASSETS

As has been noted earlier, there is a strong, though often times implicit, tendency in the literature to treat the stock of money as something apart from the level of economic activity. A point I have emphasized in these pages is that this is not the case. The nominal stock of money can obviously be any quantity, but the real stock is always constrained by the pool of fluid capital, for it is the latter that is available to be monetized. Nevertheless, it might be thought that the stock of produced means of production is also available to be monetized, as assets are frequently mortgaged or provided as collateral in order to obtain loans that are used to purchase other assets or to finance current consumption.

In a world of perfect information and perfect crystal balls, there would never be a need to collateralize loans. Production loans would be self-liquidating, while consumption loans would be retired out of future income. If bankers were 'prudent' in such a world, inflation would never be a problem because the amount of money created would never exceed the value in current prices of the pool of fluid capital. In the real world of uncertainty and imperfect information, however, most loans are collateralized. If all goes well, loans will be repaid out of quasi-rents or revenues, and those that are not (because expectations are not

---

[8] Since some production decisions take place at each point in time, the two pools defining aggregate demand and aggregate supply change continuously. Conceptually, therefore, changes in the general price level are also best viewed as occurring continuously, in response to the ebb and flow of the pool of purchasing power against the stock of goods embodied in the pool of fluid capital. However, as data are necessarily collected over intervals of time, rather than continuously, defining a price index that changes continuously is obviously a practical impossibility. Of existing conventional aggregate price indices, the one which comes closest to the continuously chained index which emerges from this discussion is the implicit deflator for GDP. This is because the implicit GDP deflator is, in principle, a current quantity-weighted index.

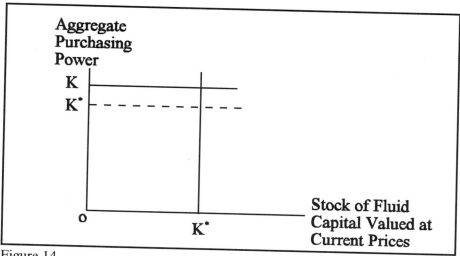

Figure 14

fulfilled) will be covered through the forfeiture of collateral. Once again, 'prudence' essentially guarantees that money creation will be bounded by the pool of fluid capital. While collateralization of loans is clearly reflective of good banking practice, there is nevertheless an associated danger, namely, that vigilance will be relaxed in assessing the expectations that drive the loan demands to begin with.

The worst danger is the situation of excessive collateralization of loans for purchasing *existing* assets, rather than for financing current production or investment in newly produced means of production. Excessive monetization of assets is virtually certain to lead to problems because, as asset prices begin to rise -- as they must in the short run because of a fixed supply -- the ground is laid for new loans to be made using the newly emergent capital gains as collateral. A speculative bubble in asset prices is accordingly created.[9]

The question now becomes: what happens when the speculative bubble in asset prices bursts, as it eventually must? Clearly, there will be a deflation in asset prices, but will there be a spillover into the goods market as well? Whether or not this is the case will depend primarily upon what happens to expectations. If expectations are adversely affected, then investment will almost certainly be depressed, and consumption may become depressed as well, as a consequence

---

[9] So long as the money that is created by an excessive collateralization of assets remains in the asset markets, goods prices will not be affected. But there is the obvious danger that this will not remain the case, so that there could be inflation in the goods market as well.

of an increased desire to save. The result will almost certainly be unemployment and possibly depressed goods prices -- in short, a situation not unlike what occurred in the U.S. during the late 1980s and early 1990s.

One of the implications of the foregoing is a need, when speaking about inflation, to distinguish between inflation in asset prices and inflation in goods prices. Ordinarily, when economists speak of inflation, it is with reference to the goods market. When inflation is viewed just in terms of changes in the general price level for finished goods, it would seem (in view of the experience since WWII) that deflation is a thing of the past. But this is too narrow a view of how money and monetization impinge upon the economy. For it is clear that, while downward flexibility may be (currently) absent from goods prices, this is not the case with respect to asset prices. For speculative bubbles in asset prices that are induced by excessive monetization of assets (both real assets and financial) must necessarily burst, leading to a fall in asset prices to a level consistent with the current value of the pool of fluid capital.[10]

One of the consequences of an asset price deflation following the bursting of a speculative bubble is a forced transfer of assets from debtors to creditors. Not only do debtors face disaster, but many creditors as well, because many loans collateralized by the capital gains that accompanied the run-up in asset prices will themselves have a failure of collateral (i.e., a liquidation value that is less than the face value of the loan). The speculative bubbles in Midwestern agricultural land during the late 1970s and commercial office properties in the late 1980s in the U.S. are clear cases in point.

One of the conclusions of all this is that, in the aggregate, monetization of produced means of production involves an illusion. Although monetization of non-monetary assets is possible for an individual, this is not the case in the aggregate, for once again a fallacy of composition is involved. Loans secured against the value of produced means of production are, in effect, secured against both current and future income, not just current income as is the case with loans secured against the pool of fluid capital. Money as a means of payment that arises out of monetization of produced means of production is, therefore, potentially extremely inflationary if it flows onto the goods side of the pool of fluid capital. This is because (to emphasize again) the real value of the pool of current purchasing power is necessarily constrained (in a closed system) by the pool of fluid capital valued in current prices. If the pool of fluid capital is fully

---

[10] Another way of stating this is that, in equilibrium, asset prices are tied to goods prices, and that causation in fact runs from goods prices to asset prices, rather than vice versa. The deflation of asset prices that occurred in Japan in the early 1990s seems a good case in point.

monetized, then any monetization of produced means of production that adds to the stock of money as a means of payment (as opposed to the stock of money as an asset) is necessarily inflationary.

THE GENERAL PRICE LEVEL AND THE NATURAL RATE OF INTEREST

The natural rate of interest has been defined in terms of the market-clearing price in the market for fluid capital. In the discussion of inflation and the general price level, we have defined changes in the general price level in terms of aggregate demand and aggregate supply, both of which are also associated with the pool of fluid capital. Does this mean that the natural rate of interest is simply another way of looking at the general price level, and visa versa?

The natural interest rate and general price level are closely related, but they are different prices in different markets. As has constantly been emphasized, the pool of fluid capital has two sides. In a sense, it is like a coin. One side, the obverse (or 'heads'), represents the remnants of past saving that are not tied up in produced means of production. It is what is available to finance new investment, current production, and current consumption in excess of current income. This is the 'capital' side of the pool of fluid capital. The natural rate of interest is the price which clears demand and supply in this 'capital' market.

The second side of the pool of fluid capital, the reverse (or 'tails'), represents the inventories of unconsumed consumables, intermediate goods, and investment goods. This is the stock that is consumed or used as input into current production -- food that is consumed by labor, fuel to power machines, raw materials, intermediate goods, etc. In a monetary economy, this stock of goods is purchased (or absorbed) by the pool of purchasing power that is created through monetization of the 'capital' side of the pool of fluid capital. In a monetary economy, goods are transferred through money prices. These prices are established through the interaction of myriad markets, with the general (or absolute) level of prices being determined by the volume of general purchasing power that flows from the 'capital' side of the pool of fluid capital onto the goods side.

The general price level, as we have seen, can be defined only implicitly, and really has meaning only in terms of changes. The general price level can be viewed as changing when the volume of purchasing power emanating from the 'capital' side of the pool of fluid capital is different from the value (at current prices) of the stock of unconsumed consumables and investment goods. The general price level accordingly represents the 'price' (interpreted as an index) which adjusts aggregate demand to aggregate supply on the goods side of the pool of fluid capital.

The implication of all this is that, since the two sides of the pool of fluid capital obviously have to be in equilibrium with one another when the economy is in equilibrium, equilibrium on the 'capital' side implies equilibrium on the goods side. Three equivalent conditions for macroeconomic equilibrium accordingly emerge:

1. Equilibrium of supply and demand in the market for fluid capital;

2. Equilibrium of aggregate demand and aggregate supply;

3. A stable general price level.

EQUILIBRIUM IN THE NATURAL AND MONEY RATES OF INTEREST

Let us now turn our attention to the question of how the money rate of interest is related to the natural rate of interest and the general price level and whether, in equilibrium, the money and natural rates of interest are equal. The money rate of interest, to recall, represents the price at which the pool of fluid capital is monetized, while the natural rate of interest represents the price that adjusts the demand for claims on the pool of fluid capital with the supply of claims. These are different prices in different markets, and it is clear that, in real time, there is no simple mechanical connection between them. On the other hand, it is equally clear that what goes on in one of the markets influences what goes on in the other.

We begin with demands for goods from the pool of fluid capital.[11] These demands initially have to be pursued with money, so that in general the first price that demanders of goods see is the price of acquiring claims to money. The needed money can be obtained either through bank loans or by inducing owners of existing money to give up their holdings. The price charged by banks is clearly a money rate of interest, for loans represent the creation of new money.

---

[11] The demands in question are those which arise from the funding of current production, investment in newly produced means of production, and consumption in excess of current income. Current consumption demands are not included because these demands are funded out of current income, which is paid in money.

However, the price paid to individuals is not a money rate of interest, but a natural rate of interest, because the transactions involved are the transfer of existing claims on the pool of fluid capital (which happen to be in the form of money), rather than the creation of new money. Since the liquidity premium on money sets the lower bound to the price at which holders of money will relinquish their claims, this means that the natural rate of interest must ultimately adjust to liquidity preference.

In a fractional reserve banking system, however, banks can obtain reserves from the central bank as well as from holders of money. This means, accordingly, that the money rate of interest is constrained by liquidity preference only when the cheapest way for banks to obtain reserves is by inducing holders of money to transfer some of their holdings to the banks. In this situation, there is a direct link between the money and natural rates of interest. This is because the money rate of interest is being determined by the liquidity premium on money, which is itself a natural rate. The link is broken, however, when banks are able to obtain reserves from the central bank at a price which is less than the liquidity premium on money. And when this occurs, the stage is set for a 'cumulative process' of inflation to come into existence *a la* Wicksell.

The problem is that a money rate of interest that is less than the natural rate of interest can fuel the creation of an aggregate demand that is greater than aggregate supply. The result, in line with the discussion earlier in this chapter, will be an increase in the general price level. Once begun, the inflation can feed upon itself, as a new pool of purchasing power is created in anticipation of higher prices, the anticipated inflation is realized, and so on.

From this, it is clear that an economy cannot be in equilibrium with a money rate of interest that is less than the liquidity premium on money. Since in equilibrium the natural rate of interest and the liquidity premium must be equal,[12] it follows that the money rate of interest in equilibrium can never be less than the natural rate. The only question, then, is whether in equilibrium the money rate can ever be greater than the natural rate. If the money rate of interest is greater than the natural rate, this means that demanders of current purchasing power can obtain the money needed directly from the 'capital' market cheaper than it can be obtained from banks. This will obviously put upward pressure on the natural rate of interest, driving it toward the money rate. The conclusion from all this,

---

[12] This follows from portfolio adjustment in which yields on different assets, including money, are equalized.

consequently, is that money and natural rates of interest will be equal in equilibrium.[13]

* * *

Although it has not previously been described in these terms, the results of this chapter can be interpreted as representing the equilibrium, or steady-state implications, of the conservation laws that are imposed on a closed economy by the pool of fluid capital. We have seen how the pool of fluid capital provides for natural (and consistent) definitions of aggregate demand and aggregate supply, how aggregate supply in turn provides for a natural (although implicit) definition of the general price level, and how inflation or deflation then results from adjustment of aggregate demand to aggregate supply. An equilibrium price level is then defined in terms of aggregate demand being in equilibrium with aggregate supply. From here, we go on to show that associated with an equilibrium price level is an equilibrium natural rate of interest equal to an equilibrium money rate of interest. All of these are, in essence, equivalent implications of an equilibrium in the market for fluid capital in which inflows into the pool of fluid capital are in balance with outflows.

What is meant by equilibrium in this context is a steady-state equilibrium in which the expectations driving the levels of current production, consumption, saving, and investment in newly produced means of production are harmonized. In real time, such harmonization of expectations is obviously never achieved, and real-world economies will always be in disequilibrium. The key question is whether the behavioral relationships which embody the expectations are dynamically stable. If they are, then the steady-state relationships between aggregate demand, aggregate supply, and the natural and money rates of interests can be seen as 'magnets' (or 'attractors') towards which actual economies are drawn.

---

[13] This might accordingly seem to imply a horizontal equilibrium yield curve, but this is not necessarily the case. The conventional view at present (at least in elementary money and banking textbooks) seems to be that long-term interest rates are determined as geometric means of expected short-term rates. [Cf., for example, Burton and Lombra (2000).] The normally positive slope of the yield curve is then seen as a consequence of the greater uncertainty which attaches to expectations the further they lie in the future. Another factor to be taken into account is the option loss associated with a long-term security as opposed to a short-term one. Since the future is unknown, an 'investor' unexpectedly needing money might have to sell a long-term security at a loss before its maturity. To compensate for this possibility, long-term rates will need to be higher than short-term rates. An additional liquidity premium will accordingly attach to short-term rates. For an analysis of this option effect, see Hlusek (1999).

CHAPTER 7

CAPITAL VALUES, WEALTH, AND RELATED TOPICS

In this chapter, I want to discuss implications of the conservation laws associated with the pool of fluid capital as they relate to asset values in an economy. Specific topics to be discussed include aggregate wealth, real-balance (or wealth) effects, the burden of government debt, taxation of capital gains, gold standards, monetization and demonetization of economies, and economic growth and deflation.

THE AGGREGATE WEALTH OF AN ECONOMY

A term that has been used sparingly to this point is wealth. Wealth at the individual level can properly be viewed as the current flow of income plus the value of all real and financial assets (including Old Masters, rare stamps and coins, and other collectibles). Real and financial assets represent wealth for an individual because their value can be realized for money through sale. For an economy as a whole, however, to represent wealth as the sum total of all individual wealth involves a fallacy of composition. In a closed system, the value of real and financial assets cannot be converted to money in the aggregate because everyone would be trying to sell at the same time so that there would be no buyers.[1]

As we have seen, the sum total of asset values in an economy is bounded by the pool of fluid capital valued in current prices. This means, accordingly, that the aggregate wealth for an economy is simply the economy's pool of fluid capital. Alternatively (and equivalently), aggregate wealth is represented by the current flow of income, plus existing inventories of finished goods valued at

---

[1] The October 1987 stock market crash provides a striking manifestation of this fallacy of composition in operation.

current prices. From the latter, it then follows that in steady-state equilibrium the aggregate wealth of an economy can be characterized in terms of the economy's capacity to consume today without impairing its capacity to consume tomorrow.[2]

MONEY AS WEALTH AND REAL-BALANCE EFFECTS

We now turn to the question of whether money is a component of wealth. Money obviously represents wealth for an individual, but to treat the aggregate stock of money as a component of aggregate wealth once again entails a fallacy of composition. Since the stock of money is created out of the pool of fluid capital, its real value (as we have seen) is clearly bounded by this pool. Hence, to include the stock of money as well as the pool of fluid capital in aggregate wealth would represent double counting.[3]

There is an important implication of this analysis for real-balance effects. Since the real stock of money is bounded by the pool of fluid capital valued in current prices, the stock of money cannot have a value that is independent of the size of this pool. In the aggregate, accordingly, there can be no such thing as Pigou (or real-balance) effects. There can be real-balance effects for individuals, but to posit one in the aggregate again entails a fallacy of composition. *Moreover, this conclusion does not depend upon an absence of fiat money, for the total real stock of money is bounded by the pool of fluid capital, not just the real stock of inside money.*[4]

---

[2] This will be recognized as the Hicksian definition of income [Hicks (1946, p.173)]. It also represents one of the conventional definitions of permanent income [See Friedman (1957, Chapter 3)]. Even with the Permanent Income Hypothesis, one nevertheless has to be wary of a fallacy of composition. For an individual, permanent income is defined by Friedman as rW, where r is an interest rate and W represents the individual's stock of capital, including human capital. Clearly, one cannot define aggregate permanent income as rW^*, where $W^* = \Sigma W$, because of the fallacy of composition mentioned in the text. To describe permanent income in the aggregate as rW^* entails nothing other than defining aggregate wealth as the capitalized value of permanent income, where permanent income is defined to begin with as the capacity to consume today without impairing the capacity to consume tomorrow. To treat aggregate wealth as something apart from aggregate income is simply to play a word game with no substance.

[3] Money clearly makes an extremely important contribution to the wealth of an economy, but it does so as a *social institution* -- an institution which facilitates exchange and reduces uncertainty, thereby contributing to a much higher level of economic activity than would be possible in its absence. However, this is the only sense that money contributes to aggregate wealth.

[4] The implications of real-balance effects for individuals for equilibrium at less than full employment will be discussed in Chapter 8.

SOME IMPLICATIONS OF OLD MASTERS AS A STORE OF VALUE

In Chapter 3 (as well as in the Prologue), we described how Old Masters can emerge as a store of value and how this value depends upon and relates to the pool of fluid capital.[5] In this section, we shall consider how the existence of Old Masters as an asset affects other asset prices, interest rates, and saving and investment.

To begin with, we should clarify just how it is that an Old Master, viewed strictly as a financial investment, yields a return. As already noted, since Old Masters are barren in terms of income, the yield has to result through price appreciation. Specifically, let P_h denote the price expected to obtain for an Old Master at a time h periods in the future, and let P be its current price. Then, a necessary condition for purchase of the Old Master to be attractive as an investment is for:

$$(1) \quad \frac{P_h}{(1 + r)^h} > P,$$

where r represents an appropriate interest rate, for some investment horizon h. Alternatively, this necessary condition can be expressed in terms of the internal rate of return, ρ:

$$(2) \quad P = \frac{P_h}{(1 + \rho)^h}.$$

For the Old Master to be attractive as an investment, it is obviously necessary (in the present context) for ρ to be at least as great as the rate-of-return on equities.[6]

Since, as vehicles for transferring purchasing power over time, Old Masters and equities are substitutes, the emergence of Old Masters as a store of value will clearly put upward pressure on the rate-of-return on equities, and therefore upward pressure on the natural rate of interest. While this might call forth

---

[5] Again, readers are reminded that Old Masters in this context are meant to stand for collectibles in general.

[6] Whether or not investment in Old Masters turns out to be good investments *ex post* is obviously another question. Markets for Old Masters tend to be extremely thin, and willingnesses-to-pay for them are subject to considerable whim, fancy, and fashion. Investment in them is accordingly subject to considerable risk and uncertainty.

additional saving, it might also dampen investment in newly produced means of production. Whether or not there will be upward pressure on the money rate of interest will depend upon what the sellers of Old Masters do with the proceeds. If they purchase equities, then the transaction can be viewed as exchange of Old Masters for equities. In this case, there need be no effect at all on the money rate of interest. By the same token, if the buyers of Old Masters financed their purchases through the sale of equities, then there need not be an effect on the return to equities. Also, there need not be an effect on rates of return if purchase of an Old Master is either out of current income at the expense of current consumption, or out of current saving if the proceeds are used to purchase equities (which is a case that has already been considered). If the seller of an Old Master were to hold the proceeds as money, and the reason for doing so was because of an increase in liquidity preference, both money and natural rates of interest would be subjected to upward pressure.

An alternative way of analyzing the effects of Old Masters as a store of value is in terms of the impact (if any) on the pool of fluid capital. As was noted earlier, the actual creation of the Old Masters requires financing from the pool of fluid capital just as for any other good that is currently produced. Once they are created, Old Masters do not depreciate in the usual sense of the word, but they do give rise to carrying costs which are charged against current income (or, more generally, against the pool of fluid capital). When an existing Old Master is exchanged for money, this is simply an exchange of existing assets and accordingly does not affect either the pool of fluid capital or the capacity of the economy to produce. Production of Old Masters is another matter, however, and the real economy can be affected in two ways. The first is a direct effect arising from the fact that creation of Old Masters does not lead to an increase in the produced means of production, so that investment in Old Masters does not add to the economy's capacity to generate money income --at least not in the way that investment in capacity to produce automobiles does.[7] What Old Masters produce is streams of consumption enjoyment, most of which accrues to their owners without the payment of fees. The only way that Old Masters would generate money income would be if fees were charged for their viewing. Old Masters increase the psychic wealth of an economy, but not wealth as measured by the pool of fluid capital. This is because the capital expended in the original creation of an Old Master is not (in general) returned to the pool of fluid capital through charges against quasi-rents. Investment in the production of Old Masters must accordingly be seen as leading to a diminution of the pool of fluid capital

---

[7] I am abstracting from the fact that it takes time for Old Masters to acquire an 'investment' value. At the time of actual production and purchase, an Old Master is just like any other durable consumption good.

relative to what it would be if the investment had been in newly produced means of production.

The second way that creation of Old Masters can adversely affect the real economy is through an increase in rates of return and a possible increase in the money rate of interest. Since production of Old Masters permanently reduces the stock of fluid capital, the natural rate of interest may be increased. The largest effect, however, is likely to be on incentives to invest in produced means of production. For if firms see an increasing amount of income being spent on Old Masters, as opposed to traditional consumption goods, this may cause an increase in the required return on investment in newly produced means of production.

Does it follow, therefore, that the production of Old Masters must be viewed as a drag on an economy? Obviously, this is not the case, for the emergence of Old Masters as a store of value is the result of voluntary exchange between demanders and suppliers, so that welfare (as usually conceived by economists) has to be higher with their presence than in their absence. What it points out is an increasing divergence, as an economy becomes more and more wealthy, between welfare and money income. Old Masters are included in income only at the time of their production. The streams of consumption enjoyment that they produce over long periods of time do not appear as income. Economies in which Old Masters (or, more generally, works of art) acquire great money value are wealthy economies indeed, for although income does not have to be high for an Old Master to be produced, it does have to be high for Old Masters to have great value. Also, the wealth of such an economy in terms of psychic welfare will be much higher than what is measured by money income.[8]

TAXATION OF CAPITAL GAINS

I turn now to questions concerning the taxation of capital, or more specifically, the taxation of capital gains. A capital gains tax is a tax on the difference between two capital values, or more generally, between two asset values. The asset in question can be a financial asset, as well as a direct claim (i.e., ownership claim), on produced means of production. The first question I wish to address is whether in any meaningful sense, a capital gain represents income.

---

[8] Old Masters as examples of position goods will be discussed in Chapter 12.

Let us begin with the reminder that for an asset that generates income, the value of the asset is the present value of the asset's prospective stream of quasi-rents. For an Old Master (which in general does not generate income) viewed as a store of value, the value of the asset is the discounted price that a buyer today foresees some buyer being willing to pay at some point in the future. In both cases, the capital value of the asset has two determinants:

1. The current stock of fluid capital and,

2. The prospective capacity to produce (or equivalently, the prospective capacity to generate income or to command money in exchange).

The current stock of fluid capital is what provides the *means* to pay, while the prospective capacity to generate a stream of income is what provides the *motivation* to purchase an asset.

How is it that an existing asset can experience a gain in capital value? There are two ways in which this can happen:

1. Through an increase in the prospective stream of income (or, more particularly, an increase in the stream of prospective quasi-rents);

2. Through a decrease in the discount rate used in the calculation of present value.

While (1) is clearly associated with increased income, the increase in asset value represents the capitalized value of this income, rather than income *per se*. A tax on the capital gain would accordingly represent, in part, a tax on current income (assuming that current income is included in the stream of prospective quasi-rents) and, in part, a tax on future income. If income is also taxed directly, then a capital gains tax in addition to the income tax quite clearly represents a double taxation of income. On the other hand, an increase in capital value that is the result of a decrease in the discount rate does not, in any real sense, represent an increase in income at all. A tax on this component of capital gains accordingly amounts to nothing more than an increased tax on future income (because a lower discount rate increases the present value of future quasi-rents).

Advocates of capital-gains taxation see capital gains as income, but this is a mistaken view. The reason that it is incorrect is that, since capital value represents the present value of future income flows, any change in capital values represents changed perceptions of these flows, either because the size of the flows are seen as changed or because the rate at which the flows are discounted is changed. *A capital gains tax is therefore a tax on future incomes.* Only in small part is it a tax on current income. Moreover, the mistake is compounded by the view that capital gains represent an independent source of income. This is simply not the case, for we have just seen that capital gains derive from changed perceptions concerning future income. To tax a capital gain is potentially to tax income multiple times -- *before* it is earned, *each time* a capital gain is realized, and then possibly *twice more* through corporate and personal income taxes (as under current tax laws in the U.S.) as the income is actually realized.

Since a capital gains tax is basically a tax on future income, the burden of the tax is on the owners of the current pool of fluid capital. This is because the tax is paid by those who realize the capital gain, and there is no place to which the tax can be shifted. Since the sale that realizes the capital gain involves an exchange of existing assets -- money in exchange for the asset in question -- the final burden has to be on the current pool of fluid capital. On the other hand, the final outcome obviously depends upon how the tax proceeds are used. If they are used for current consumption, then the final effect of a capital gains tax is in fact a consumption of capital.[9]

The foregoing is with reference to an income-producing asset. What about an Old Master? Suppose an Old Master is sold for a capital gain and a tax is imposed on the gain. In this case, it is very clear that the burden of the tax will again be on the current pool of fluid capital. This is because no income (in the sense of income generation) is involved in the sale/purchase of the Old Master (except possibly for some transactions fees), only an exchange of an existing asset (money) for another. The Old Master has a new value, but all that has taken place is a reshuffling of claims on the existing pool of fluid capital.[10] The burden of the capital gains tax thus must necessarily fall on the current pool of fluid capital.

Consider, next, an empty parcel of land whose value has increased because it is in the expansion path of a nearby city. Suppose, in line with Henry George, that a lump-sum tax is placed on the increase in capital value. Where will the burden of the tax fall in this case? To begin with, it might seem that, because the

---

[9] Similar conclusions apply to the taxation of estates and inheritances.

[10] If the Old Master now has a higher value, while no other asset has a lower value, this simply means that the current pool of fluid capital is larger than when the Old Master was previously valued.

increase in capital value arose from an externality, the current value of the land is independent of the value of the pool of fluid capital. This cannot be the case, however, because aggregate asset values are bounded by the pool of fluid capital. The increased value for the land reflects an increase in willingness-to-pay on the part of at least one party holding claims on the pool of fluid capital, an increase that could arise from either of two sources. If the pool of fluid capital has not changed since the land was originally valued, then any increase in the willingness-to-pay for the land would have to be offset by a decrease in the willingness-to-pay for at least one other asset. On the other hand, if the pool of fluid capital has increased since the land was originally valued, then an increased willingness-to-pay for the land could simply reflect this now larger pool. In short, an increase in capital value for the land has to be the result either of a reallocation of willingnesses-to-pay among assets or an enlargement of the pool of fluid capital.

But whatever the origin of the increased capital value for the land, a lump-sum tax on a capital gain in this situation must, as with any capital gain, be paid out of the current pool of fluid capital. Since in this case the capital gain is not associated with any current flow of income, the result, at least in terms of its initial impact, will be a transfer of already existing claims in the pool of fluid capital to the government. If the tax proceeds support current consumption, then as before the tax will result in a consumption of capital.

FORCED SAVING AND INVESTMENT

I want now to turn to an old controversy between Keynes and Robertson concerning forced saving and investment. In his 1926 book, *Banking Policy and The Price Level*, Robertson (who had collaborated extensively with Keynes in its writing) took as a point of departure that saving had to precede investment, or alternatively that saving had to finance investment. Saving, for Robertson, was therefore seen to consist of two components, voluntary saving, which represented the saving that would voluntarily be forthcoming (out of last period's income) at the current rate of interest, and involuntary (or forced) saving.

For Robertson, forced saving arose when current investment was larger than voluntary saving. Since investment for Robertson *had* to be financed by saving, the shortfall was assumed to be made up by an increase in prices that was sufficient to bid the resources needed by investment away from consumers. Keynes seemed to accept this at the time that *Banking Policy* was being written, but expressed himself otherwise soon after its publication. Keynes did not accept forced saving in the *Treatise*, and rejected it with vehemence in the *General*

Theory. That investment has to be financed by savings is obvious, but the key point is that the savings need not be current. So long as the amount required is resident in the pool of fluid capital, investment can be funded out of past savings. This is not to deny that investment in excess of current voluntary saving can on occasion cause forced saving, only that it is not a necessary consequence.[11]

A view widely held in discussions related to capital theory is that capital goods are different from consumer goods.[12] This is obviously true for the finished goods, but in terms of inputs the difference is much less evident. Certainly, capital goods include machine tools, electronics, and heavy equipment as inputs that consumer goods do not, but much of investment expenditure is for wages and salaries, most of which is in turn spent on consumer goods. This relates to the point made repeatedly in these pages that the pool of fluid capital funds the consumption expenditures of the labor engaged in constructing produced means of production. At the most basic level, the consumer goods that must be available to sustain the labor engaged in constructing produced means of production are food and shelter. As illustrated in the Prologue, escape from an economic state of nature accordingly clearly requires a buildup of food stocks. Shelter is more subtle, in that because of its durability, housing services can be provided from the existing stock of housing for long periods, even in the absence of current additions to the stock. Indeed, with regard to the role of shelter in investment, much of the 'finance' can in principle be provided by workers themselves, especially those who own their housing outright.[13]

Does all of this mean that investment has to be funded by *prior* saving, or can it be funded by current saving as well?[14] The answer to the latter is clearly yes, for it is easily seen that claims that are not exercised on current production allow goods not claimed to be instantaneously available to fund current

---

[11] Keynes, both in the *General Theory* and especially in its defense, was adamant that investment does not require prior saving. Indeed, for Keynes, investment (through adjustment in income via the multiplier) always creates an amount of saving that is just equal to the amount of the investment. As far as I can tell, however, Keynes never paid any attention to the fact that the initial funding of investment has to come out of the pool of fluid capital. In the absence of such a pool, it would seem that Keynes was implicitly assuming that the goods subsumed in investment are instantaneously produced.

[12] Except when the focus is a simple one-sector growth model.

[13] This paragraph clearly identifies a gray area in identifying what is to be included in the pool of fluid capital, specifically with regard to durable goods owned by consumers. These and related questions of measurement are discussed in Appendix 4.

[14] For Robertson, current saving is assumed to be out of last period's income. This is now usually referred to as Robertsonian Saving.

investment. A decision, for example, by a couple to curb their consumption expenditures by foregoing an evening out makes the resources that they would have consumed available to a worker employed on a current investment project.[15]

MORE ON EXCESS MONETIZATION OF ASSETS

Once it is accepted that the real value of the stock of tangible assets is constrained by the stock of fluid capital (valued in current prices), the dangers of loans made on the basis of tangible assets as collateral become apparent. For, in effect, this amounts to a monetization of these assets, and can (as noted in Chapter 6) lead to excess monetization of the pool of fluid capital. The usual type of commercial loan may be secured by claims to produced means of production, but the claims involved are really claims against current production. So long as the amount of purchasing power that is created does not exceed the current value of the pool of fluid capital, inflation cannot be a problem (except in the sense that expectations are in error). However, if the value of assets is monetized as well as the current production that these assets produce, then (as has been noted) there is great danger that too much purchasing power will be created.

The best that might happen is an inflation of asset prices. This would be the case when one asset is mortgaged to buy another asset. If the newly created money stays within the asset market, the general price level for goods will not be affected. However, money that is created for the purpose of purchasing existing assets contains the seeds of its own destruction, for asset price increases often give rise to expected future increases, which can lead to a speculative spiral which can be sustained only by a Ponzi-type scheme of finance. Once the spiral starts and new loans are made on the basis of increased capital values, the only way that interest on the loans can be paid is through further capital gains. Once the money creation stops, the bubble must necessarily burst.

As the bubble bursts, asset values can fall precipitously, leading to the 'destruction' of wealth. While this is a destruction of an individual's wealth, it is not a destruction of the economy's wealth unless something also happens that reduces the pool of fluid capital. With the deflation in asset values, there will be loan defaults. The money that would have been extinguished by the repayment of loans will remain in the economy, and in general will be held by those who were the last to sell the assets in question. The result is a transfer of real wealth

---

[15] Among other things, this illustrates the point that, in terms of production, there is little difference between capital goods and consumer goods, as both require labor and intermediate goods as inputs.

(in the sense of claims on the pool of fluid capital) from banks that had loans defaulted upon and from those with capital losses to holders of money. An important implication of all this is to beware of asset price inflation in a period of stagnation in the real economy, for the inflation of asset prices is almost certainly being fueled through a monetization of assets.[16]

LOAN DEFAULTS AND THE STOCK OF MONEY

As we have seen, prudent application of the Banking Principle of Money Creation implies that the amount of money created -- at least on an expected value basis -- will be consistent with the constraint on the real stock of money that is imposed by the pool of fluid capital. Because of uncertainty, however, some bank loans will not be repaid even with the most prudent application of the principle. In event of defaulted loans, the money that the loans originally created will obviously continue to exist. Does this mean that defaulted loans, in effect, become fiat money? Also, who ultimately bears the burden of defaults? To answer these questions, several cases have to be considered, depending upon whether collateral is involved, and, if so, whether the collateral is sufficient to cover the amount of the loan.

The first (and easiest) case occurs when a defaulted loan lacks collateral and the bank has no recourse against other assets of the defaulting party. In this case, the bank would charge the loss against its capital account, but the money originally created by the defaulted loan will continue to exist.[17] On the other

---

[16] A market in which asset price inflation was spurred, at least in part, by monetization of the assets involved fine art in the late 1980s. The purchase of van Gogh's *Sunflowers* by the Australian Alan Bond for $53m, for which $27m was borrowed from Sothebys, is a prime example. Although the loan to Bond from Sothebys did not involve the direct creation of money, it probably did indirectly because Sothebys almost certainly had borrowed the money from a bank.

Coins represent still another example. The rare (and not-so-rare) coin market is sufficiently thin that a few million dollars can cause prices to shoot upward. Several rare coin funds involving upwards of $100m of 'Wall Street' money were set up in the second half of the 1980s and clearly had a major impact on coin prices. Although these funds were not themselves bank financed, a number of banks started making loans to finance 'investment' in rare coins. At least one of these, the West Coast Bank of Encino, CA went under, resulting in the acquisition by the FDIC of portfolios of coins that had provided collateral for loans that had gone sour when the bubble in the rare coin market burst in 1990 and 1991.

The conclusion from these last two examples is that money creation for the purpose of investing in collectibles is extremely imprudent, for the only way that collectibles (or any position good, for that matter) can earn a return is through appreciation in prices that are sustained by increases in the pool of fluid capital.

[17] The only exception to this would be if the money in question were strictly a liability of the bank involved (as could have occurred in the U.S. in the nineteenth century), in which case the 'bank notes' would eventually be presented for redemption in 'lawful' money.

hand, if the defaulted loan was collateralized, the pledged assets will pass to the bank and the money that was originally created by the loan will be extinguished when the pledged assets are sold by the bank. In this case, the burden will be borne by the defaulter rather than by the bank. Suppose, however, that the amount obtained by sale of the collateral does not cover the original loan. In this case, an amount of money equal only to the sales proceeds from the collateral will be extinguished. The bank will charge the difference against its capital account, and this difference will also continue to exist as money. In this case, the burden of the default will be shared proportionately between the bank and the defaulter.

Of the money originally created by the defaulted loan, a part will continue in existence that is equal to the difference (if positive) between the amount of the loan and the sales proceeds of the pledged collateral. If no collateral was pledged, the entire amount of the defaulted loan will continue to exist as money. Since, in normal circumstances, bank money is convertible into fiat money at the option of the holder, the money in question may therefore eventually take the form of fiat money. The conclusion, accordingly, is that the part of defaulted loans not covered by collateral can become a net addition to the stock of fiat money.[18]

CROWDING-OUT

I want to turn now to the financing of public expenditures and the insights that the present framework might have regarding 'crowding-out'. Crowding-out, to recall, refers to public expenditure that is financed by debt at the expense of private investment. This view, which is periodically recycled, is most prominently associated in this century with the British 'Treasury View' of the late 1920s and early 1930s.[19]

The standard argument regarding crowding-out is that it occurs through an increase in the rate of interest. The view seems to be that there is a fixed amount available to finance investment, the public sector has first crack, and what remains (if any) is then rationed to the private sector through a higher rate of

---

[18] However, it does not follow from this that the total stock of money will necessarily be increased, for when banks obtain fiat money (i.e., currency) from the central bank their reserves are correspondingly reduced.

[19] The 'Treasury View' was the response of the British Treasury to the views, proposed by Keynes and Hubert Henderson in *Can Lloyd George Do It?*, to combat unemployment through debt-financed public works. An excellent account of the debate is given by Clarke (1988).

interest. A key ingredient in this argument is the assumption (usually implicit) that investment can be financed (in a closed system) only out of current saving.

To begin with, the assumption that investment (whether public or private) *has* to be funded out of current saving is incorrect. As we have seen, the only time when this is the case is at the time of escape from an economic state of nature. When a non-empty pool of fluid capital exists, investment can be funded from the pool even in the absence of current saving. In itself, however, this does not dispose of the crowding-out argument, for it only says that we have to focus on the total pool of fluid capital, not just on inflows into it. In assessing whether crowding-out can occur, a number of factors need to be taken into account, including:

1. How the deficit is financed;

2. Whether the deficit finances public investment in produced means of production, current operations, or transfer payments to individuals;

3   Effects on the *money* rate of interest;

4   Effects on the *natural* rate of interest;

5. Effects on the general price level.

There are three possible ways that a government deficit can be financed: (1) through sale of bonds to the domestic public; (2) through sale of bonds to foreign purchasers; (3) through the sale of bonds to the central bank. For now, it will be assumed that bonds are sold to the domestic public. Since the bonds are sold for money, the first question to ask is from where does the money come. Two possibilities have to be considered:

1. If the bonds are sold to the non-bank public, the money has to come from the stock of money being held as an asset. Obviously, this requires that the bonds be priced such that some individuals be willing to substitute money for bonds. *Ceteris paribus*, this will put downward pressure on the prices of financial assets.

2. If the bonds are sold to commercial banks, the initial effect will be to reduce the free reserves of the banking system. The banking system, accordingly, has reduced capacity to lend,

therefore less capacity to create money. For bankers to be
induced to buy the bonds, the price of the bonds must be low
enough that banks are willing to hold them in lieu of loans. In
this case, the public sector can be seen as competing directly
with the private sector for use of bank reserves.

If the central bank is not accommodative, the end result in either situation
will almost certainly be upward pressure on the money rate of interest. The effect
will be direct for the case in which the bonds are sold to banks, but indirect in the
case in which the bonds are sold to the non-bank public. In the latter case, there
need not be any upward pressure at all if the banking system has sufficient
reserves that it does not have to raise the money rate of interest in order to attract
additional reserves from the public's holdings of money as an asset.

So much for the moment about the money rate of interest, what about the
natural rate of interest? Since equilibrium for the natural rate of interest can be
identified with a stable general price level, I will focus the discussion in terms of
the latter. What ultimately happens depends upon the impact of the public deficit
on the pool of fluid capital. At this point, we need to distinguish among the uses
to which the proceeds from the sales of bonds are put. There are three possibilities:

1. Investment in public-produced means of production. In terms of
    the effect on the pool of fluid capital, there is no difference
    between public investment and private investment. Both
    represent direct draws from the pool. If, everything else being
    constant, this results in upward pressure on the general price
    level, which in turn causes private firms to reduce the amount
    that they invest, one can clearly identify a crowding-out effect.

2. Funding of current governmental operations (wages, salaries,
    etc.). This situation represents a borrowing to fund the current
    output of government for which there is no revenue stream (i.e.,
    no inflow of taxes). Since consumption out of private-sector
    income is likely to be larger than what would be the case if
    taxes were larger, consumption in the aggregate is likely to be
    larger, which will put upward pressure on the general price
    level. In this case, however, price increases are more likely to
    be concentrated in consumption goods than in investment
    goods, so that investment plans of private firms may not be
    adversely affected. Still, this is not necessarily the case, so that
    once again there exists a possibility of some crowding-out.

3. Transfer payments to individuals in the private sector. This situation differs from the preceding one in that the public sector makes no purchases from the pool of fluid capital. Since (at least on Keynesian grounds) the presumption is that recipients of transfer payments have a high marginal propensity to consume, the final process can be interpreted as a loan to finance consumption. Indeed, even if the recipients of the transfers have marginal propensities to consume equal to the average marginal propensity to consume for the economy as a whole, the net effect will be a stimulus to consumption. This is because the proceeds from the sale of bonds in general are drawn from (the claims side of) the pool of fluid capital rather than out of current income. The result, accordingly, is some likely upward pressure on the general price level and therefore possibly some crowding-out.

The important point in all this is what ultimately happens to the economy's capacity to produce. Public investment obviously leads to an increase in the stock of produced means of production and therefore to an increase in the capacity to produce. In this case, even if there is some crowding-out, it can be viewed as a substitution of public for private investment, and it is possible that public investment is the more productive. Borrowing to finance public investment is very different in this regard than borrowing to finance current government operations and transfer payments. While it may be that the stimulation to consume that the latter activities entail may induce private firms to increase investment, this is not likely. Failing this, the only way that these activities could add to the capacity to produce would be if the expenditures were to result in the creation of human capital. A conclusion accordingly seems clear: *Public borrowing to finance current governmental operations and transfer payments is almost certainly a drag on economic growth.*

Let us now consider the situation in which the public deficit is monetized immediately through sale of bonds to the central bank. The obvious difference between this case, and that in which bonds are sold to the public is a net addition from the start to the stock of money. Any inflationary tendencies will accordingly be magnified, especially in the case of transfer payments. And any crowding-out tendencies will be magnified as well. Whether or not there will be inflation in the circumstances depends upon how fully monetized is the pool of fluid capital. If the money created by purchasing bonds by the central bank over-monetizes the pool, there will be inflation, and this will be the case independent of the use to which the proceeds are put. For a given degree of over-monetization, however, inflation pressures will be highest for transfer payments and lowest for public investment.

The final possibility is sale of bonds abroad. Since the proceeds are to be used domestically, they must ultimately be converted into domestic currency. There are obviously a number of mechanisms through which this could occur, but whichever is used it is clear that once converted the proceeds will represent an addition to the active stock of domestic currency. *Ceteris paribus*, this means that, as before, any over-monetization of the pool of fluid capital will lead to upward pressure on the general price level.

There is one other factor to be considered, however, the possibility that any excess monetization of the pool of fluid capital will spill over onto imports. Indeed, with free trade this will almost certainly happen. With free trade and convertible currencies, the pool of fluid capital relevant to an economy is not just the domestic pool, but the pools of fluid capital of all of the economy's trading partners.[20]

BURDEN OF THE NATIONAL DEBT

Many years ago, Franco Modigliani pointed out that the burden of the National Debt (in a closed system) on future generations is not the higher taxes they will have to pay, but rather the taxes that must be paid out of an income that may be lower than it otherwise would be.[21] Actually, the debt *per se* is not the issue, but the uses to which the proceeds of the debt are put. If the debt funds investment in newly produced means of production (including human capital), then (assuming that the investment is productive) the capacity of the economy to produce will be increased. Income will be higher and the debt can be 'repaid' from the resulting quasi-rents with no burden on the generation involved.

However, if proceeds from the debt are used to fund current government operations or transfer payments, there is clearly a problem, for in general it is

---

[20] Statements that borrowing from abroad has financed a U.S. consumption 'binge' during the 1980s and much of the 1990s would thus appear to have some validity. The deficit in the balance of payments during these years would appear to be a direct consequence of the Federal Government's decision to fund current operations and transfer payments through borrowing. These decisions have stimulated consumption (at the expense of investment), and upward pressures on the domestic price level have been alleviated by a virtually infinitely elastic supply of imported consumption goods at current prices. This was possible, even with the deterioration in exchange rates *vis-a-vis* the dollar, because of strong productivity gains abroad.

[21] See Modigliani (1961).

consumption that is being funded rather than investment. Unless this somehow results in a stimulus to private investment, future generations are clearly made worse off because the capacity of the economy will be smaller than if the public debt were used to fund investment.[22] This is the essential thrust of Modigliani's point, and it is completely consistent with the framework of this book.[23]

RICARDIAN EQUIVALENCE

One of the tenets of the 'New' Classical Economics is the Ricardian Equivalence Theorem -- due originally to Ricardo, but most recently rediscovered by Barro (1973) -- which states that, under certain conditions, the public is indifferent to whether a public expenditure is financed by debt or by taxes. The conditions are that taxpayers have an infinite horizon and that the future is discounted at the same rate of interest as applies to the debt. Under these conditions, the discounted value of the stream of future interest payments on the debt is equal to a current equivalent tax. Tobin (1980) provides a detailed critique of Barro's analysis and conclusion, especially with regard to distribution effects (in connection with varying marginal propensities to consume) and the assumption that taxpayers discount the future at the same rate the government pays interest on the debt. Here, I want to comment briefly on a different kind of distribution effect, namely, whether public borrowing affects private investment differently than does taxation.

In general, it is to be expected that a different group of people will buy bonds than would pay an equivalent amount of taxes.[24] If the debt is purchased by the non-bank public, then the proceeds will be drawn from the stock of money being held as an asset, and this will tend to put upward pressure on both the natural and money rates of interest. If, on the other hand, the debt is purchased by banks, reserves of the banking system will be reduced, again putting upward pressure on the money rate of interest. In either case, private investment could be adversely affected. What, however, if the public expenditure is tax financed? The

---

[22] A similar conclusion applies to a tax 'fund' that is built up avowedly to 'finance' future social security payments, but which in reality is simply used to cover what would otherwise would be a deficit in current spending. This will be discussed in Chapter 12.

[23] My own view in all this is that the driving force of the problem is the continuing decisions of the Federal Government to fund consumption rather than investment. When this is juxtaposed with the anti-investment bias of the current tax system (the existence of a capital gains tax, the corporate income tax, and estate and inheritance taxes), investment clearly receives a double whammy.

[24] I am assuming here that the debt is sold to the public, rather than to the central bank. I am also assuming that the public expenditure in question is for current operations rather than investment.

key consideration, here, is that taxes are paid out of current income and are likely to be (in part, anyway) at the expense of current consumption. This being the case, there will be less upward pressure on the natural and money rates of interest than if the public expenditure is financed by debt. The conclusion thus seems to be that debt finance is more disruptive of private investment than tax finance. If this is the case, then a forward-looking economy should not be indifferent between taxation and debt finance, for there is a prospect of a larger future capacity to produce with tax finance.[25]

COMMODITY MONEY

The focus throughout the discussion to this point has been on bank and fiat money. Nothing really has been said about commodity money. Money, as has been emphasized, is a social invention that enables specific property rights to be converted into general property rights through the creation of general purchasing power. To state the obvious, commodity money differs from fiat money in that commodity money has value as a commodity as well as money. For concreteness in the discussion that follows, the commodity money will be assumed to be gold.

The first question to ask is how it is that gold acquires a value in the first place. Just as the basis for value for bank and fiat money is the pool of fluid capital, so too for commodity money. As seen in the Prologue, gold acquires value in exactly the same way as do Old Masters: someone with claims to goods in the pool of fluid capital finds gold desirable and is willing to exchange these claims for it. If there is no fiat money in the economy, so that all exchange is by barter, a set of relative (prices) will be established, which gives the prices at which gold can be exchanged against the goods in the pool of fluid capital. If the desirability of gold is widespread, people will be willing to exchange goods for gold and gold for goods, so that gold can be used as a medium of exchange. The prices of goods in terms of gold simply become the 'prices' in the economy. The important thing in all this is that gold's value as a commodity is not intrinsic, but arises out of the pool of fluid capital, just as with Old Masters. The social invention in this case, although not as apparent as for fiat or bank money, is the implicit agreement amongst participants in the economy to use gold as a medium of exchange, and therefore as general purchasing power.

Although gold is sufficiently desirable in relation to its supply that it has high value in relation to weight/volume, it is nevertheless cumbersome to carry

---

[25] Again, this is the case for public expenditure for current operations. The situation can obviously be different if the expenditure is for public investment.

around in large quantities, and security is required when it is held as a store of value. Gold would thus come to be stored in a secure place under lock and key, with receipts being issued to owners. With 'confidence' that the amount of gold registered on the receipt could be redeemed on demand, the receipts could, and would, be used in exchange in place of the gold that they represented. These claims on money come to function as money themselves. Since in a period of confidence little of the gold would be actually withdrawn from depositories, it is a simple step for custodians of gold to begin making loans and then to begin to function as bankers. 'Reserves' in this case would be hard money, rather than central bank credit, as with bank money.

Since the commodity value of gold is dependent upon the size of the pool of fluid capital, it is clear that, as with bank and fiat money, the real value of the stock of gold money is bounded by this pool, only in this case the connection is more transparent, since all of the quantities are real commodities. Yet, there should be no mistake in thinking that the connection of the stock of money to the pool of fluid capital is any less real with bank or fiat money. Concerning inflation and deflation, goods prices will rise in terms of gold whenever the pool of purchasing power represented by the stock of gold (functioning as media of exchange) is greater than the stock of goods valued in current prices. Deflation will ensue in the opposite case. Changes in the general price level thus occur in the same way with commodity money as with bank and fiat money.

FLUID CAPITAL AND THE GOLD STANDARD

I want now to examine the theory of capital and money that is being developed in these pages in the context of a gold standard. Two forms of the constraint imposed by a gold standard need to be considered. The first is where the amount of money in the economy is fixed by the amount of gold that is available -- i.e., gold is the only type of money. The second form of constraint is where other types of money also exist, bank money in particular. Although the first form is clearly unrealistic, it represents an important extreme to examine.

Consequently, let us assume that there is a fixed quantity of gold in an economy that somehow came to be regarded as money. There are a number of ways this might occur, but let us assume that the gold was simply imported into a previously purely barter economy. Specifically, assume that the gold was imported as payment for goods that had been exported. Payment for the exported goods by gold establishes a price for those goods in terms of gold. Through the barter exchange rates of the goods exported with the other goods in the economy, gold prices for all the goods in the economy are established as well. Since the gold represents current production that is not consumed by residents of the economy, it also represents current saving and therefore represents an addition to the stock of fluid capital (at least in terms of purchasing power). Assume that the gold immediately acquires the mantle of being money.

Assume, next, that the owners/holders of the gold are besieged with requests for loans, either for investment in newly produced means of production or for the finance of current production. As loans are made in gold, the gold disperses throughout the economy and begins functioning as a medium of exchange. As economic activity proceeds, the gold prices of some goods can increase in response to increased demands, but any increases must be offset (in value) by decreases elsewhere. The reason for this is that the general price level was established by the gold price of the goods that were exported for the gold to begin with, and so long as the quantity of gold does not change, neither can the general price level -- except possibly to decrease in the event that some goods are sold at a loss. The key point is that, with a fixed quantity of gold, the general price level cannot increase -- i.e., there can be no inflation.

Suppose, now, that one of the holders of gold makes a loan in the form of a slip of paper that represents a claim on gold rather than literally transferring gold to the person getting the loan. Assume that the claim begins to circulate as a medium of exchange. What are the inflationary implications in this situation? So long as both the gold and its claim ticket do not circulate simultaneously -- i.e., there is a 100% gold reserve -- the situation is no different than before; the general price level can go down, but can never go up. The situation will clearly be different, however, if the holders of gold were to create claim-ticket loans in excess of the amount of gold that is held. In this case, inflation is quite clearly a possibility. This situation obviously corresponds to a fractional reserve banking system, with gold acting as the 'high-powered' money.

At the point that gold enters the economy as payment for the goods that are exported, the general price level is established, as already noted, in terms of the gold price of the exports and the barter rates of exchange of the exports with the other goods in the economy. Let us suppose that through investment in produced means of production the economy begins to grow. What will happen to the general price level, assuming that the amount of gold remains fixed? If all loans are made in gold or claim-tickets to gold with 100% reserve, it is clear that the general price level must fall, for the value of production in terms of gold cannot change (since the amount of gold is fixed), but the volume of output is increasing. The general price level *has* to fall.[26]

The important question concerning an economy with a fixed amount of gold circulating as money, is whether this will permit the economy to function properly -- i.e., can both current production and investment in new capacity be financed in ways that allow the economy to grow? To deal with this question, we need to consider two cases, the first being where the stock of gold represents all of fluid capital and the second being the more normal case in which the gold is only a part of fluid capital. In the first case, it is clear that the gold is adequate to finance both investment and current production, although most probably at low levels. However, this will not be true in the second case, unless the structure of transactions were such that the gold could have a high velocity of circulation or unless there remained a lot of barter. In general, other forms of money would be needed, either in the form of a fractional reserve banking system based on the gold or in the form of trade credit or bills of exchange.

It might seem in this (the second) case that the 'shortage' of gold at the prices established by the gold price of the exports (that created the gold stock to begin with) could be dealt with simply by an upward revaluation of the stock of gold (i.e., by proportional decreases in all prices). Assuming that this could somehow be done, would it work? It seems that the only way it could work would be if the economy were to be closed to external trade. For if the trade that led to the import of gold to begin with were to continue, it is hard to see how the price level could be made to fall by the proper amount, the problem being that the price level (in terms of gold) is established by the gold price of exports.[27]

It has been stressed repeatedly that the pool of fluid capital has two sides, a claims side and a goods side. If gold represents the claims side, what balances the gold on the goods side? Unless the gold is seen as also representing a good, there would seem to be a problem, for since the gold's existence arose in exchange for exports, it lacks a counterpart in goods. In this case, it seems pretty clear that consistency with the definition of the pool of fluid capital that has been advanced does require that the gold be a good as well as representing a claim. Nevertheless, there still seems to be a problem, for with gold as the good that is monetized, where are the goods that the gold can come up against when it is

---

[26] Obviously, this need not be the case if more gold is imported (or is produced domestically) or if the holders of gold begin to function as bankers operating under a fractional reserve.

[27] If the general price level should somehow be reduced, then exports would become less expensive, and there would be an influx of gold, which in turn should eventually lead to increases in the price level.

expended? For there would appear to be a shortfall of goods in the pool of fluid capital equal to the value of the gold. If the gold were expended in a forward market -- i.e., if the goods purchased are for forward delivery -- there would be no need for prices to increase. However, this would not be the case if the spending were for goods for current delivery; some prices would have to go up.

On the other hand, suppose that the gold were in the economy all of the time, but had never functioned as money. Owners of it had simply desired it for its beauty (i.e., as an Old Master). Assume that via some form of social revelation, people suddenly see the use of gold as a medium of exchange to overcome the inefficiencies of barter. The first question to ask is what will determine the level of prices. If gold has previously been traded, it is clear that prices will be determined in terms of the barter exchange rates for gold. If gold has never traded, then prices will be determined in terms of the *highest* reservation price for exchanging gold for goods among owners of gold. The general price level in effect will be determined by the reservation supply price of a single person. As gold begins to function as a medium of exchange, it obviously acquires a use which it did not have before. In an important sense, it has become part of the economy's capacity to produce. Its marginal (or incremental) product is the increased output that is made possible by the elimination of barter. This added output is clearly a public good.[28] If gold is part of the economy's produced means of production, does this mean that it is not to be counted in the pool of fluid capital? The answer is no, for being money, the gold is fluid capital *par excellence*. In short, gold is *both* produced means of production and fluid capital. Moreover, as produced means of production, gold has one exceptionally desirable characteristic -- it is extremely durable and rarely has to be replaced. In addition, with gold being both produced means of production and fluid capital, the initial investment in it does not have to be charged against revenues in order to be returned to fluid capital.[29]

As has been emphasized throughout these pages, the pool of fluid capital provides an upper bound to the real stock of money in an economy. A gold standard does not alter this, but in the presence of prices that are inflexible downward, a gold standard can impose a bound to the real stock of money that is lower than that imposed by the pool of fluid capital. With flexible prices, the

---

[28] It should be noted that once gold starts circulating as a medium of exchange, it cannot also simultaneously continue to function as an Old Master. People can, of course, hold gold as an asset, but any return would be dependent upon changes in the general price level. The return would be negative in the case of inflation, positive in the case of deflation.

[29] Gold is not peculiar in this regard. Any highly desirable form of money has this characteristic. The extreme is electronic money (i.e., numbers in accounts) which obviously never wears out.

general price level can adjust so as to bring the stocks of gold and fluid capital into equilibrium with one another. With inflexibly downward prices, however, a loss of gold can result in a price level that is too high for the gold that remains in relation to the pool of fluid capital.

DEMONETIZATION & MONETIZATION OF ECONOMIES

It was just noted in connection with the gold standard that monetization of an economy is clearly a public good, in that the efficiency gains that accompany the escape from a barter system accrue to the economy at large and are shared by everyone. The flip side is that there are efficiency losses when an economy demonetizes. The standard case of demonetization is when the currency begins to break down because of inflation. As this happens, an economy (in the absence of gold or an external currency assuming the role of money) will begin to resort to barter, and productivity will necessarily fall.

I now want to consider a somewhat different case, namely, the monetization of the economies of Eastern Europe. The problem that these countries had to face is usually posed in terms of moving from a socialist command economy to a capitalist one, but implicit in this is a movement from a non-monetary to a monetary economy. It is not that money did not exist in a socialist command economy. However, its essential function was as a claim ticket to a discretionary portion of the social dividend. Because Eastern European economies saved and invested, pools of fluid capital existed, but these pools were directed to end uses (i.e., investment in produced means of production, current production, or consumption) by command, rather than through monetization and a market price system. With break up of the Soviet system came a breakdown in the command system, and institutions and experience were not in place to monetize the stocks of fluid capital and organize production and investment through market-based price systems.

Since monetization essentially had to begin from scratch, one would almost certainly have to expect a fall in productivity from what was the case in the command economies. This is almost certainly what occurred in Russia during 1991 and 1992. The problem was not an absence of money, but an absence of money in the right places. Getting money into the right places requires the creation of a banking system that will facilitate, on a prudent basis, the monetization of the pool of fluid capital.[30] The loss in productivity as an economy ceases being command and begins to monetize is in principle temporary, but there is another factor to be taken into account. This is that the goods the economy is structured to produce under a centrally directed command system may not -- indeed, almost certainly will not -- be the goods that consumers will demand when they are able to freely choose according to their tastes and preferences. If the produced means of production cannot be converted to produce what consumers want, then there is obviously a problem, and much of the existing capacity to produce will have to be abandoned, with the capital that remains embodied in it lost forever.

While the foregoing is likely a problem to some extent in Russia, what appears more so is that much of the physical capital stock of the economy is either technologically obsolete or nearly worn out (or both). Additionally, the capital embodied in it has not, through appropriate charges against production, been repatriated back into the pool of fluid capital. The capital, instead, has been consumed. In short, while the capacity of Russia to produce at the time of the breakup of the Soviet system appeared to be large on paper, its pool of fluid capital may, in fact, have been small.

Let me now turn to the question of monetization of what has previously been a command economy. By monetization in this context, I have in mind both the emergence of a set of financial institutions for monetizing the pool of fluid capital and the emergence of a system of relative prices for guiding production, investment, and consumption decisions. While money and prices obviously exist in a command economy, prices are not formed on the basis of relative scarcities and consumer/investor willingnesses-to-pay. An interesting question is how will the general price level become established in an economy such as Russia's. In a western economy, a question such as this is, in general, only of interest to philosophers; price levels already exist, so that the first emergence (or creation) of a general price level is not a question of practical interest. This is not the case, however, for an economy emerging from central direction.

The first question that has to be asked is whether there are any prices in the economy that genuinely reflect relative scarcities. The only real candidates for this are goods traded internationally at international prices. Traded goods will have both an internal price and an international price, but the price that really

---

[30] Obviously, creation of a financial system is only one of the tasks. Markets and meaningful relative (and absolute) prices must be created, and participants must acquire experience in their use. [For a discussion, see McKinnon(1991)]. This has especially been the case in Russia, where a meaningful market economy last operated in 1917.

matters is the international price. All that is needed for a starter is that there be one such traded good (it does not matter whether it is an import or an export), but this is just the starter. There must also come into existence a credible primary money, by which I mean a money that not only is acceptable as money internally, but is freely convertible into western currency. Domestic money usually does not qualify at this point, because it is not freely convertible, so candidates are western currencies (such as the dollar, mark, or now the euro) or gold.[31]

Once a primary money is in place, monetization of the pool of fluid capital can begin in a meaningful manner. The primary money and domestic money must be convertible into one another at an exchange rate that is freely determined. Loans should be made in domestic currency, but the domestic currency must be convertible into the primary money on demand. It is especially important that loans be short-term and satisfy strict commercial banking criteria. As the exchange rate between domestic currency and the primary money becomes established and stabilizes, there will emerge a general price level (measured in units of domestic currency) that has really been determined by the primary-money prices of traded goods. In the circumstances, it is obvious that it will take some time (possibly even a considerable period) for relative prices to stabilize, but in general this will not affect the general price level so long as there is no change in the primary-money prices of traded goods, and there is no marked change in the domestic-currency/primary-money exchange rate.

It is important, of course, that financial institutions -- specifically, a banking system based upon the primary money -- come into existence and foster orderly, prudent monetization of the pool of fluid capital. Since convertible western currencies can function as the primary money, an evident institutional arrangement to consider is the establishment of a currency board. The thing that has to be accomplished is to develop confidence on the part of Eastern European populations in their domestic currencies as money. A way of accelerating this is to take the dollar or euro or gold as the primary money, tie the domestic currency to the primary money by making gold freely convertible into the other, and then tie creation of domestic currency to holding of the primary money. Above all, the creation of domestic currency through loans must be guided by strict commercial prudence. Loans must be short-term and self-liquidating.[32]

---

[31] For a detailed analysis of the points in this paragraph, see McKinnon (1991).

[32] The absence of a viable fiducial structure has been especially apparent in Russia in the 1990s. Among other things, the economy lacks a banking system that allows for the funding of current production by the creation of money through self-liquidating short-term loans. As a consequence, much of the economy is barter driven. For a discussion and analysis, see [Woodruff (1999)].

ECONOMIC GROWTH WITH DEFLATION: THE PERIOD 1873 - 1896 IN THE UNITED STATES

A period of U.S. economic history that has always been fascinating to me is 1873-1896, a period of strong economic growth with steadily decreasing prices. Because economic growth combined with deflation is a somewhat unusual phenomenon, I want now to explore its accommodation within the present framework. As discussed earlier, changes in the general price level are approached in a supply/demand framework in which supply is defined in terms of the goods embodied in the pool of fluid capital, while demand is defined in terms of the pool of purchasing power actively seeking to purchase goods and services. As noted earlier, current income, since it is implicitly valued (or measured) in current prices, cannot, in itself, be the basis for inflation, although saving that is not offset by investment can be the basis for deflation.

As inflation has already been discussed, I want now to look at deflation. Let me consider first the case of where the banking system is fractional reserve, with gold as the primary money. In order to keep things simple yet realistic, assume that there are only two types of goods in the economy, agricultural products and manufactures. Assume, as was the case during 1873-1896, that productivity is increasing in both sectors. Simply as a matter of arithmetic, we know that, with increasing productivity, the growth in real income can occur through a combination of constant money wages and a falling price level, as well as through a combination of rising money wages and a constant price level. My concern is to identify a set of circumstances that allows for the former to occur.

Let us consider first the case where gold is being exported in payment for imports of capital goods. With a fractional reserve banking system that is tied to gold, the import of goods necessarily means that the amount of money that the banking system can create is reduced. This means that the pool of purchasing power that confronts the goods in the pool of fluid capital valued in current prices will be less than that value. Prices will fall, but can they fall in a way that does not harm the suppliers of the goods? For harm not to occur, relative prices must not be changed. As we have seen, the general price level in an economy on a gold standard is (in the absence of excess creation of money) determined by the gold price of exports. Alternatively, we can see the general price level being determined by the gold price of imports. If gold is exported because the gold price of imports has fallen, then in order to keep the relative price of imports and domestic goods constant, the gold prices of domestic goods must fall as well --

in short, there must be a general deflation, with no change in relative prices.[33]

The second case to be considered is where there is not an export of gold, or more specifically, where there is no foreign trade. Can growth and deflation occur in a closed economy? While the arithmetic of increasing productivity makes it clear that this could in fact occur, it is difficult to think of a mechanism that would bring it about, the problem being that it is not clear what the incentives would be for producers and bankers to create a reduced pool of purchasing power. With a loss of gold through exports as just considered, the amount of money that can be created is necessarily reduced, but loss of gold is not at issue in a closed economy. A mechanism that might do the trick is through productivity gains in agriculture. These could lead to lower food prices, which in turn might induce laborers to reduce money labor-supply prices, which in turn could lead manufacturers to reduce the money prices of manufactures. All of this could in principle occur without affecting relative prices. In this case, the general price level would, in effect, be determined by the gold price of agricultural goods.

---

[33] An obvious question at this point is whether the U.S. was in fact exporting gold during the period 1873-1896.

CHAPTER 8

MACROECONOMIC EQUILIBRIUM AND EMPLOYMENT

I now turn to a perennial question in macroeconomics since the time the *General Theory* was published: Can an economy be in equilibrium at less than full employment? Keynes's answer in the *General Theory* was a clear yes. His reasoning (and mechanism) was that aggregate output and income are determined by the Principle of Effective Demand. Aggregate expenditure (and therefore income) is equal to the sum of consumption and investment expenditures, consumption (and therefore saving) is primarily determined by the level of income, investment is determined by the interest rate, and the interest rate is determined by Liquidity Preference. Savings and investment are brought into equilibrium through adjustments in the level of income, rather than through adjustments in the rate of interest. The resulting equilibrium level of output determines the level of employment, and there is no necessity for this to be at the full-employment level. Full employment could be foreclosed, for Keynes, either because of the 'liquidity trap' or because of a depressed marginal efficiency of capital.

Although Keynes claimed he was attacking a classical doctrine that could be traced to Ricardo, it is clear now that the doctrine he was attacking was what is at present referred to as the neoclassical orthodoxy of Walras, Jevons, and Menger, as extended by J.B. Clark, Wicksell and (in Keynes's time) Pigou. The idea that Keynes was attacking is at base a simple one, namely, that in a competitive general-equilibrium system, all markets clear, factor markets as well as product markets. All that is required for the labor market to clear is for the capital and labor markets to be competitive and for capital and labor to be substitutable in production or consumption. The prices in question are the real interest rate and the real wage rate.

The first attack on Keynes's conclusion of a less-than-full-employment equilibrium emerged in the form of the Haberler-Pigou-Scitovsky wealth effect (or what Patinkin subsequently called the real-balance effect).[1] Suppose that in an economy with perfectly flexible prices and wages the money rate of interest is in the liquidity trap, but suppose that there is a fiat money component in the stock of money. The real-balance argument is then that as prices fall the real value of the stock of fiat money will increase sufficiently that the consumption function will shift upward to a point where saving is reduced to equality with investment at full employment.[2]

The real-balance effect has been an accepted part of neoclassical theorizing for years, and because of it Keynes is viewed as simply being wrong in his conclusion that an economy could be in equilibrium at less than full employment. In my view, however, it is the neoclassicists who are in error. For, while there can be real-balance effects for individuals, extending a real-balance effect to an economy as a whole entails a fallacy of composition. As discussed in Chapters 3 and 7, the real value of the stock of money (no matter what its origin or type, inside or outside) is constrained by the pool of fluid capital valued in current prices. Since price changes *per se* cannot affect the real value of this pool, a real-balance effect on the aggregate stock of money is simply impossible. Keynes may have been wrong about equilibrium at less than full employment, but not because of the existence of real-balance effects.

The general-equilibrium neoclassical conclusion requires not only that there be substitution between capital and labor in production or consumption, but that

---

[1] See Patinkin (1948, 1965).

[2] See Haberler (1937), Pigou (1941, 1943, 1947), Patinkin (1965), and Metzler (1951). Not only is the real-balance effect critical to equilibrium at full employment in neoclassical theorizing, but it is also viewed as being fundamental to monetary theory. According to Patinkin:

> It must also be emphasized that, for the simple exchange economy with which we are now dealing, the assumption that there exists a real-balance effect in the commodity markets is the *sine qua non* of monetary theory. For as we shall see below, in the absence of this effect the absolute level of money prices in such an economy is indeterminate: that is, no market forces exist to stabilize it at a specific level. It follows that though approximations which neglect the real-balance effect may -- because of the smallness of this effect -- be useful in the theory of the determination of relative prices, such "approximations" ignore a basic analytical factor in the theory of the determination of the absolute price level. Thus, whatever the justification for neglecting the real-balance effect in value theory, there can be no justification for neglecting it in monetary theory. [Patinkin (1965, p. 21).]

In the framework of this book, there is no justification for this view, for as was discussed in Chapter 6 the general price level is determined by the interaction of aggregate demand and aggregate supply, where aggregate demand is represented by the current pool of purchasing power and aggregate supply is represented by the pool of fluid capital valued in current prices. Since it is impossible (in a closed system) to have a real-balance effect in the aggregate, real-balance effects cannot influence aggregate demand and therefore cannot be a factor in determining the general price level.

there also be a negative relationship between capital and the rate of interest. The latter assumption (which was accepted uncritically by Keynes in defining the investment function in terms of the marginal efficiency of capital) has been challenged extensively by the Cambridge (England) capital theorists, most notably by Pierangelo Garegnani.[3] Garegnani's criticism takes two forms. The first is based upon the standard Cambridge (England) criticism of neoclassical growth theory, that capital can be treated as a factor of production measured in physical units. The gist of Garegnani's criticism is as follows: Capital can be measured only as a value. Since a value requires prices, prices have to be determined before the amount of capital can be determined. Therefore, how can the price of capital (i.e., the interest rate) be determined *jointly* with other prices? This accordingly to the Cantabridgians makes nonsense of the interest rate and real wage rate adjusting mutually in a fashion that causes the labor market to clear. In my view, this is a valid criticism.

The second point of Garegnani's criticism relates to a negative relationship between investment and the rate of interest. This point is based on the reswitching controversy of the 1960s and 1970s which occupied the capital theorists of the two Cambridges.[4] Capital, in this context, is defined in terms of a book of blueprints of production techniques that employ labor and capital goods in varying proportions. A technique that is optimal at a low interest rate may be optimal again at a high interest rate, but not at intermediate interest rates.[5] This means that there is not necessarily a monotonically negative relation between the amount of 'capital' used in production and the interest rate (defined as the rate of return on capital). Strictly speaking, the foregoing refers to the relationship between the stock of capital (however defined) and the rate of interest, so the fact that capital and the interest rate may not be negatively related does not mean the relationship between investment and the interest rate is not negative. But Garegnani argues that this is not necessarily the case either.

For present purposes, there is no need to get caught up in Garegnani's argument, for I want to approach the questions involved in terms of the

---

[3] See Garegnani (1983).

[4] See, *inter alia*, the papers in the November 1966 issue of the *Quarterly Journal of Economics*, particularly the "Summing Up" by Samuelson. See also Harcourt (1972), Robinson (1953, 1956, 1975), Samuelson (1975), and Solow (1967).

[5] See Samuelson (1966) for some simple arithmetical examples.

framework developed in this book.[6] Within the present framework, the tradeoff between 'capital' and labor in production has to be viewed in terms of the stock of produced means of production. While it is meaningful to think of this stock as representing an amalgam of capital-labor ratios, it is better, in my view, to interpret it in terms of an output-labor ratio, or equivalently as an income-labor ratio, measured as value per unit of labor. Clearly the only way that the stock of produced means of production can be altered in response to changes in the relative prices of capital and labor is through investment.[7]

It must be kept in mind, however, that not only does fluid capital finance investment, it also finances production. As a consequence, interest rates enter into the present value calculations driving investment decisions at two points, rather than one -- in the discount factor in the denominator *and* as a component of short-run production cost in the numerator. This reflects that interest not only has to be paid on the purchase price of the investment but also on the short-term loans that will fund production over the lifetime of the investment. For a firm contemplating expansion of capacity, there accordingly will be a tradeoff between the amount invested in newly produced means of production and the length of the period-of-production (once the new capacity is in place). A long period-of-production can entail a substantial burden of interest, so that an increase in the rate of interest can cause a firm to *shorten* its period-of-production by investing in a more capital-intensive structure of production. In this case, there would be a *positive* relationship between investment and the rate of interest, and also between the 'capital-intensity' of the produced means of production and the rate of interest.[8]

Let me now turn to the labor market and examine how it fits into the framework of this book. The conventional definition of the demand function for labor is in terms of the marginal revenue product that the employment of an additional unit of labor can be expected to generate. For present purposes, marginal revenue product is assumed to be measured with respect to a firm's current period-of-production, under the assumption that the capacity to produce is fixed. In the output market, it is assumed that firms face a demand function

---

[6] It should be evident at this point that, of the two Cambridge views of capital, the concept that has been suggested in this book is closer to Cambridge, England, than to Cambridge, Massachusetts. My primary problem with Cambridge, Massachusetts, is that capital is essentially identified with the stock of produced means of production, rather than the pool of fluid capital. Cambridge, England, clearly includes fluid capital in their concept of capital, but I am unsympathetic to their method of valuation.

[7] Capital is now taken to refer to fluid capital and the price of capital is assumed to be the natural rate of interest as defined earlier.

[8] The details of all of this are presented in Appendix 2.

with some elasticity and that the decision variable in determining the rate of short-run production is price. Firms are assumed to peer into their crystal balls regarding the demand functions they face, choose prices which maximize expected quasi-rents, plan production accordingly, and then make plans to purchase the necessary inputs (including labor).

Maximization of quasi-rents obviously requires knowledge of short-run marginal cost curves, as these were defined in Chapter 5. The important question now is how much substitution in the short run exists between labor and other inputs. Since the overall capacity to produce is constant, there can be no substitution between labor and produced means of production for an economy as a whole, but an individual firm may not face such a constraint. Such would be the case for a firm that hires some (or all) of its productive capacity.[9] For most firms, though, this is not an option, and inputs will be purchased (including labor), more or less in fixed proportions, as determined by the planned scale of production.

We now turn to a derivation of the demand curve for labor. Let a firm's quasi-rents be given by

(1) $\pi = R - C$,

where R denotes revenue and C denotes total short-run cost, as short-run cost was defined in Chapter 5. Assuming that the firm plans production so as to maximize quasi-rents, then with respect to the employment of labor, we will have for $\partial \pi / \partial L$,

(2) $\dfrac{\partial R}{\partial L} - \dfrac{\partial C}{\partial L} = 0$,

where L denotes the amount of labor employed. Assuming that labor is purchased in a competitive market, it follows that

(3) $\dfrac{\partial C}{\partial L} = w$,

where w denotes the money wage rate.

Since $R = pq$, where p denotes the price of output and q planned output, both with reference to the 'crystal-ball' (i.e., expected) demand function, we will have

---

[9] An example would be a vegetable grower who can decide at the time of harvest whether to have the crop picked by hand or by machine.

(4) $\dfrac{\partial R}{\partial L} = p\dfrac{\partial q}{\partial L} + q\dfrac{\partial p}{\partial L}$

$$= p\dfrac{\partial q}{\partial p}\dfrac{\partial p}{\partial L} + q\dfrac{\partial p}{\partial L}$$

$$= q(1 + \eta_p)\dfrac{\partial p}{\partial L} \; ,$$

where $\eta_p = \dfrac{p}{q}\dfrac{\partial q}{\partial p}$ denotes the price elasticity of demand.

For $\partial p/\partial L$, we can write

(5) $\dfrac{\partial p}{\partial L} = \dfrac{\partial p}{\partial C}\cdot\dfrac{\partial C}{\partial L}$

$$= \dfrac{\partial p}{\partial C} w \; ,$$

since $\partial C/\partial L = w$. For $\partial p/\partial C$, on the other hand:

(6) $\dfrac{\partial p}{\partial C} = \dfrac{\partial p}{\partial (mc)}\cdot\dfrac{\partial (mc)}{\partial C}$,

where mc $= \partial C/\partial q$ (i.e., short-run marginal cost).

At this point, it is necessary to make an assumption as to how price is set. My assumption will be that price is set at prospective short-run marginal cost (whether in anticipation of competition, because of regulation, or whatever, is immaterial), so that

(7) $\partial p/\partial (mc) = 1$.

Also, $\partial C/\partial (mc) = 1$, hence,

(8) $\partial p/\partial C = 1$.

Consequently,

(9) $\dfrac{\partial R}{\partial L} = qw(1 + \eta_p)$.

This last expression represents the willingness-to-pay function (i.e., the demand function) for labor. Note that, under the pricing assumption that has been made (i.e., price equal to expected short-run marginal cost), the slope of this function depends upon the price elasticity of demand. Only in the case of an elastic demand -- i.e., $\eta_p < -1$ -- will the demand function be downward-sloping! From this, we can conclude that in an economy with both competitive product markets (so that $\eta_p < -1$) and competitive labor markets, the demand function for labor for the economy as a whole would seem to be downward-sloping. We can also take the supply function to be upward-sloping. Does it follow, accordingly, that the natural tendency for the economy in the short run is for the labor market to clear?

To analyze this question it is necessary to derive an aggregate demand function for labor (which is not the same as the labor demand function alluded to in the preceding paragraph). To this end, refer to Figure 15, which describes the short-run production decision for a typical firm in the economy. My assumption will be that the area defined by opq represents the *minimum* receipts that the firm feels that it has to have in order to produce an output q. The firm may see its output and price driven to q and p by prospective competition or by regulation.[10] Let L represent the labor input associated with the production of q, and let R denote the associated gross revenue (i.e., opq in the figure). Hence, we can write

(10) $L = Q(R)$

for an individual firm, and

(11) $L^* = \Phi(R^*)$

for all firms in the aggregate, where $L^* = \Sigma L$ and $R^* = \Sigma R$.

The economy's labor market can be described by Figure 16. The upward-sloping curve labeled S represents labor supply as a function of the real wage, while L^* denotes the maximum amount of labor that will be demanded (as just described) for a prospective real wage w/p^*, where w is the money wage and p^* represents the price of consumption goods. In the situation described, there will be involuntary unemployment equal to $L^* - L^F$.

---

[10] If market power were to allow the firm to entertain a feasible price above q, it may do so if this were to imply higher prospective quasi-rents. The essential point is that the firm would not intentionally plan to set a price lower than p, so that q is the maximum output the firm would plan to produce.

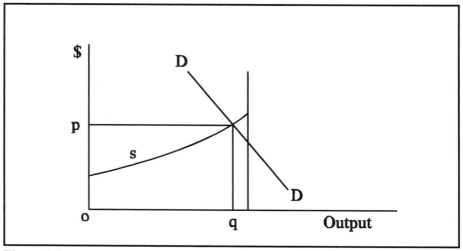

Figure 15

The question is whether there will be forces operating to eliminate this unemployment. Assuming competition in the labor market, we can reasonably imagine that the initial effect of the unemployment will be for the money wage rate to fall, leading to a decrease in the real wage rate. This will lead to a decrease in the short-run marginal cost curve for a firm and, *ceteris paribus*, to an increase in the maximum prospective output, from q to q′ in Figure 17. However, for q′ to be produced price would have to fall to p′, so that the impact on output of the initial fall in the real wage will be moderated. For a firm facing an elastic demand, the maximum prospective receipts would increase, assuming that the demand curve D is not affected. The maximum prospective amount of labor demanded would go up, however, no matter what the elasticity of demand (so long as it is not zero). Since this would appear to be true for every firm, it would seem that L^* would increase and that unemployment would therefore be decreased.

Generally speaking, however, goods demand functions would be affected by both the fall in the money wage and the fall in prices. Almost certainly demand functions would shift to the left, as depicted by the demand function D′ in Figure 17. Figure 17 shows the new demand function as cutting the short-run marginal cost curve S at q as before, so there would appear to be no change in the maximum prospective output. This is *not* a necessary implication of the analysis, for there can clearly exist a q′ that lies to the right of q. If this were uniformly the case, then it would seem that the new maximum prospective employment for the economy overall could be larger than L, so a fall in the real wage could lead to an increase in employment.

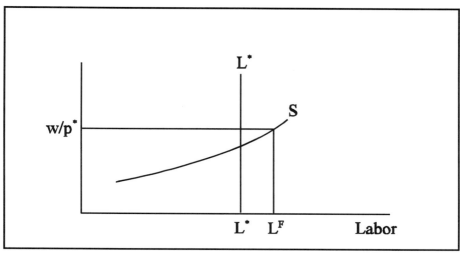

Figure 16

Still, this is not the end of the story. With reference to Figure 17, the critical consideration would seem to be the size of price elasticities of demand in relation to the backward shifts in demand functions. For individual firms, price elasticity can be interpreted in terms of substitution of the firm's product against the products of other firms, but this type of substitution obviously washes out for an economy as a whole. For an entire economy, the only form of substitution that is possible is of current consumption against future consumption. This being the case, the only way that a fall in the money wage and prices can lead to an increase in the maximum prospective employment is if firms, in gazing into their crystal balls, see consumers spending a higher proportion of their prospective incomes on consumables -- i.e., if the saving rate is seen as falling.

In the conventional neoclassical framework, the way that this would come about is through a real-balance effect on the stock of fiat (or outside) money, which shifts the consumption function upward to the point where saving is equal to investment at full employment. As has already been discussed, however, an aggregate real-balance effect is a will-o'-the-wisp. For, while falling prices will increase the real value of money for individuals, this cannot be the case in the aggregate because the real value of the aggregate stock of money is bounded by the real value of the pool of fluid capital. Since the real value of the pool of fluid capital is determined entirely by the goods embodied in it, its real value is therefore independent of the nominal level of prices. Even so, it might seem that if, because of *individual* real-balance effects, everyone begins to increase their purchases of goods, the aggregate consumption function must necessarily shift upward. This is an illusion, however. For if prices are flexible downward, they

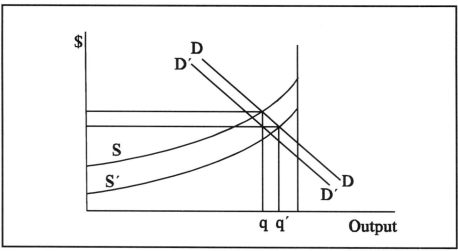

Figure 17

must be flexible upward as well, so that once additional purchasing power begins to flood into the goods market, the aggregate price level will begin to increase, and real-balance effects will operate in reverse. There is no escaping the constraint that is imposed on the real value of the stock of money. *In short, there can be no real-balance effect in the aggregate.*

My conclusion at this point from all of this is that there are no automatic forces that are set in motion by an excess supply of labor at the existing real-wage rate that will lead to a clearing of the short-run labor market. Keynes, in my view, was correct in his conclusion in this regard, and largely for the reasons that he argued.

CHAPTER 9

CAPITAL THEORY IN PERSPECTIVE

At several points in earlier chapters, reference has been made concerning the relationship of fluid capital to the capital notions of Hayek, Keynes, Schumpeter, and others. The purpose of this chapter is to examine these connections in greater detail. In doing this, I hope to provide readers not only with a better understanding of what is meant by fluid capital, but also to convince them that capital theory is still an extremely interesting and fruitful subject for research.[1]

SCHUMPETER

I shall begin with Schumpeter's concept of money. Schumpeter at base had a credit theory of money, in that he saw most money (as a means of payment) as being generated through creation (or extension) of credit by banks. In the *Theory of Economic Development*, Schumpeter distinguished between *normal* credit and *abnormal* credit:

> Normal credit creates claims to the social dividend, which represents and may be thought of as certifying services rendered and previous delivery of existing goods. That kind of credit, which is designated by traditional opinion as abnormal, also creates claims to the social product, which, however, in the absence of past productive services could only be described as certificates of future services or of goods yet to be delivered. [Schumpeter (1934, p. 101).]

---

[1] The current younger generation of economists, at least on the U.S. side of the Atlantic, might think that conceptual problems involving capital have been solved, comfortable with the idea that capital is simply the argument 'K' in the aggregate production function. In my opinion, this is an incorrect reading of what finally emerged from the capital controversy of the 1960s and 1970s. Despite the apparent agreement on reswitching, Cambridge, U.S., no more convinced Cambridge, U.K., of the correctness of its position than Cambridge, U.K., convinced Cambridge, U.S. Moreover, as has been pointed out by Mirowski (1989, Chapter 6), the concepts of capital of the two sides were simply too incompatible for there to have been any meaningful compromise. What happened (at least in my view) was that both sides simply tired of the debate, and went on to other things.

Schumpeter always viewed credit as the creation of generalized purchasing power, which enabled resources to be transferred to the hands of entrepreneurs for the creation of new combinations of production. For Schumpeter, the creation of credit was absolutely essential for economic development. Additionally, he makes the point that, in principle, the entrepreneur is the only one who needs credit.[2] The businessman has purchasing power (and therefore resources) flowing towards him through the sale of product, but this is not the case for the entrepreneur. The only way that the entrepreneur can acquire resources is through the creation of new credit granted to his control. This is the abnormal credit referred to above. By its nature, this type of credit cannot be secured by a flow of current goods (as with normal credit), but is secured by future goods. This does not mean that credit granted to entrepreneurs may not be secured by existing assets, but even if it were, the credit is nevertheless unsecured in terms of current output.[3]

The point of departure for Schumpeter (in the *Theory*) was always a circular-flow equilibrium, which was assumed to be at full employment. Since the economy is at full employment, entrepreneurs can get the resources needed to effect new combinations only by bidding them away from existing uses with the newly created entrepreneurial credit. This results in what Schumpeter referred to as 'forced saving'.[4] With the economy at full employment, the bidding away of resources by entrepreneurs requires an increase in prices. The inflation, however, is only temporary, since prices will fall once the output from the new combination of production comes into the market. Indeed, the price level, once equilibrium is reestablished, will actually be lower than before because of the increased productivity of the new combination.[5]

Schumpeter's essential point concerning entrepreneurial credit is that credit is necessary for an entrepreneur to acquire the resources to effect new combinations. As he puts it, the entrepreneur has no prior claims on resources within the

---

[2] Schumpeter (1934, p. 102).

[3] Schumpeter notes (*Theory*, p. 101) that the entrepreneur may mortgage goods acquired with the newly created purchasing power, but there is still a time interval, if only an instant, in which the entrepreneur's credit is unsecured.

[4] Since the *Theory* was first published (in German) in 1911, Schumpeter's concept of forced saving clearly predated the debate between Keynes and Robertson regarding forced saving.

[5] It should be noted that if the economy is at less than full employment when credit is created to finance a new combination, forced saving is not necessary because the resources to be transferred to entrepreneurs can come out of existing stocks. Moreover, there is no necessity of a temporary increase in prices. Since Keynes saw unemployment as the norm, this is obviously an important difference between Schumpeter and Keynes.

current circular flow and credit acquisition is the only way that he can obtain the purchasing power to bid resources away from their existing uses.[6] Schumpeter viewed money as a 'claim ticket' to a portion of the social dividend. His analogy was to the claim on space in a theater that a ticket holder has to a play to be given in the theater.[7] For Schumpeter, the key thing about entrepreneurial credit was the creation of purchasing power where none had previously existed. He did not view the money that is created through the monetization of bills of exchange, bills of lading, etc., as the creation of new purchasing power, but only as monetization of purchasing power that already exists in the circular flow.[8]

Turning now to Schumpeter's concept of capital:

Capital is nothing but the lever by which the entrepreneur subjects to his control the concrete goods which he needs, nothing but a means of diverting the factors of production to new uses, or of dictating a new direction to production. [Schumpeter (1934, p. 116); italics in original.]

The function of capital consists in procuring for the entrepreneur the means with which to produce. It stands as a third agent necessary to production in an exchange economy *between* the entrepreneur and the world of goods. It constitutes the bridge between them. It does not take part directly in production, it is not itself 'worked up'; on the contrary it performs a task which must begin before technical production can begin. [Schumpeter (1934, p. 117); italics in original.]

Schumpeter's concept of capital is very similar to the one that is used in this book -- similar, yet not the same. The concept of capital employed in this book is that capital is a surplus consisting of all goods in process of production plus all stocks of finished goods. This is what has been referred to as (the goods side of) the pool of fluid capital. For Schumpeter, on the other hand, capital consists of the ability (as represented by newly created purchasing power) to divert resources contained in the pool from existing uses to new uses. Schumpeter's

---

[6] The only problem I have with Schumpeter's view regarding the creation of entrepreneurial credit is the implication that purchasing power cannot be borrowed, but must be created *de novo*. This was necessary for Schumpeter because of his assumption that innovation always begins from a position of full employment.

[7] At various points in his writings, Schumpeter extended his concept of 'claim ticket' to income by viewing income as representing a pool of claims to the social dividend. This characterizes the definition of income adopted in this book.

[8] At his death, Schumpeter left an unpublished manuscript on money, which was subsequently published in German [Schumpeter (1970)]. As far as I know, the only part of this book that has been translated into English is the editor's introduction. This is found in a Ph.D. thesis by Michael Reclam (1984) at the University of California at Riverside.

concept of capital is thus a disequilibrium concept in that capital exists only when resources are being diverted from existing uses to new uses. My concept of capital is a stock that exists at all points in time (although it can obviously be undergoing change). The relationship between the two concepts of capital is that my concept represents the pool from which Schumpeter's capital is drawn.

Let me now turn to Schumpeter's treatment of interest. In Schumpeter's scheme, investment is undertaken because of the prospect of making a profit. In order to acquire the capital necessary to effect the new combination, interest has to be paid to the bank which creates the entrepreneurial credit. The interest is paid out of the profit. Profit disappears, however, once the economy settles into a new circular-flow equilibrium, which means that, for Schumpeter, the equilibrium rate of interest is zero.[9]

KEYNES

In essentials, Keynes had much the same view of money as Schumpeter, in that he saw most money as being created by banks through the extension of loans.[10] Keynes had virtually no discussion of how money was created in the *General Theory* -- the stock of money was treated as exogenous, controlled by the monetary authority -- so that Keynes's most developed views on money are to be found in the *Tract on Monetary Reform* and the *Treatise on Money*. However, Keynes's view of money that is of most interest for present purposes is the one implicit in his discussion of the 'finance' motive for holding money. In one of his 1937 *Economic Journal* articles, Keynes states:

> . . . the finance required during the interregnum between the intention to invest and its achievement is mainly supplied by specialists, in particular by the banks, which organise and manage a revolving fund of liquid finance. . . . For 'finance' is essentially a revolving fund. It employs no savings. It is,

[9] This is in marked contrast to Keynes, for whom the rate of interest was determined, in normal circumstances, by the unwillingness of individuals to give up the liquidity of money. In assessing this difference between Keynes and Schumpeter, however, it must be kept in mind that their two points of reference are very different. Schumpeter's equilibrium was a stationary state in which the circular flow endlessly repeated itself, and there was no uncertainty. In disequilibrium -- i.e., when investment was occurring -- when the interest rate for Schumpeter is non-zero, there is not much difference between their two views on interest. Also, in the very long run, Keynes had the marginal efficiency of capital falling to zero, which, in the absence of uncertainty, would imply a zero rate of interest as well.

[10] In general, Schumpeter had a very critical view of Keynes. He had admiration for the *Treatise on Money*, but none at all for the *General Theory*. Schumpeter undoubtedly viewed Keynes as his rival as the "World's Greatest Economist", whereas Keynes did not reciprocate. I doubt that it ever crossed Keynes's mind that the world's greatest economist was anyone other than himself!

for the community as a whole, only a bookkeeping transaction. As soon as it is 'used' in the sense of being expended, the lack of liquidity is automatically made good and the readiness to become temporarily unliquid is available to be used over again. Finance covering the interregnum is, to use a phrase employed by bankers in a more limited context, necessarily 'self-liquidating' for the community taken as a whole at the end of the interregnum period. [Keynes (1937b, p. 615).]

And then in an oft-quoted passage later in the same article:

This means that, in general, the banks hold the key position in the transition from a lower to a higher scale of activity. If they refuse to relax, the growing congestion of the short-term loan market or of the new issue market, as the case may be, will inhibit the improvement, no matter how thrifty the public purpose to be out of their future incomes. On the other hand, there will always be *exactly* enough *ex post* saving to take up the *ex post* investment and so release the finance which the latter had been previously employing. The investment market can become congested through shortage of cash. It can never become congested through shortage of saving. This is the most fundamental of my conclusions within this field. [Keynes (1937b, pp. 618-619); italics in original.]

While Keynes's focus in the article from which these passages come was on the equality of saving and investment, it is clear that, in seeing 'finance' as a revolving fund that is created and extinguished independently of saving, his views of money and money creation are similar to those adopted in this book. If the concept of 'finance' is extended to the financing of current production, as well as to the 'interregnum' between the intent to invest and its achievement, then the 'revolving fund' in question can be interpreted in the present context in terms of the stock of transactions balances. The only essential difference between Keynes's view of money in these passages and that of this book is that Keynes appears to make the 'revolving fund' independent of all saving, past as well as current. In this book, the revolving fund can be independent of current saving, but not of past saving, because an existing pool of savings must be in existence in order for monetization to occur.

Like many, Keynes employed a variety of concepts of capital in his arguments, usually without formal definition or explanation. The precise meaning was meant to be supplied by the particular context. In the *General Theory*, he seemed to slip back and forth between capital as working capital and capital as physical capital, depending upon whether reference was to finance or to investment. In the *Treatise*, on the other hand, capital most of the time appears to refer to working capital. As Keynes was a pragmatist at base, I do not think he ever really concerned himself with the question of what capital is. To him, it was simply a fact that capital existed, and how it was to be defined and treated was to be determined by the question at issue. Keynes nowhere seems to work with the concept of fluid capital as defined in these pages, yet fluid capital would seem to be implicit, as just noted, in his discussion of the 'finance' motive for holding money.

IRVING FISHER

Let me now turn to Irving Fisher, who is generally acclaimed to be the premier capital theorist of this century. In *The Nature of Capital and Interest*, Fisher defines *wealth* as anything material that is owned. *Capital* is then defined as the stock of wealth at a point in time, while *income* is defined as the flows of services generated from wealth. Fisher's definition of capital is thus extremely broad, in that anything that generates a service which yields a benefit (whether paid for or not) is viewed as capital. In general, I find Fisher's confounding of capital with *capital value* to be unsatisfactory for at least four reasons:

1. The stock of capital becomes dependent upon the discount rate used in calculating present values;

2. Capital is treated as unrealized future consumption;

3. Any distinction between the capital expended in creating produced means of production and capital value of the latter is foreclosed;

4. Finally, foreclosed, too, are conservation laws imposed by the stock of fluid capital on the total of capital values and the real stock of money.

Since produced means of production are durable, today's stock of produced means of production will obviously also be capable of producing output and income tomorrow. But it is not useful, in my view, to interpret this capacity to produce tomorrow as deferred consumption. And it makes no sense at all, in my opinion, to measure this deferred consumption in terms of capital value. While the present value of an existing capital good depends upon future quasi-rents, which clearly depend upon expected future incomes, the actual willingness-to-pay depends upon *current* income, except in the case of a bank or other lender willing to lend on the basis of the expected future income.[11] In my view, it is much better to distinguish between fluid capital and produced means of production, and then to see the stock of produced means of production (in conjunction with the pool of fluid capital) as determining the current capacity to produce and the facility to generate income. Fisher's concept of capital might have merit in terms of describing the wealth of an individual, but it is too inclusive to be usefully applied to an entire economy.[12]

BOHM-BAWERK

In the first several chapters in Volume 2 of the *Positive Theory of Capital*, Bohm-Bawerk reviews and critiques a number of concepts of capital in the literature, and also offers and defends his own definitions. Specifically, he defines capital as:

> *Let us call capital, in general, an aggregate of products which serve as a means of acquiring goods.* [Bohm-Bawerk (1959, p. 32); italics in original.]

Later, Bohm-Bawerk identifies capital as consisting of intermediate goods. The more intermediate goods that are employed in production, the more capital that is used, and the more indirect -- or roundabout -- is production[13]. In general, what Bohm-Bawerk calls capital is what I have referred to as physical capital or produced means of production. However, Bohm-Bawerk is also adamant at one point in stating that saving must precede the formation of capital, but then sees capital as arising out of both saving and production.[14] In doing this, he very clearly merges fluid capital and produced means of production.

While Bohm-Bawerk identifies capital with intermediate goods, he does not

---

[11] And even in this case, it would seem that (in normal circumstances) the *ability* to lend is constrained by current income (or more generally by the current pool of fluid capital).

[12] Before leaving this discussion of Fisher's concept of capital, it is interesting to note that, at one point in *The Nature of Capital and Interest*, Fisher describes capital in terms of the stock of all goods in existence. Assuming that this includes goods-in-process as well as finished goods, it corresponds to the goods side of the pool of fluid capital as defined in this book.

[13] There is a tendency in the literature to equate roundaboutness with the period of production and to associate more roundabout techniques with a longer period of production. This is a mistake. Although Bohm-Bawerk, himself, seems guilty of this at times, his intent, it is pretty clear, was to identify roundaboutness with division of labor, which in most cases leads to a shortening, rather than a lengthening, of the period of production.

[14] Bohm-Bawerk (1959, p. 102).

distinguish between capital embodied (or sunk) in produced means of production and capital that has a counterpart in goods-in-process and stocks of finished goods. By distinguishing produced means of production from fluid capital, we are able to understand and keep separate, in a fundamental way, the two most important attributes of capital: (1) its contribution to enhanced production and (2) its fluidity or ability to flow from one use to another. Capital that is embodied in produced means of production is not fluid. It becomes fluid only as it is recovered through charges against revenues.

By not distinguishing between sunk and fluid capital, Bohm-Bawerk does not allow for these mechanics of capital formation -- i.e., that capital is not only initially formed through saving, but is 'reformed' through myros recovery charges against quasi-rents. Also, Bohm-Bawerk's definition of capital does not allow for us to see in a straightforward way that not all capital (in Bohm-Bawerk's sense) is mobile -- only fluid capital (and produced means of production which are perfectly fungible) is mobile.

Bohm-Bawerk's concept of capital also does not allow in a transparent way for the fact that current production in general must be funded out of the pool of fluid capital, not just investment in newly produced means of production. Capital embodied in produced means of production cannot do this. Finally, a last benefit of separating physical and fluid capital is that it allows for the proper place for money in an economy, in that it allows one to see that money (or, more properly, monetization) is tied to the pool of fluid capital, rather than the total of physical and fluid capital.

JEVONS AND WICKSELL

I now turn to Jevons and Wicksell, whose notions of capital (along with those of Hayek), as noted in Chapter 2, clearly inspire the conception of capital that is advanced in this book. In the *Theory of Political Economy*, Jevons states:

> . . . Capital, as I regard it, consists merely in the *aggregate of those commodities which are required for sustaining labourers of any kind or class engaged in work.* A stock of food is the main element of capital; but supplies of clothes, furniture, and all the other articles in common daily use are also necessary parts of capital. The *current means of sustenance constitute capital in its free or uninvested form.* The single and all-important function of capital is to enable the labourer to await the result of any long-lasting work -- to put an interval between the beginning and the end of an enterprise. [Jevons (1871, 5th ed., pp. 223-224); italics in original.]

In *Interest and Prices*, Wicksell commented on this conceptualization of capital by Jevons as follows:

> Fundamentally this line of approach is certainly correct. But Jevons commits the error of confusing the part with the whole. Even if it is agreed that fixed capacity is merely the temporary product of labour and free capital, the costs of production which are advanced out of the latter can never be resolved *entirely* into wages. The rewards of the other factors of production, and particularly of land, must be taken into account. . . .
>
> Capital in its "free and uninvested form" consists not only of the means of sustenance by which labourers can defray their consumption, but it also provides for the owners of other factors of production, above all for the owners of land. In its essence it is not merely a "wages fund" but also a "wages and rent fund". [Wicksell (1936, pp. 122-123); italics in original.]

Wicksell is surely correct in his criticism of Jevons, in that production obviously requires expenditures for inputs other than labor. If Wicksell's "wages and rent fund" is interpreted to include provision for the intermediate goods used in production, it is clear that Wicksell's conception of capital in "free and uninvested form" is essentially the same as the concept of fluid capital of this book.

Despite this apparent equivalence, "free and uninvested" capital does not play the role in Wicksell's analysis that fluid capital does in this book. Specifically missing from Wicksell's analysis is a functional separation between the goods side of 'free' capital and the claims side. By not making this distinction, Wicksell (in my view) was led to too narrow a conception of the market (i.e., the 'capital' market) in which the natural rate of interest is determined. In this book, the natural rate of interest is determined in the market which transfers claims on the pool of fluid capital from suppliers to demanders. For Wicksell, in contrast, determination of the natural rate of interest is confined to the market for saving and investment. No account is taken of the supply of claims from past saving or of demands arising from the need to fund current production. Moreover, Wicksell's analysis also does not take into account the macroeconomic constraints that the stock of 'free'capital imposes on capital values and the real stock of money.

CAPITAL AS EMBEDDED (OR STORED) LABOR

It is common in capital theory to interpret physical capital as representing embodied, or stored, labor. Saving is similarly viewed as representing deferred consumption. The deferred consumption is then ultimately seen as being produced by the labor that is 'stored' in the physical capital. In my view, this is not a useful conception of what physical capital represents, for among other things it encourages the overly sophisticated treatment of depreciation that is now an integral part of capital theory. In the framework of this book, depreciation is viewed simply as a device whereby the capital embodied in physical capital is returned to the pool of fluid capital through charges against revenues. The current conventional view in economics, however, is that depreciation is an element of cost.[15] Included in depreciation (at least in the view of many) will be a return to capital, so that, *inter alia*, optimal economic depreciation will make investors whole on the original investment. I do not mean to imply by this that optimization with regard to depreciation is not a meaningful concept. Since there are many depreciation schemes that can, in terms of out-of-pocket cost, make an investment whole, it is perfectly reasonable for a firm to choose the one that is in some sense best. But I think it is misguided to identify optimal depreciation with the 'correct' definition of long-run marginal cost, which then becomes the basis, in some contexts, for a socially optimal price.[16]

As discussed earlier in these pages, long-run marginal cost drives investment decisions and is relevant in guiding pricing in long-term contracts, but is not relevant to decisions regarding current output and pricing. The idea that price at times (specifically, during times of peak demand for goods and services subject to time-varying demands) should reflect a depreciation component (unless the price is negotiated in a long-run contract) is simply wrong in my view. If the expectations that drive an investment in the first place are in fact realized, then the investment will be made whole through the quasi-rents that the investment generates. Long-run marginal cost is reflected in the price that is paid for the investment, not in the quasi-rents the investment is expected to generate. The present value of these quasi-rents must, for the investment to be pursued, be at least as great as the price (or cost) of the investment. That is all. Once the investment is undertaken, one cannot then turn around and reinterpret the quasi-rents as depreciation. Depreciation (in the form of myros recovery charges) will be charged against the quasi-rents in repatriating the fluid capital that was originally embodied in the investment back into the pool of fluid capital, but quasi-rents are not depreciation *per se*.

---

[15] See Baumol (1971). Cf., also, the discussion in Chapter 2 above.

[16] See Turvey (1968, Chapter 8).

CAPITAL THEORY AS THE ECONOMICS OF TIME

Related to the foregoing is the widely shared view amongst current-day capital theorists that capital theory, at base, is simply the economics of time. Hirshleifer, for example, characterizes capital theory as the optimal intertemporal allocation of resources,[17] while Samuelson, similarly but a bit more narrowly, describes "what used to be loosely called capital theory" in terms of the economics of "time-phased production".[18] However, of all the modern neoclassical capital theorists, the one who probably has focused most deeply on the question of the "proper scope of capital theory" is Robert Solow. In his de Vries lectures in 1963, Solow states:

> There is a highbrow answer to this question and a lowbrow one. The highbrow answer is that the theory of capital is after all just a part of the fundamentally microeconomic theory of the allocation of resources, necessary to allow for the fact that commodities can be transformed into other commodities over time. Just as the theory of resource allocation has as its 'dual' a theory of competitive pricing, so the theory of capital has as its 'dual' a theory of intertemporal pricing involving rentals, interest rates, present values and the like.

> The lowbrow answer, I suppose, is that theory is supposed to help us understand real problems, and the problems that cannot be understood without capital-theoretic notions are those connected with saving and investment. Therefore the proper scope of capital theory is the elucidation of the causes and consequences of acts of saving and investment. Where the highbrow approach tends to be technical, disaggregated, and exact, the lowbrow view tends to be pecuniary, aggregative, and approximate.

> A middlebrow like myself sees virtue in each of these ways of looking at capital theory. I am personally attracted by what I have described as the lowbrow view of the function of capital theory. But as so often happens, I think the highbrow view offers indispensable help in achieving the lowbrow objective. In particular, the suggestion that capital theory is an extension of ordinary resource allocation and price theory reminds one that modern microeconomics has two aspects which might be called the descriptive and the normative. . . .

> Capital theory, too, has a technocratic and a descriptive side. I believe that the easiest and safest route to a simple but rigorous view of the subject is to

[17] Hirshleifer (1970).

[18] Samuelson (1976, p. 11).

begin technocratically. By asking planning questions, allocation questions, we, as I hope to show, dodge many embarrassing questions of definition and ideological overtones. . . . [Solow (1965, pp. 14-15).]

After additional discussion, Solow then states:

> Thinking about saving and investment from this technocratic point of view has convinced me that the central concept in capital theory should be *the rate of return on investment.* In short, we really want a theory of interest rates, not a theory of capital. [Solow (1965, p. 16); italics in original.]

By focusing on the rate of return on investment, one is able (according to Solow) to avoid:

> . . . most or all of the real or imaginary 'problems' that have beset this branch of economics for so long. In particular, to calculate the rate of return in my sense requires no measurement of the stock of 'capital'. What is more, a careful person will see that the whole process can be described without even mentioning the word 'capital'. [Solow (1965, p. 25).]

Solow's conviction that one can banish 'capital' from the lexicon is illusion in my opinion, for a well-defined concept of capital is never far from the surface in Solow's analysis. That this is the case is evident when he follows the above passage with:

> If there are concrete capital goods, or inventories, or delay periods, these will all of course affect the rate at which bundles of current consumption goods can be transformed into bundles of future consumption goods. But unless it is a natural thing to do under the technological circumstances there is no need to identify or measure a stock of generalized capital. If the economy throws up market prices or if the process of analysis yields some kind of efficiency prices, then there is no harm in adding up various value sums which may correspond to the market (or other) value of the stock of capital goods. *But such value sums are not 'capital' in the sense of something that belongs in a production function and has a marginal product.* . . . I am content with the point that the problem of measuring 'capital' simply does not arise in my way of looking at the theory. [Solow (1965, pp. 25-26); italics added.]

There is one overarching problem with the (highbrow) neoclassical view that capital theory is the extension of ordinary price theory to intertemporal allocation of resources and consumption. This problem is that it requires that capital, however defined, be a substance whose value is conserved over time. Fluid capital, as it has been defined in this book, clearly has a substantive dimension, in that, on the one hand, it consists of goods. On the other hand, it also has a value dimension, in that its components can be aggregated only as values, so that fluid capital can be represented only in the aggregate as a value.

As we have seen, the aggregate value of fluid capital imposes a variety of constraints on macroeconomic activity, so that fluid capital can certainly be seen to be conservative at a point in time. However, it does not follow from this that fluid capital is conservative over time. For this to be the case, it would be necessary either (1) that a substance theory of value be in place or (2) that the tastes and preferences determining individual values be time-invariant. Since neoclassical price theory is based upon a subjective field theory of value, (1) is clearly rejected. As for (2), it was argued earlier in this book that there is simply no way in the real world that this condition can ever hope to be satisfied.[19] Neoclassical capital theory accordingly contains an unremovable inconsistency: in order for capital to be treated as a substance that is conserved over time, a substance theory of value is required, but value in neoclassical price theory is determined subjectively.[20]

CAPITAL ACCOUNTING

In my view, much of the confusion involving capital and capital-related concepts can be alleviated through the development of an appropriate framework for capital accounting. By an accounting framework for capital, I simply mean the establishment of a set of simple rules for describing the evolution of capital in response to behavioral decisions which add to or subtract from its quantity.

As noted at the outset of this book, the literature contains many concepts of capital, with the same author often mixing them in vague and inconsistent ways. My approach throughout this work has been to distinguish among three types of capital:

1. *Produced Means of Production*, which comes into being through investment and combines with permanent resources and labor to define an economy's capacity to produce goods and generate income.

[19] See Appendix 1.

[20] That neoclassical growth theory is bedeviled by a fusing of inconsistent theories of value is discussed in detail by Mirowski (1989, Chapters 5 and 6).

2. *The Pool of Fluid Capital*, which can be viewed as representing two equivalent stocks. On one side it represents, at any point in time, the stock of goods in existence, at all stages of production, both consumables and physical capital goods, measured in current prices.[21] On the other side, it can be seen as consisting, again at any point in time, of the uncommitted residue from past savings -- i.e., the uncommitted surplus of an economy -- again valued in current prices.

3. *Financial capital*, which in general represents the current market valuations of the property rights in the stocks of produced means of production and fluid capital.

The focus throughout the discussion has been on the pool of fluid capital, for this is the critical quantity that drives *any* economy, no matter what its social and political structure or how its economic activity is organized. An economy simply cannot grow in absence of enlargement of this pool through saving and investment from it in produced means of production. The pool of fluid capital is what allows produced means of production in one form to be transformed into another form. It is the 'putty' of the 'putty-clay' discussions of the 1960s and 1970s.

The capital originally expended on produced means of production is recovered back into the pool of fluid capital through (myros recovery) charges against quasi-rents generated by the produced means of production. As has been noted, the timing of these charges is discretionary. A firm with a short investment horizon (for whatever reason) will insist upon the prospect of much larger early-on quasi-rents than a firm with a long investment horizon. It is to be emphasized that the decision as to timing of myros recovery charges does not bear any necessary relationship to 'economic' depreciation as this term is usually understood by economists.[22]

'Economic' depreciation refers to changes in capital values, and is therefore prospective, whereas the 'depreciation' at issue here refers to the recovery of fluid capital that has been expended in the past. What matters for capital recovery is that the quasi-rents envisioned at the time the capital was invested be more-or-less realized on schedule, not the current valuation of the quasi-rents yet

---

[21] The physical capital goods in reference are those in inventory, not those already *in situ* through investment. The latter are represented in the stock of produced means of production.

[22] Cf. the discussion in Chapter 2.

to be realized. A substantial increase in the discount rate used in valuing these quasi-rents can make their 'present value' look small -- and therefore 'economic' depreciation large -- even though the actual size of the quasi-rents are totally on track with what was originally envisioned.

The foregoing emphasizes the importance of deriving an accounting framework to accurately record the capital structure of an economy. Five accounts are needed:

1. An account recording the pool of fluid capital;

2. An account recording the stock of undepreciated produced means of production;[23]

3. An account recording the flow into the pool of fluid capital from saving out of current income;

4. An account recording the flow into the pool of fluid capital through myros recovery charges against current quasi-rents;

5. An account recording the flow out of the pool of fluid capital through investment in newly produced means of production.

All entries in these accounts are values. As has been emphasized throughout this book, there should be no pretense that capital is to be represented in the accounts as a physical quantity. Accounts 1, 3, and 5, will be in current prices, while accounts 2 and 4 will be in historical prices (i.e., a dollar is a dollar no matter what point in time the investment was made or the myros recovery charge was taken).

In general, the capital-accounting framework just outlined is pretty much in line with standard accounting practices, but only at the micro level (i.e., for firms). The focus here, however, is macro, specifically on the pool of fluid capital. I am not aware of any country that attempts to measure this quantity. Some countries have capital accounts in their national accounts, but the focus is on produced means of production, rather than fluid capital. The U.S. has no official capital accounts at all.

---

[23] By *undepreciated*, I mean original cost of investment minus accumulated myros recovery charges.

The absence of capital accounts is unfortunate, for by not focusing on the pool of fluid capital, bad things can be happening to an economy's stock of physical capital without policymakers even being aware of it. A case in point may be the recurrent debate in the U.S. concerning the state of the public physical capital stock (as represented in bridges, highways, streets, water and sewer systems, etc.). In principle, there is no difference between public and private physical capital in an economy. Investment in both must come from the pool of fluid capital, and both can be recovered only through charges against current income. For private firms, this is done simply as a matter of fiducial prudence through charges against quasi-rents. For public physical capital, however, this is generally not the case, for in general there are no public quasi-rents to make myros recovery charges against. Proper capital accounting would require the establishment of capital sinking funds to be charged against general tax revenues, but this is almost never done. The result may be that the U.S. in recent decades has, indeed, been consuming its public capital.

CAPITAL AND NONRENEWABLE NATURAL RESOURCES[24]

At the start of this work, capital was defined as temporary resources, as opposed to permanent resources (such as land and basic labor). This leaves up in the air how nonrenewable natural resources, such as minerals, are to be treated. Consider an oilfield. Assume that the oilfield has been developed so that it is ready to begin producing oil, but production has not yet started. The field is expected to contain one billion barrels of recoverable oil. What is the capital represented in this oilfield and how is it to be treated in the capital account?

To begin with, it is clear that every dollar spent, for whatever reason, including interest, in developing the oilfield represents investment of capital from the pool of fluid capital, and it is obviously expected that these expenditures will be returned to the pool through charges against quasi-rents. The question really concerns the one billion barrels of oil to be pumped from the field. Once the oil is pumped and consumed, it is gone forever. Should this loss also be charged against quasi-rents?

In my view, the answer is no. For one thing, it is not clear just what the capital would be that is to be charged off. Some would advocate using economic depreciation (i.e., the difference in the present values of the prospective quasi-rents between not pumping the oil and pumping), but this would make the

[24] For a detailed elaboration of the points in this section with reference to nonrenewable natural resources, see Taylor (1998).

amount to be charged a function of (among other things) the interest rate used in calculating the present values.[25] As I see it, there should be no charges against quasi-rents for the disappearance of the oil because, *with regard to the oil as such, no fluid capital was expended in bringing it into existence.* The oil *per se* is a gift of nature, just like land. The only difference is that oil depletes.

However, what about the case where the oilfield is sold to another firm just before it begins to produce? The oilfield clearly has a capital value, so does this value not represent an expenditure of capital? Again, in my view, this is not the case, for the development expenditure of the oilfield will be included in the supply price of the field, and therefore will be expected to be recouped by the original developer in sales proceeds. The new owners of the oilfield will expect to have their investment made whole through the stream of prospective quasi-rents, but (once the development costs are recovered) the pool of fluid capital will be no smaller once the oilfield is depleted than what it would have been if the oilfield had never been discovered in the first place. Should the new owners decide that they want to remain in the oil business after the field is depleted, they will set up a sinking fund to be funded by 'depletion' of the oilfield. These depletion charges will clearly be additions to the pool of fluid capital, so that in this case the pool will be *larger* after the oilfield is depleted than what it would have been had the field never been discovered. The conclusion, therefore, is that *depletion reserves on non-renewable resources provide a powerful vehicle for capital formation.*

Economic depreciation in this situation, since it is calculated as the difference between present values of two stream of prospective yields, informs the decision of how much to produce today as opposed to how much to produce tomorrow. In short, economic depreciation in this case would determine the *time path* of depletion of the oilfield.

---

[25] The case where the oilfield is sold after development, but before production begins, will be considered in a moment.

CHAPTER 10

OPPORTUNITY AND SUNK COSTS

In the preceding chapter, it was noted how the view that capital is stored (or embedded) labor can lead to problems in interpreting depreciation and whether or not depreciation is a component of long-run marginal cost. In this chapter, we shall look at some related questions involving opportunity costs and sunk costs, especially as they relate to costing and pricing issues in the regulated industries. The focus for the discussion will be questions raised by Richard Emmerson in a paper in a recent volume on marginal cost techniques in the telephone industry sponsored by the National Regulatory Research Institute.[1]

OPPORTUNITY COSTS

On p. 161 of the NRRI volume, Emmerson makes the statement:

This nature of capital creates a "time problem", resources are committed now, precluding their alternative uses (and thereby causing an opportunity cost), while at least some of the intended output is created later. A *per unit* calculation of "costs" requires a current cost to be divided by later quantities of output. Such arithmetic cannot be performed until either the costs are aligned with output or vice versa. By attending to proper time alignment, we account for the opportunity cost of the resources between the time of their commitment to production and the results of their production. [Emmerson (1991, p. 161); italics in original.]

This statement, it seems to me, is symptomatic of a confusion that is widespread amongst economists, namely, that opportunity cost is somehow to be

[1] I want to thank Rick Emmerson for being such a good sport in letting me use statements from his NRRI paper as foils in this chapter. Rick has been an enthusiastic supporter of the ideas in this book for many years, and our many and long discussions have led to considerable improvement and refinement.

treated as an objective cost of an investment. The decision to invest is seen as causing a subsequent opportunity cost by precluding the resources from alternative uses. However, this is an improper view of opportunity cost. Opportunity costs, which in general are subjective, are what drive choice and decisions.[2] Once an investment decision is made, the stream of costs that the decision gives rise to are the objective costs of the decision. Once the investment is in place, the opportunity cost that drove the investment decision to begin with is no longer relevant.[3]

In addition, it is mistaken in my view to attempt to line up output at various points in time with the cost of the investment. Long-run marginal cost (which probably should be called long-run average incremental cost) is measured by the cost of the investment divided by some appropriate measure of the capacity of the plant represented in the investment. This could be either rated capacity, or rated capacity multiplied by some average 'fill' factor. However, to attempt to identify components of the cost of the plant with specific units of output generated by the plant is nothing more than an arbitrary cost allocation.[4]

Closely related to the foregoing is the widely accepted view in the literature that those who cause a cost to be incurred should pay for that cost. This is a laudable sentiment, but this is all it is, a sentiment, especially in the context of pricing the output where highly durable physical capital is involved. Standard economic efficiency requires that price be equal to marginal cost, but the marginal cost in question is short-run marginal cost, not long-run marginal cost. For a good sold in a spot market, long-run marginal cost, as was discussed in Chapter 5, informs investment decisions, but not pricing decisions. For operating rates short of full capacity utilization, the relevant guide to price is short-run avoidable cost. In this situation, it is clearly meaningful to say that those who cause costs to occur ought to pay those costs, but this is with respect to short-run operating costs, not capital costs. On the other hand, if capacity is fully utilized,

---

[2] James Buchanan in his book, *Cost and Choice* (1969), provides convincing discussion of this point. See also Buchanan and Thirlby (1981).

[3] Once an investment is made, the relevant opportunity cost for subsequent decisions involving that investment is the quasi-rents from the best alternative use to which the investment can be put. The opportunity cost which drove the investment is not the objective cost that has to be amortized out of the quasi-rents generated by the investment. The cost to be amortized is the price that was paid for the investment.

[4] The motivation involved is a noble one, namely, to confront those adding to quantity demanded with the long-run costs of those decisions. The problem is that, except in the case where the demand decisions are embodied in long-term contracts, there is no meaningful objective way for this to be done. For output sold in a spot market, the relevant cost-guide for pricing is short-run avoidable cost, and this bears no necessary relationship at all to long-run marginal (or incremental cost).

price should be set at the point where output is allocated to those with the highest willingness-to-pay. In this case, the only thing that can be said about price in relation to cost is it will be above short-run avoidable cost. Again, there is no reference to long-run cost.

So much for a good sold in a spot market. What about goods like telephone services and electricity, which have historically been sold under socially negotiated tariffs? As was noted in Chapter 5, when output is sold under a long-term contract, it is perfectly reasonable and appropriate for capital costs to be represented in the negotiated price. Indeed, if the time period of the contract should coincide with the payback horizon of the underlying plant producing the output, the floor to price should, in fact, be long-run marginal cost. However, this is the only circumstance in which it is plausible to identify cost causers (i.e., the demanders in the contract) with cost payers.

The problem with trying to accomplish this for telephone and electricity rate payers in the circumstances of the real world are threefold:

1. With a mix of plants of different vintages, long-run marginal cost is inherently ambiguous, which means that any procedure to identify a single number as *the* long-run marginal cost will be arbitrary.

2. Tariffs are periodically, if not regularly, renegotiated, so that long-run marginal cost is, in effect, a moving target.

3. People and customers come and go, so that a customer whose current demands cause a capacity-augmenting investment today may not still be a customer when the new capacity comes on line.

In my view, the problems discussed in this section can be attributed to an illusion, an illusion that it is meaningful to decompose the price of a good into the costs of its various production inputs, including capital. Capital costs drive investment decisions, but once an investment is made, the capital costs incurred become financial obligations that have to be covered out of the quasi-rents from the sale of current production. Whether or not the quasi-rents will, in fact, cover the capital costs will depend on short-run demand in relation to the short-run avoidable cost curve.[5]

THE MEASUREMENT OF UNIT INCREMENTAL COST

On p. 160 of his paper in the NRRI volume, Emmerson defines *unit incremental cost* (UIC) as the ratio of two differences in present value:

$$(1) \quad UIC = \frac{PV[C(y_t + \Delta y_t)] - PV[C(y_t)]}{PV[y_t + \Delta y_t] - PV[y_t]} ,$$

where y_t denotes output at time t and $C(y_t)$ denotes the cost of producing y_t. My misgivings about the denominator have already been noted, so nothing further needs to be said about the discounting of output.

The numerator defines the incremental cost of adding Δy_t to output using the framework of Turvey (1968). That is, incremental cost is defined as the difference in the present values of two infinite-horizon cost streams, one for producing $y_t + \Delta y_t$ and the second for producing y_t. In my opinion, this is not the proper way of measuring the incremental cost of capacity. The cost of additional capacity should be defined simply as the objective cost of the capacity in question. This is then converted to a unit incremental cost by dividing by the amount of capacity involved. Moreover, Turvey's procedure includes in the stream of costs of producing a particular output, the costs of periodic replacement of the underlying plant. A firm calculating the cost of a prospective investment does not, it seems to me, look beyond the expected useful life of the investment, for there is no need *today* to decide whether a decision to replace will be made *tomorrow*. That decision will be made when tomorrow comes. What the firm looks at in contemplating an investment today is whether (on an expected value basis, with allowances for risk) the quasi-rents generated by the investment

---

[5] The idea of identifying price in the long run with costs of production is, of course, a residual legacy of Classical economics. However, in the present context, the sentiment to make those who cause costs pay those costs is clearly helped along by the classic peak-load pricing papers of Steiner (1957) and Boiteux (1960). The conclusion of their papers is that peak demanders should pay all capital costs, while off-peak demanders should pay only operating costs. The Steiner and Boiteux papers are beautiful pieces of analysis, but they have in my opinion led to a lot of mischief because practitioners have tended to overlook the strong assumptions which yield the result. In general, what the Steiner-Boiteux analysis shows is that the peak price should be such as to allocate existing capacity output to those with the highest willingnesses-to-pay. The fact that this peak price equates to operating cost plus unit capital cost in the Steiner-Boiteux analysis is simply an artifact of the strong stationarity assumptions that are made: There is a single stationary technology, and demand is both stationary and known with certainty. None of these assumptions is even remotely close to being fulfilled in reality.

will make the investment whole in relation to its cost. If the answer is yes, the investment will be undertaken (or capacity will be added to), and the cost of the increment of capacity is simply the objective cost of this capacity.

As noted in footnote 4, the desire on the part of Emmerson and others is a noble one, namely, to confront those adding to quantity demanded with the long-run costs of those decisions. As just discussed, however, the problem is that, except in the case where the demand decisions are embodied in long-term contracts, there is no meaningful objective way for this to be done. The relevant cost-guide for pricing in a spot market is short-run avoidable cost, and this bears no necessary relationship to long-run marginal (or incremental) cost.

SUNK COSTS

Later in the same paper in the NRRI volume, there is the statement:

A cost is a sunk cost if, once committed, the cost cannot be avoided even by terminating business altogether. Equivalently, the cost of a resource is sunk if, once committed, to a specific purpose it [the resource] has no opportunity cost. [Emmerson (1991, p. 186).]

These are, I imagine, pretty standard statements (or definitions) of sunk cost. I do not have a problem with them as they stand, but I do not think that they clear up all of the confusion that surrounds the concept of sunk cost. To begin with, I think that the term sunk cost is unfortunate. To convey the idea intended, a much better term in my view would be sunk resources or sunk plant, for this is what is really involved -- i.e., resources (or plant) that have a specific use and which cannot be transferred, on short notice, into another use.

One must also distinguish between non-transferability of plant and non-transferability of the fluid capital that is embodied in the plant. Not being able to transfer physical capital to another use is something entirely different from not being able to transfer the capital embodied in the physical capital to another use. As was discussed in Chapter 2 and again in Chapter 5, the capital that is embodied in physical capital is transformed back into fluid capital through charges against quasi-rents. Plant that is completely sunk may nevertheless be perfectly fungible in terms of the capital that was embodied in it, because the capital has been entirely returned to the pool of fluid capital through myros recovery charges. The worst case scenario for 'sunkness', obviously, is when plant which has never generated any quasi-rents, with no prospects for ever doing so, has no alternative use. The Washington Public Power Supply System

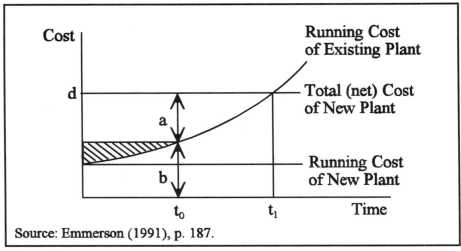

Source: Emmerson (1991), p. 187.

Figure 18

nuclear power generating plants in the state of Washington, which were started in the 1970s but never finished, provide a prime example.[6]

In another passage in his paper in the NRRI volume, Emmerson states that the current value of a perfectly fungible old plant with characteristics identical to those of new plant will be based on the cost of the new plant:

> Today, the running cost of the old plant is b [cf. Figure 18]. Because the old plant is perfectly fungible, the old plant has an imputed capital cost equal to a. That is, were the old plant to be made available due to declining demand, the cost of new plant (d) could be avoided by incurring running cost (b) to reuse the old plant. The imputed capital cost of the old plant is the amount (a) and the total cost of the old plant is a + b (= d). Thus, for perfectly fungible old plant (which is fungibly equivalent to new plant), a cost study which assumes all new plant is correct. [Emmerson (1991, p. 188)].

I have the following problems with this view of things:

---

[6] The standard view in economics concerning sunk costs is that they are bygones and are, therefore, irrelevant for current decisions. This may be true for sunk costs, but not for sunk plant. For the existence of plant that is used and useful can convey a powerful competitive advantage to the firm that owns it *vis-a-vis* firms that are contemplating producing from plant that would have to be constructed from scratch. This is because the total costs of production from new plant have to compete with only the avoidable costs of production from old plant. The capital costs of old plant, being sunk, do not figure into the floor to price for production from the old plant. This is why sunk plant can provide a barrier to entry.

1. To begin with, let us suppose that, at time t_0, the old plant in question was being purchased from another firm. What would be the maximum price that the purchasing firm would be willing to pay? It is clear that the maximum would be given by the present value of the cross-hatched area in Figure 18. If a capital value is to be imputed, it seems that it ought to be this number, rather than a, as stated by Emmerson.

2. However, it is not clear why there should be an imputation to begin with. If the purpose is to get the 'capital' account of the firm right, I do not think this is the proper way to do it. When the plant was originally purchased, a certain price was paid for it, and this is the number that would be represented in the capital account of the firm's books.

3. Further to the preceding point: the 'capital' embodied in the plant (as represented by the price that is paid for the plant) will be 'recovered' -- i.e., returned to the pool of fluid capital -- through myros recovery charges against quasi-rents. If there is a failure of demand before the capital is fully recovered, but the plant is still usable and 100% fungible, then the capital cost of diverting the plant to a new use is what remains in the capital account of the original cost of the plant (plus, of course, any costs of conversion).

4. The essential point is that opportunity costs should not be capitalized. The discounted value of the cross-hatched area in Figure 18 is a genuine opportunity cost that drives the decision to reuse old plant rather than invest in new plant, but it is not a capital cost in the sense of embodied fluid capital that must be recovered from quasi-rents.

CHAPTER 11

TRADE, TRANSFERS, AND MONETARY OVERHANGS

In this chapter, we turn to questions involving international trade and the transfer of wealth from one country to another or from one region within a country to another. The focus, initially, will be on the emergence of trade between two previously closed monetary economies and the factors which influence the exchange rate established between their respective currencies. Following this, we will turn to transfer questions involving 'monetary overhangs' and how they are related to the conservation laws imposed by the pool of fluid capital. Two examples will be considered, the first the 'capital levy' proposed by Schumpeter for Austria at the end of WWI, the second the reunification of Germany in 1990 following collapse of the Berlin Wall.

TRADE AND EXCHANGE RATES

In this section, we explore the factors that determine the exchange rate between currencies of two countries that engage in trade with one another. For convenience, assume that the two countries are Germany and the United States, so that the currencies in question are the deutschmark (DM) and the dollar. Assume, also, that these are the only countries in the world, and that they initially form two closed systems. Our procedure will be to trace out what happens when exchange between the two countries first emerges.

As a point of departure, assume that Germany is in macroeconomic equilibrium and that the U.S. is as well, except for one individual who wishes to purchase a good produced in Germany. Payment for the good has to be in DM, so the individual must first find someone in Germany who is willing to give up DM in exchange for dollars. Assume that this is, in fact, accomplished and that the necessary DM are purchased at a rate of κDM per dollar. The German good is purchased, makes its way to the U.S., and is consumed. We want now to trace out what happens in the financial and goods markets in both countries as a result of these transactions.

Let us begin with the U.S. Assume that the dollars used to purchase the DM are dollars that have been received as current income. Since these dollars are diverted to the purchase of a German good, it follows that a like value of U.S. goods (valued in current prices) will not be sold, so (assuming that investment is not affected) there will be downward pressure on goods prices in the U.S. Initially, there will no effect on asset prices in the U.S.

Things will be more complicated in Germany. Let us assume, to start with, that the DM which are exchanged for dollars were being held as an asset. With the exchange, these DM are transformed into media of exchange, so there will be an increase in the volume of spending in Germany. Since the total stock of goods is fixed in the short run, the result will be upward pressure on goods prices in Germany. However, this is not the end of the story, for unlike in the U.S., there will also be an effect on German interest rates and asset prices.

Since it is assumed that the DM that are purchased are DM being held as an asset, and the fact (also by assumption) that Germany is in macroeconomic equilibrium, then the value for κ must be high enough to overcome the liquidity preference of the marginal holder of DM. The resulting reduction in the amount of DM that are available to be held as an asset will put upward pressure on the money rate of interest and, through portfolio adjustments, on other interest rates as well (unless, of course, the German Bundesbank should take offsetting action).

Assuming that the DM/dollar exchange rate κ somehow gets determined, all of this seems straightforward. The important question, however, is how κ is determined. To begin with, it has to be a truism that the German who gives up DM for dollars must see some benefits of holding dollars. What might these benefits be? There are three possibilities:

1. Interest rates are higher in the U.S. than in Germany, so that, while the German was a holder of money in Germany, he/she can be a holder of interest-bearing dollar-denominated assets. (This assumes, of course, that the German does not expect a sufficiently adverse movement in the exchange rate during the period of an investment in dollar-denominated assets so as to negate the interest rate differential.)

2. The German holder of dollars expects the exchange rate to appreciate sufficiently that a profit in DM will be made when the dollars are converted back into DM.

3. Although the German was a holder of money as an asset in Germany, he/she could decide to use the dollars to purchase U.S. goods because U.S. goods appear to be a bargain in relation to the price of German goods.

Three determining variables for the exchange rate between two currencies emerge from this list: (1) interest rate differentials, (2) expectations of changes in the exchange rate, and (3) Purchasing Power Parity differences between the relative purchasing powers (in terms of domestic versus foreign goods) of the two currencies. The first two factors will primarily affect flows of financial capital between the countries, while the third factor -- i.e., Purchasing Power Parity -- will primarily affect trade flows. However, since a single exchange rate governs both types of flows, the exchange rate which emerges will be the result of all three factors.

MONETARY OVERHANGS AND CAPITAL LEVIES

In a paper written in 1916, but not available to English readers until relatively recently, Schumpeter (1954), anticipating the monetary problem that would accompany the end of the ongoing great war in Europe, proposed a capital levy as the best method of dealing with these problems. The problem, as described by Schumpeter, was as follows:[1]

> The first problem is fiscal. It is, in concrete terms, a matter of *money*: money which the state needs to fulfill its obligations and to get rid of its deficit. It is not a matter of goods, such as war materials, food and clothing for the army, etc. To be sure, the true costs of the war lie in the goods sphere: the used-up goods, the devastation of parts of the country, the loss of manpower, these are the real "cost" of war to the economies. It was the procurement of the mass of goods needed for the conduct of the war that was the great problem within which the raising of the necessary sums of money was a relatively subordinate problem of fiscal technique. However, this problem is already solved. What the armies and the peoples needed for warfare in the way of goods, we have

---

[1] Schumpeter's specific focus was Austria, but the problem he was concerned with is a very general one and, as we shall see in a moment, can be identified with the 'monetary overhangs' that plagued the Eastern European economies in 1989 and 1990.

raised already by hook or by crook and we shall continue to raise it during the war.

The problem which *then* remains is merely a "question of money". We shall be in the position of a businessman whose factory has burned down and who now faces the task of expressing this loss in his books. Like a huge conflagration the war has devoured a large part of our national wealth, the economy has become poorer. This has already happened, nothing can change it, and whatever goods were necessary for the purposes of war will have been supplied by the end of the war. However, in money terms, the economy has not become poorer. How is this possible? Simply so that claims on the state and money tokens have taken the place of stocks of goods in the private economies. The state cannot replace the goods it has taken out of the private economies -- it could after all only take them from the economy itself. What is needed is simply an adjustment of money values which would return them to harmony with the world of goods, that is to say, a large-scale writing-down of book values. And this can be done only by the state covering its monetary obligations out of the money claims and money stocks of the economy. . . . [Schumpeter, "The Crisis of the Tax State," in Swedberg (1991), pp.118-19; italics in original.]

The problem described by Schumpeter is one in which, because of the destruction pursuant to war and the manner of its finance, the real value of national wealth is considerably smaller than the money value of the same. Since real wealth cannot be created *en vacuo*, the only way that the two values can be brought into "harmony" with one another is through a destruction of monetary claims, whether directly (as per a capital levy) or indirectly through inflation. As it turned out, the destruction in Austria occurred through a hyperinflation, following a failure on the part of Schumpeter, during the six months in 1919 that he was Finance Minister, to convince the Austrian government that a capital levy was the better route to take.[2]

The focus in the present section is not on Austria and Schumpeter *per se*, but rather on the modern day 'monetary overhangs' that characterized the Eastern European economies in 1989 and 1990 on the eve of their transformations from centrally directed command economies into market economies. My purpose in this section is to draw parallels between the problems posed by these monetary overhangs and the problem addressed by Schumpeter, to discuss methods (other than inflation) of dealing with them, and to show that the solution taken in the reunification of Germany amounted, in essence, to a Schumpeterian capital levy.

---

[2] For a chronicle and detailed analysis of Schumpeter's ill-fated attempt to effect the capital levy, see Stolper (1994, Chapters 14-19).

For purposes of discussion, a monetary overhang will be defined as a (positive) divergence between the stock of monetary claims on the pool of fluid capital and the goods represented in the pool valued in current prices. While there are a number of ways in which monetary overhangs can come into existence, the ones of present interest are the finance of war expenditures through the sale of debt and the accumulation of savings in an economy in which the only private asset is money. The former is what motivated Schumpeter's analysis, while the latter will be assumed as a stylized fact characterizing the Eastern European economies during the years of communist rule.

As ably described by Schumpeter, a monetary overhang emerges with war financed by debt because of the simple fact that the goods that the debt finances are for the most part destroyed, whereas the monetary claims continue to exist. The divergence in values between the claims and goods sides of the pool of fluid capital is both direct and unmistakable, and the only way that the divergence can be eliminated without an inflation in goods prices is through destruction of an appropriate amount of monetary claims. Schumpeter's solution was through a levy on financial assets whose proceeds could be used *only* to retire debt.[3]

The monetary overhangs that characterized the Eastern European economies on the eve of their conversions to market economies had a much different origin than war debt, as the primary cause of these overhangs was an absence of assets other than money in which private savings could be held. To see what is involved, let us consider the polar case of an economy in which the only asset that can be privately owned is money. Income is received as money, and the claim tickets it represents can either be exercised in the purchase of consumer goods or saved.[4] If saved, the unexercised claim tickets can be held either as cash or as deposits in a bank. Real assets are owned by the state, so that there are no equities or bonds. Houses are not owned, but are rented (or provided free) by the state, so that there are no mortgages. There are no precious metals, 'Old Masters', or other stores of value. In short, it is either money or nothing.[5]

---

[3] The fact that the war debt in Austria was internal made a capital levy, in principle, feasible. The levy was to have been paid in either money or bonds. In the case of payment in bonds, the bonds would obviously have ceased to exist once they were received by the Treasury. In the case of payment in money, the money was to have been used to repay government loans from commercial banks as well as the central bank.

[4] This is an obvious stylization of how income was received in the communist command economies, for much of income was received in kind in the form of nonmarket prices for housing, food, public transportation and free medical care, etc.

[5] In East Germany, homes could be owned, as could small craft-type businesses, and there were small amounts of privately owned life insurances policies in force at the time of the monetary union with West Germany. Also, states cannot completely eliminate the values placed on privately created

In this situation, the pool of fluid capital is co-extensive (on the claims side) with the stock of money held as an asset. On the goods side, things are more complicated, for most (if not all) of the goods left 'unclaimed' by saving are ultimately consumed as investment in produced means of production (i.e., physical capital), whose ownership resides with the state. The result is the creation of a monetary overhang, though of a different type than that created by war debt.

What monetary overhang means in these circumstances is that, compared with a 'normal' economy in which there are private property rights and many forms of assets (both real and financial) in which savings can be held, there is too much latent liquidity. This latent excess liquidity would become manifest if an economy with such an overhang were suddenly to be merged with a normal economy at a currency conversion which left the overhang intact. The economy of East Germany at the time of its integration into West Germany in 1990 provides a precise case in point, and it is to this that we will now turn. However, in order to establish the central ideas, it will be useful initially to consider the transfer problems involved in terms of two stylized economies.

WEALTH TRANSFERS AND MONETARY OVERHANGS: A STYLIZED ANALYSIS

In the present section, we shall lay the groundwork for analyzing the purely economic problems of integrating the two German economies, using the macroeconomic framework which has been developed in this book. Social and cultural problems associated with the integration will not be addressed except in passing. The procedure in this section will be to set up two stylized economies, one with high levels of income and productivity and the other with low levels of the same. Complete integration of the two economies will then be analyzed, taking into the account the conservation laws imposed by the pool of fluid capital.

Let the two economies being merged be denoted by D1 and D2, respectively, each with the following characteristics at the time of merger:

1. D1 has high levels of income and productivity, while D2 has low levels of the same.

---

works of art, etc. Yet the fact remains that, at the time of the monetary union, the bulk of private Eastern savings was held as money.

2. The population of D1 is four times that of D2, 64m in D1 and 16m in D2.

3. Produced means of production are privately owned in D1, but owned by the state in D2.

4. The economy in D2 is command, while the economy in D1 is market-driven. The newly integrated economy will be market-driven and its social welfare system will be that of D1.

5. Although the currencies in D1 and D2 share the same name (mark), assume that the 'market' exchange rate for D2 goods exported to D1 is four D2 marks for each D1 mark.

6. Assume that the value of the pool of fluid capital in D1 is 250b D1 marks, while the value of the pool of fluid capital in D2 is 28b D2 marks.

7. Assume that residents of D1 hold 200b D1 marks as an asset and that residents of D2 hold 48b D2 marks.

The terms of the merger are assumed to specify that, within the borders of the 'new' country (D), all restrictions on the movement of goods, human resources, and capital (whether fluid or otherwise) are eliminated immediately and completely. Secondly, it is assumed that the D2 mark is placed at parity with the D1 mark. Finally, it is assumed that the two economies are closed in terms of capital movements.

With these assumptions, we now turn to an analysis of some of the macroeconomic consequences of the merger of the two economies, specifically as regards:

a. The immediate effects on the residents of D1;

b. The immediate effects on the residents of D2;

c. The longer-run effects on investment;

d The longer-run effects on the pool of fluid capital;

e. The longer-run effects on the growth of income;

f.   The consequences for inflation;

g.   The period of time that might reasonably be expected for full integration of the two economies to occur.

At the point in time that the exchange rate between the two currencies was pegged at par, there would be a transfer of wealth from holders of D1 marks to holders of D2 marks. This would not have been the case had the exchange rate been established at the 'market' exchange rate for goods of four D2 marks for each D1 mark. This conclusion is a straightforward consequence of the conservation laws imposed by the pool of fluid capital. Specifically, at the time of the currency merger, the stock of fluid capital in the two economies was (per our assumptions) equal to 257b marks evaluated in D1 marks (using the assumed 'market' exchange rate of four to one). The amount of money held as an asset in the two economies is 248b marks in total, but only 212b evaluated in D1 marks. Pegging of the two currencies at par accordingly accords the holders of D2 marks the equivalent of a windfall of 36b D1 marks.

Because the real value of the pool of fluid capital for the two economies is set by the market exchange rate of the two currencies, it is invariant to the pegged exchange rate. Since the number of D1 marks held by D1 residents does not change, but (with the pegging at par) the number of D1 marks held by residents of D2 is in essence increased by 36b, the number of 'new' marks held by residents of D2 is increased relative to the number held by the residents of D1. Since the aggregate amount of wealth in the two economies is constrained by the real value of the combined pools of fluid capital, and because this is invariant to the pegged exchange rate, there is necessarily a transfer of real wealth from the residents of D1 to the residents of D2.

The foregoing conclusion is a purely formal consequence of the invariance of the real value of the pool of fluid capital. As such, it does not say anything about how the transfer of wealth might actually be effected. Since pegging of the exchange rate between the two currencies at par rather than at the market rate of four to one amounts, in effect, to an autonomous increase in the stock of money held as an asset of 36b marks, and since there is no offsetting increase in the capacity of the 'new' economy to produce, the transfer necessarily has to take place through inflation in some form or another.[6] There are several mechanisms by which this could occur, and I will single out two for discussion:

---

[6] I am assuming at this point that there are no assets to be held in D2 except for money and goods. A different conclusion could emerge if, at the time of the currency merger, D2 residents were also to acquire property rights in D2's produced means of production. This will be discussed below.

inflation in the goods market and inflation in the asset market.

The most obvious and direct way for the transfer of wealth to occur would be through price inflation in the goods market, as residents of D2 (who now have free movement into D1) spend at least part of their windfall of 36b marks on goods produced in D1. The result would be a once-and-for-all increase in the general price level.[7] A transfer through asset inflation, on the other hand, is more indirect. Assume that residents of D2 decide to hold part of their 36b-mark windfall as an asset, though not necessarily in the form of money. Since equities in produced means of production could not be owned in D2, but could in D1, residents of D2 held a larger proportion of their wealth in the form of money than did residents of D1. Since with merger (but before privatization of D2's produced means of production) D2 residents can now purchase D1 equities, it would be reasonable for them to do so, not only out of their windfall of 36b marks, but out of their equivalent 'original' holdings of 12b D1 marks as well. The result will be an increase in the price of D1 equities.

Since the D1 equities purchased by residents of D2 were held by residents of D1, the mark balances of the latter will be increased. If all or part of these increased balances is spent on goods, then goods prices will also increase, and there will once again be a transfer of wealth through inflation. On the other hand, if the residents of D1 choose to hold their increased mark balances as an asset, goods prices will not be immediately affected, and it might seem that there has been no transfer of wealth. This is not the case, however. Because the real value of the stock of money is always constrained by the pool of fluid capital evaluated in current prices, the fact that the stock of money has increased, whereas the general price level has not, simply means that the inflation is latent. Holders of the increased mark balances may *individually* feel that their wealth has not changed, but *as a group* their wealth has necessarily been reduced. This will be manifested by the latent inflation becoming open inflation whenever there is an attempt to convert the increased mark balances into goods. Until this occurs, the holders of these increased mark balances (again as a group) will live under an illusion that their real wealth is the same as it was before the merger.

---

[7] Since goods produced in D2 would almost certainly be less desirable than goods produced in D1, it might seem that inflation could be contained by price decreases for D2 goods. This would not be the case, however, so long as the windfall to D2 residents leads to a net increase for the newly combined economies in the desire to consume, for a now larger pool of purchasing power is coming up against the same amount of goods. Prices of D2 goods may very well decrease, but any decreases will necessarily be more than offset by price increases in D1. Also, it should be noted that it is implicitly being assumed that the economy of D1 is operating at full capacity. If this should not be the case, then some of the increased demand for D1 goods could be accommodated by an increase in utilization with little or no inflation. I am grateful to Dieter Elixmann for pointing this out.

For the illustrative numbers which are being used, pegging the exchange rate at par effectively transfers 36b D1 marks of wealth from residents of D1 to residents of D2. Since the total wealth of D1 prior to the merger was 250b D1 marks (the value in current prices of the pool of fluid capital in D1), a transfer of 36b marks is equivalent to a *capital levy* on D1's residents of about 14%.

Pegging the exchange rate at par also has implications for the real purchasing power of current income. Prior to the merger, each mark of income in D2 was the equivalent of one-fourth of a mark of income in D1, whereas after the merger the two marks are at par in purchasing power.[8] By assumption, real income per capita is much higher in D1 than in D2, but the disparity was much larger prior to the merger than after. Prior to the merger, per capita income in D2 was only 11% of that in D1, whereas after the merger it is 43%.[9] Since, initially anyway, there will be no increase in the amount of goods available, the increased real purchasing power of the D2 residents, occasioned by the pegging of the two currencies at par, will lead to an inflation in goods prices, thereby causing a reduction in the real purchasing power of incomes in D1. In terms of the numbers we have been using, goods valued in pre-merger prices of 257b marks will be confronted by a pool of post-merger purchasing power of 278b marks, which implies an increase in the general price level of 8.2% and a reduction in the real purchasing power of D1 incomes of 7.6%.[10] The conclusion from this analysis is clear. *The decision to peg the two currencies at par results in substantial transfers of both wealth and real purchasing power of income from the residents of D1 to the residents of D2. The enabling mechanism in both cases is inflation.*

In view of this, let us now ask what would happen if the monetary authority were to seek to contain the inflation. In particular, let us suppose that the central bank attempts to kill the inflationary potential caused by the pegging of the two

[8] This is with respect to the consumption by D2 residents of D1 goods, and accordingly does not take into account the much lower prices of non-traded goods in D2. In terms of purchasing-power parity, therefore, the 'market' exchange rate will understate the real purchasing power of the pre-merger D2 mark. The implications of this will be discussed below.

[9] Although illustrative numbers for total income in the two economies have not been provided, total income will always be of the same order of magnitude as the value of the pool of fluid capital. The numbers in the text are accordingly derived using 250b and 28b as the total incomes for the two economies in conjunction with the populations of 64m and 16m.

[10] This 8.2% inflation in goods prices is in addition to that triggered by the increase in real value of the D2 marks held as an asset which is caused by the pegging of the two currencies at par. The analysis assumes that D2 goods continue to be desirable at pre-merger prices. If this were not so, then the inflation in D1 goods would be greater than 8.2%, in which case the decrease in real incomes in D1 would be even larger.

currencies at par through a 32b-mark reduction in the total stock of money. This could, in principle, be accomplished within one period of production by forcing the banking system (by whatever means) not to renew 32b marks of existing loans. Since most loans represent working capital for financing current production, the result would almost certainly be a major recession. Inflation might be contained, but at a cost of substantial unemployment and loss of income. In fact, with fewer goods available as a consequence of the reduced availability of working capital, the most likely outcome would be *both* inflation *and* unemployment!

While the transfers of wealth and real purchasing power caused by pegging the currencies of D1 and D2 at par at the time of merger is one thing, the effects of these transfers on the morale of the people involved is something else. The residents of D2, being the recipients of substantial windfalls, would almost certainly be elated. But this will not be the case for the residents of D1, for they are on receiving ends of substantial capital and income levies, which for the most part are hidden since these levies take the form of an inflation tax. While increases in real income and wealth can boost morale, decreases never do.

The analysis to this point has dealt entirely with the wealth and real income transfers implied by the conservation laws imposed by the pool of fluid capital as a consequence of conversion of the two currencies at par. We now turn to questions involving the longer-term effects of the integration of the two economies on levels of investment, productivity, and income. The effects in all three instances depend upon what happens to the size of the pool of fluid capital. Before going into details, however, several points concerning transitory economic forces which would come into play at the time of integration need to be discussed.

The first point concerns the elimination of all restrictions on the movement of labor. Since the pre-merger real wage in D2 is substantially below that in D1, lifting the restrictions on the movement of labor will obviously encourage labor to migrate from D2 to D1. Pegging the two marks at par clearly counteracts these forces, however, for (as already noted) conversion at par increases the D2 real wage (in terms of D1 prices) from about 10% of the D1 pre-merger level to about 40% post-merger. Taking non-traded goods into account (assuming that their nominal prices remain at pre-merger levels) moves the D2 real wage even closer to the D1 level. Conversion at par accordingly might foreclose labor migration altogether.

A second point concerns the produced means of production in the dowry of D2, for it is highly unlikely that these will have all that much to contribute to the overall productive capacity of the newly combined economies. Two factors are at issue. The first relates to the general desirability of the goods produced in D2, while the second relates to the strong likelihood that, desirability aside, much of D2's produced means of production is economically obsolete. Since D2 was a command economy, both the quality and the range of goods that D2's productive structure is capable of producing will not likely be in accord with choice-driven market demands.[11] The upshot is a serious mismatch, at least in the short run, between goods that will be demanded in the newly integrated economy and the goods which D2's produced means of production are capable of supplying. Even if such a mismatch were not a problem, it would be likely in the circumstances that D2's productive capacity is so technologically obsolete that, with the higher real wage rates induced by the decisions to peg the two currencies at par, much of the capacity is economically obsolete as well. Because of these factors, much of the productive capacity in place in D2 at the time of merger will be of little or no value as it stands, and the capital which remains sunk in it will be unrecoverable -- unrecoverable in the sense that there will be no revenues against which myros recovery charges can be taken which would transform the capital remaining in this productive capacity back into the pool of fluid capital. Among other things, an implication of all this is that the goods inflation caused by pegging of the two currencies at par will be exacerbated because of a decreased supply of goods (in relation to the *apparent* productive capacity of the combined economies).

Obviously, a major goal of integration is to bring the levels of income and productivity in the two economies into parity, where parity is presumed to mean increasing income levels in D2 to the levels of D1, rather than vice versa. We have seen, however, that one of the immediate effects of the merger is to reduce the level of real income in D1 by a transfer of wealth from residents of D1 to those of D2. In the long run, income parity will obviously require, if morale is to be maintained, that real incomes in D2 increase more rapidly than real incomes in D1.[12]

Purely in terms of economics, the crucial consideration in the longer run concerns what happens to investment, and even more fundamentally, what happens to the pool of fluid capital. Clearly, for D2 incomes to be brought up to

---

[11] Moreover, for the real-world circumstances in question, this problem is compounded by the fact that D2's productive structure was highly geared to external markets which, for the most part, ceased to exist.

[12] Reference here is to people rather than to geography. Presumably, what is meant by parity in the long run is that the distribution of real income reflects ability rather than former place of residence in D1 or D2.

the levels of D1, investment not only has to take place, but in amounts well in excess of past levels. In a closed system, the only way the capital can be created to fund this investment is through a higher saving rate. However, this may be difficult because of the two circumstances: the transfer of wealth from D1 to D2 caused by pegging the two currencies at par, and extension to the residents of D2 the same welfare benefits as enjoyed by the residents of D1. Both clearly encourage consumption. The problem could be circumvented by tapping into the global pool of fluid capital, but this would require either loans from abroad, or an assessment on the part of foreign private capital holders that D is an attractive place to invest.

A major factor driving investment in the 'new' D ought to be investment in new manufacturing facilities in D2 as production, at least on the margin, is shifted to D2 in consequence of prospectively lower labor costs. However, I say 'ought to be' rather than 'will be' because labor costs may not be lower in D2 than in D1. Three factors could contribute to this not occurring: (1) inflation in D2 wage levels which moves them towards parity in nominal terms with wage levels in D1, (2) inadequate infrastructure in D2 (especially transport and communications), and (3) *ceteris paribus*, D2 workers may simply not be as productive as D1 workers.

If investment in D2 is not stimulated by the prospect of lower production costs in D2, then the only *static* factor spurring investment in D (viewing D as a closed system) would be the incentive of producing for a now larger domestic market. It is unlikely, however, that the investment forthcoming for this reason alone would be sufficient, over any reasonable period of time, to narrow the income gap in a socially acceptable manner. To fund in a non-inflationary way the investment that would be needed to achieve this would require either a substantial increase in the domestic saving rate, or healthy inflows of capital from abroad. Neither of these would seem to be probable, primarily as a consequence of a likely absence of optimism. Optimism is necessary because investment is governed by prospective yields, and if much of the population is pessimistic about the future, the 'animal spirits' of those making investment decisions will almost certainly be dampened. But why should pessimism be the norm, rather than optimism? After all, 20% of the population of the new D now face much improved economic prospects (and presumably much better social and political prospects as well).

The problem, obviously, lies with the other 80% of the population who experience the decrease in real income occasioned by the pegging of the two currencies at par. Not only are there no immediate prospects of this decrease in real income being made up, but the malaise is heightened by almost certain action (given the real-world historical circumstances) by the central bank to raise interest rates in an effort to curb the attendant inflation. As been pointed out, however, some amount of once-and-for-all inflation is inevitable as the general price level adjusts to the exogenous increase in the stock of money held as an asset caused by the currency conversion at par. The primary effect of higher interest rates will consequently be a further erosion of real income of D1 residents as the economy slides further into recession.

POLICIES FOR ELIMINATING A MONETARY OVERHANG: THE CASE OF GERMAN REUNIFICATION

With the foregoing as background, let us now turn to the reunification of the two German economies as this actually unfolded. The monetary integration of the two German economies took place on July 2, 1990, at which time all East German ostmarks were converted into deutschmarks according to the following schedule:

1. The number of marks that could be exchanged at a rate of 1:1 was limited to 2000 for children under the age of 15, to 4000 for adults under the age of 60, and to 6000 for people over 59.

2. Most of the rest of the money stock was converted at a rate of 2:1, except for money acquired for speculation in the year of unification, which could only be exchanged at a rate of 3:1.

3. Financial claims and debts [mainly firm's debts (260b ost-marks) and housing loans (108b)] were converted at a rate of 2:1.

4. The rate for price and wage contracts and pensions was 1:1. Pensions were to be based on East German wages, but calcu-lated according to West German formulae.

The motivations (both political and economic) for monetary conversion on these terms were primarily threefold: (1) to ensure the population that unification would proceed, (2) to make it clear to East Germans that there were no longer economic reasons for them to migrate to the West,[13] and (3) to provide the East

---

[13] As discussed at length by Sinn and Sinn (Chapter 5), the conversion of price and wage contracts at par was actually a two-edged sword. For although (per the earlier discussion) it raised the real wage in the East relative to the West, it also increased the wage costs of Eastern production to the

Germans with a fair amount of financial capital for their entry into a united Germany.

As was noted, there was a monetary overhang in the GDR that was the consequence of severely restricted private property rights and the resulting absence of financial instruments of wealth other than money. The average conversion rate of the stock of money of about 1.8:1 was designed to remove this overhang and to provide the newly combined German economies with a proper amount of liquidity.[14] In terms of the analysis in the preceding section, the monetary overhang represents the potential transfer of wealth from West to East that was discussed in connection with conversion of the two currencies at par. The decision to exchange ostmarks for deutschmarks at an average rate of about 1.8:1, rather than at 1:1, nullified a substantial part of the transfer and forestalled much of the inflation that such a transfer would have invoked.

On the other hand, while the conversion may have been successful at one level, Sinn and Sinn (1992) argue that there was also a dark side to the process, in that conversion at less than par unfairly eliminated a substantial part of private Eastern wealth. The argument turns on the severely restricted private property rights which prevailed in the GDR, and the ownerless produced means of production that came into being with the dissolution of the communist state. As was noted earlier, the fact that there were no equities and bonds for Eastern residents to own meant that private savings in the GDR had to be held mostly in the form of currency and bank deposits. This would lead to a monetary overhang, but only in the sense that money holdings are out of equilibrium from what they would be if other forms of real and financial assets were also available. One of the points made by Sinn and Sinn -- and it is an important one -- is that much, if not all, of the monetary overhang could have been neutralized without destruction of the claims it represented on the pool of fluid capital by allowing Eastern residents to give up money in exchange for equity in the East's produced means of production. Sinn and Sinn argue that, in these circumstances,

point where a rapid inflation of nominal Eastern wages towards parity with nominal Western wages would make Eastern manufactures unsalable. In the event, this is what occurred, resulting in massive Eastern unemployment.

[14] The point of reference (as determined by the Deutsche Bundesbank) for the 'proper' amount of liquidity was the ratio of M3 to GDP which prevailed in the FRG at the time of monetary union. The appropriate conversion rate accordingly became extremely sensitive to the assumption that was to be made concerning potential output in the GDR as a proportion of potential output in the FRG. In the event, it was assumed that GDR potential output was 9.5% of FRG potential output. The conversion rates chosen implied a resulting increase in the M3 money stock of 12% and a remaining monetary overhang for the combined economies of about 5%. For a detailed discussion, see Hasse (1993). Cf, also, Sinn and Sinn (1992, Chapter 3).

all of the East German money stock could have been converted into deutsch-marks at par, without great danger of inflation.[15] However, this would have required a much different process of privatization of East German industry than what, in fact, was followed.

The privatization process set in motion was for the property rights to East German industry to be transferred from the state at large to a state trust (the *Treuhandanstalt*, or simply the Treuhand), which then had the responsibility of transferring title into private hands either through restitution to previous owners or through sale. Rather than going into the multitude of problems that this process of privatization created,[16] I want, instead, to consider the implications for non-inflationary conversion if holders of ostmarks had been allowed to exchange ostmarks for marketable fractional ownerships in the East German produced means of production.

For concreteness in the discussion to follow, let us suppose that the marketable fractional ownerships in question had come into being through an initial transfer and auction process as follows:[17]

1. Up to 50% ownership in each East German enterprise is put up for auction for sale to the public with payment in ostmarks.

2. The remaining 50% ownership is retained by the Treuhand.

3. The Treuhand is organized as an investment trust. Ownership of the Treuhand is transferred to the public by granting each member of the East German population one marketable ownership share of the trust.

4. Once the initial auction and transfer of shares in the Treuhand is accomplished, trading of shares, both of businesses and of the Treuhand, including the business shares retained by the Treuhand, can be traded for any currency whatever.

---

[15] Sinn and Sinn cite evidence that the two marks were essentially at par in terms of purchasing-power parity and therefore that par was the proper conversion rate. See Sinn and Sinn (1992, especially Chapter 3).

[16] See Sinn and Sinn (1992, Chapter 4).

[17] The actual details of the initial transfer and auction of ownership rights are not key to present purposes. What is important is that property rights in the East's produced means of production become available to holders of ostmarks so that some form of portfolio adjustment could occur.

It is critical that steps (1) - (3) have been strictly internal to residents of the GDR, for the purpose of these steps would have been to create property rights in the East's produced means of production and then to transfer these property rights, part directly and part by auction, to the East German public. The auction part of the transfer would have allowed holders of ostmarks, whose savings allowed construction of much of the physical capital stock to begin with, to include equities as well as money in their portfolios of assets. In principle, such portfolio adjustments would have extinguished most, if not all, of the monetary overhang. Equally importantly, the transfer process would also have eliminated the capital overhang characteristic of communist command economies in which the real value of the stock of physical capital exceeds the value of the marketable financial assets.[18]

Let me now turn to the question of whether the monetary overhang would, in fact, have been eliminated by the privatization process just described. If holders of ostmarks did not see value in the produced means of production that were offered at auction, then at least part of the monetary overhang would have remained.[19] Because Eastern assets were not purchased when they were available does not mean that Western assets (including goods) would not have been purchased when they became available. In this situation, conversion of ostmarks into deutschmarks at par would almost certainly have resulted in some inflation in either West German goods or West German assets (or both). To completely extinguish the monetary overhang in these circumstances would, indeed, have required conversion of ostmarks into deutschmarks at something less than par.[20]

In the situation just described, destruction of a monetary overhang remaining after the transfer of property rights to the East's physical capital stock by conversion at less than par would not have been unfair to the holders of the overhang, because the real capital which the overhang initially allowed to be

---

[18] See Sinn and Sinn (1992, p. 66). I am assuming in all of this that sufficient market mentality would have existed for the East German population to meaningfully participate in the auctions of ownership shares. Obviously, this may not have been a valid assumption.

[19] What is at issue here is whether the real value of the stock of produced means of production, as measured by the prospective yields of these assets from the sale of marketable goods and services, is less than the nominal stock of savings, as represented in the holdings of ostmarks. There are many ways in which this might come about, including capital consumption and a production structure that is poorly adapted to produce the goods that will be demanded through the free exercise of tastes and preferences. The end result, in one form or another, has to be a reduction in the stock of ostmarks, so that the real stock of money is in accord with the stock of fluid capital.

[20] It is assumed that the ostmarks received by the Treuhand from the initial auction of ownership rights would have been neutralized, so that the monetary overhang was not simply transferred from individuals to the Treuhand. As will be discussed in a moment, the best form of neutralization would have been transfer of the ostmarks to a bank for 'reconstruction and development'.

constructed no longer existed. One way or another, the overhang would have been destructed, if not by conversion at less than par, then by inflation. Such is a necessary consequence of the conservation laws imposed by the pool of fluid capital.

Smooth and timely integration of the East German economy into the West required that investment to transform the production structure of Eastern industry begin immediately. Two types of investment were needed. The first type is investment that is simply to increase productive efficiency. In some cases, this can be achieved by 'Obstacle Removal',[21] while in other cases existing plant may have been so obsolete that it had to be scrapped altogether and new productive facilities created from scratch. The second type of required investment relates to a restructuring of production capacity that would have enabled the goods and services demanded by the free exercise of preferences to be produced, not only for the new domestic economy, but for export markets as well.

If privatization had proceeded according to the scenario just outlined, finance of investment in the East could have been provided, at least in part, by the money that passed to the Treuhand in the initial auction of ownership shares of Eastern industry.[22] To the extent that this occurred, finance of Eastern investment would have been provided by Eastern savings themselves, although most of the goods (except for labor) almost certainly would have had to have been purchased from the West or from abroad. However, the foregoing is not how privatization actually proceeded, and it is now clear (with hindsight) that the process which was chosen has positively hindered the transformation of Eastern industry. To begin with, effective destruction of much of the monetary overhang at the start by conversion of ostmarks into deutschmarks at less than par foreclosed any opportunity for the savings represented in the overhang to be mobilized as a source of investment finance.[23]

---

[21] 'Obstacle Removal' (from the Obstacle Removal Law) represents investment in retrofitting and upgrading of existing plant. There is a neat French word, *bricolage* -- "a cobbling together of contraptions from whatever is available" -- which is even more expressive. [The descriptive phrase is Patricia Churchland's, as quoted in Lewin (1992, p. 164).]

[22] There are several ways that the money thus collected could have been made available for financing investment. Two obvious ones are that the funds could have been transferred to a newly created bank for 'reconstruction and development', or the Treuhand itself could have functioned as a financial intermediary.

[23] It is to be emphasized that removing the monetary overhang by conversion at less than par caused no destruction of the pool of fluid capital, but only the claims on the pool that these ostmarks represented. The claims that were destroyed were transferred to those who were subsequently able to purchase ownership shares in East German businesses at prices lower than would have been the case if all ostmarks had been converted at par.

Secondly, about the only thing that has been accomplished by the privatization policy followed by the Treuhand was to create uncertainty and delay. By choosing, wherever possible, to restore property rights to original owners, rather than simply compensating these owners for their losses, the whole matter of property-rights transfer was considerably delayed because of problems of determining who original owners were. Even worse than the delay that this entailed was the creation of uncertainty sufficient to forestall sale of large numbers of businesses from the Treuhand inventory.

Contributing to the delay in transformation of Eastern industry, moreover, was the rapid increase in nominal wages in the East, the reasons for and implications of which are well-documented in Chapter 5 of Sinn and Sinn (1992). Although the ostmark may have been at par with the deutschmark in purchasing-power parity at the time of the monetary union, its 'market' exchange rate in terms of traded goods was more of the order of 4:1. In the circumstances, competitiveness of Eastern goods required that Eastern wages rise no faster in relation to Western wages than the rate at which Eastern productivity increased towards parity with the West. Eastern money wages rising faster than the rate at which the productivity gap was closed obviously meant that Eastern traded goods became unsalable, and the only possible result was the massive unemployment that in fact occurred.

THE GERMAN REUNIFICATION: AN ASSESSMENT

The primary purpose of the last two sections has been to analyze (using the conservation laws imposed by the pool of fluid capital) the transfer problems posed by the reunification of Germany following the fall of the Berlin Wall. The principal conclusions of the earlier theoretical analysis were that, because of the monetary overhang in the East, conversion of the two currencies at par would have implied a wealth transfer from West to East that would have led to inflation in both goods and asset prices, higher interest rates, reduced morale in the West, depression in the East, and most probably a recession in the West.

In the event, only part of these conclusions has been borne out. By removing much, if not all, of the monetary overhang by converting ostmarks into deutschmarks at a rate of about 1.8:1, rather than at 1:1, the wealth transfer from West to East was largely averted. However, as is pointed out by Sinn and Sinn (1992), and analyzed at length above, much of the same outcome almost certainly could have been obtained by a privatization process which allowed for the accumulated savings represented in the monetary overhang to be exchanged for ownership shares in the East's produced means of production. To the extent that such ownership shares commanded value, four things would have been accomplished: (1) property rights to the East's productive capacity would have been established and transferred; (2) the monetary overhang would have been removed without its destruction; (3) holders of ostmarks would not have been deprived of a good part of their savings; (4) the stage would have been set, through the establishment of a 'reconstruction and development' bank in one form or another, for Eastern savings to be mobilized for the finance of new investment.[24] Primarily because of the rapid rise of Eastern wages in relation to wages in the West, Eastern traded goods lost whatever cost advantage that they may have had, and the result was a depression with cosmic levels of unemployment. Moreover, the depression in the East was greatly exacerbated by the failure of an investment boom to materialize, in great part because of the delays and uncertainties created by the processes of privatization followed by the Treuhand.

All considered, however, the capital market in the West appears to have worked exceptionally well. As expected, interest rates increased, imports rose sharply relative to exports, and Germany turned from being capital-exporting to capital-importing.[25] Because of substantial income transfers from West to East, spending in the East was maintained despite the massive unemployment. Moreover, because of the rapid rise in Eastern wages coupled with unemployment benefits calculated according to Western formulae, the East's unemployed have largely remained at home, so that unemployment in the East has not been exported in a major way to the West.

---

[24] I do not mean to imply that Eastern savings would have been sufficient to finance all of the investment that was needed in the East. Obviously, this would have been far from the case. Nevertheless, Eastern savings could have made an important contribution and would have relieved some of the pressure on Western savings.

[25] It is not clear, however, how much of the turn in the capital account reflects (1) purely short-term financial capital movements because of the relatively higher German interest rates; (2) the finance of imported goods and services; or (3) real investment in German industry (whether in the East or the West is immaterial). (1) and (3) would be consistent with a higher exchange rate, but not (2). The higher exchange rate of the DM with the dollar in the early 1990s was, in my opinion, a consequence of U.S. domestic and international policies.

CHAPTER 12

QUESTIONS RELATED TO CONSUMPTION AND SAVING

As we have seen, decisions to save out of current income are additions to the pool of fluid capital, while decisions to consume or invest in produced means of production are subtractions. The economic drivers in an economy have been seen as owners/operators of productive capacity deciding how much of that capacity to utilize, entrepreneurs deciding how much to invest in new capacity, and households deciding how much of their income to consume. In general, this book has not been about the motivations that cause these decisions to occur, but rather about the implications of the decisions for changes in the pool of fluid capital and attendant effects upon interest rates and the general price level.

The purpose of this chapter is to take a more detailed look at questions relating to consumption and saving and how these, in turn, relate to the constraints imposed by the pool of fluid capital. Under the assumption that individuals save because they wish to transfer purchasing power from the present to sometime in the future, not only do decisions to save have implications for the current level of economic activity and the capacity of the economy to grow, but so too do the decisions to consume accumulated savings when the appropriate time arrives. The really interesting questions in this regard concern the implications for the overall economy of retirement-motivated saving and retirement consumption. In the first section of this chapter, these implications will be explored under the standard life-cycle assumption that all saving either by or for the benefit of individuals is for financing retirement consumption.

THE MACROECONOMICS OF RETIREMENT SAVING AND CONSUMPTION

Saving for retirement can take two avenues, private and social. With private saving, individuals are responsible for providing for their retirement consumption, while with social saving, the public sector has the responsibility. Private saving is voluntary, social saving is not. With social saving, saving takes the form of taxes collected by the government, while the benefits which are paid out upon retirement are usually determined according to formula. Social Security in the U.S. provides an obvious example of a socially based saving system.[1]

To begin with, let us assume that an individual who saves for retirement is able to obtain, over the period that the savings are held, a return which is in excess of the natural rate of interest. Obviously, this can be done for any individual, but it cannot be done for everyone, for in general the value of the claims on the pool of fluid capital cannot increase faster than the natural rate of interest. When individuals who have been saving for retirement finally retire and begin to consume out of their savings, the goods consumed have to be drawn from current production, as the goods which went into the pool of fluid capital at the time of initial saving will, in general, have disappeared. In short, current consumption, no matter what its source, must always be drawn from current production.

Consider now the case of a social saving system. Since the system is universal, it follows that the stock of claims associated with it cannot grow faster than the natural rate of interest. Among other things, this means that if the current recipients of social retirement payments are (as a group) receiving a total amount which (assuming no inflation) is greater than the natural rate of interest applied to the recipients' contribution (appropriately compounded), then they are drawing more than their 'share' from current production. Those in retirement obviously consume in excess of their current income, so that the goods that they consume, if the pool of fluid capital is not to be reduced, must be financed out of positive saving elsewhere in the economy.[2] Thus, to the extent that the amount spent on consumption by current recipients of social retirement payments is in excess of the contributions of the same, appropriately compounded by the natural rate of interest, there is a transfer from the presently employed to the retired.

An important difference between private and social saving is that, with social saving, there is no direct connection between the amount saved (i.e., the taxes paid) and subsequent retirement payments received. The latter are politically determined and bear no necessary relationship to the amount paid in taxes. With private saving this is not the case, for there are well-defined claim tickets

---

[1] I am ignoring retirement saving which occurs through private or public group pension plans.

[2] Financed in this context means goods released by the positive saving elsewhere in the economy.

associated with the savings, which must be reconverted to money when the savings are to be consumed. There is, accordingly, a direct link between the amount saved and the amount that can subsequently be consumed. If social retirement payments are financed on a strictly pay-as-you-go basis, the retirement consumption obviously represents transfers from those currently employed to the retired. Political considerations aside, whether or not retirement income can increase without putting a greater burden on the presently employed than what the recipients bore when they were employed, depends upon whether the per capita pool of fluid capital has increased -- i.e., whether there has been economic growth.

If, as at present in the U.S., the Social Security Fund runs a surplus, then whether the surplus can finance an increased level of retirement consumption relative to the present will depend upon what happens to the surplus. If the surplus (whether directly or indirectly) is productively invested in newly produced means of production, then increased retirement consumption is obviously possible without burdening future working generations. However, if the surplus is used to finance current government operations or for transfer payments to those with marginal propensities to consume that are greater than of those who pay the Social Security taxes, this will not be the case. Future generations will, in fact, be burdened.[3]

QUESTIONS RELATED TO POSITION GOODS

In his book, *Social Limits to Growth* (1976), Fred Hirsch introduces the notion of a position good as follows:

Certain goods and facilities from which individuals derive satisfaction are subject to absolute limitations in supply, deriving from one of a number of sources. The first though not the most significant such source of scarcity is physical availability.

Absolute physical scarcities have more usually been considered from the side of production. Thus, the limited availability of land was the centerpiece of

---

[3] In a *Newsweek* article in 1967, Paul Samuelson wrote: "The beauty about social insurance is that is *actuarially* unsound. Everyone who reaches retirement age is given benefit privileges that far exceed anything he has paid in." This beneficence is possible, Samuelson goes on to say, because "the national product is growing at compound interest and can be expected to do so for as far ahead as the eye cannot see. . . . A growing nation is the greatest Ponzi game ever contrived." [Italics in original. Quoted also in *The New York Times Magazine*, August 27, 1995, p. 56.] Samuelson's contention that the national product will continue to grow exponentially obviously requires that savings be productively invested.

classical economics as developed by David Ricardo and, from a different standpoint, by Thomas Malthus some 150 years ago. Equally, concern about the implications of limited resources of agricultural land and of natural raw materials is at the center of the contemporary environmental-ecology movement, with its stress on physical limits to growth. To economists, the implications of these physical limits are not as clear-cut as they appear to natural scientists and laymen, because of the potential -- and at any given time unknowable -- scope for substitution. . . .

Though economists do not find it possible to make positive predictions on the implications of limited natural resources for the long run future and the possibilities of human survival, there is a less apocalyptic connection between absolute scarcities and economic growth. Insofar as the scarcities are themselves objects of consumption rather than factors of production, scope for substitution on the side of production disappears. In this sense, absolute limitations on final consumption possibilities are in economic terms "more" absolute than similar limitations on factors of production. An acre of land used for the satiation of hunger can, in principle, be expanded two-, ten-, or a thousand-fold by technological advances. These advances may occur in one or all of the processes that come between the productive agricultural use of that acre and the end product in the form of nutrient. From the same productive acre, more and more food can be and has been produced. By contrast, an acre of land used as a pleasure garden for the enjoyment of a single family can never rise above its initial productivity in that use. The family may be induced or forced to take its pleasures in another way -- substitution in consumption -- but to get an acre of private seclusion, an acre will always be needed. The significance of this distinction is that it marks the existence of absolute scarcity in one economic dimension, namely consumption. It is with this type of insufficiency, stemming primarily from social rather than physical limitations, that this book is essentially concerned. [Hirsch (1976, pp. 19-20).]

In his categorization of consumption position goods, Hirsch distinguishes between consumption goods which are physically in fixed supply and consumption goods for which the scarcity is socially induced. Examples of the former would be a Rembrandt painting or exclusive access to a natural landscape which is physically unique. In these cases, consumers derive at least part of their satisfaction from just the inherent characteristics of the goods -- i.e., from the painting simply as a painting or acres simply as acres, rather than as objects that are scarce. However, with the second category of consumption position goods:

... consumer demand is concentrated on particular goods and facilities that are limited in absolute supply not by physical but by social factors, including the satisfaction engendered by scarcity as such. Such social limits exist in the sense that an increase in physical availability of these goods or facilities, either in absolute terms or in relation to dimensions such as population or physical space, changes their characteristics in such a way that a given amount of use yields less satisfaction. This is equivalent to a limitation on absolute supply of a product or facility of given "quality", and it is in this sense that it is regarded here as a social limitation.

This social limitation may be derived, most directly and most familiarly, from psychological motives of various kinds, notably envy, emulation, or pride. Satisfaction is derived from relative position alone, of being in front, or from others being behind. Command over particular goods and facilities in particular times and conditions becomes an indicator of such precedence in its emergence as a status symbol. Where the sole or main source of satisfaction derives from the symbol rather than the substance, this can be regarded as pure social scarcity.

Such satisfaction may also be associated with absolute physical scarcities. Thus to at least some people, part of the attraction of a Rembrandt, or of a particular natural landscape, is derived from its being the only one of its kind; as a result, physically scarce items such as these become the repository of pure social scarcity also.... [Hirsch (1976, pp. 20-21).]

The preceding paragraphs should suffice in establishing the basic ideas underlying position consumption goods, so that we can now turn to the factors governing their valuation. Since Old Masters are clear instances of position goods, and as the factors that determine the values of Old Masters have already been analyzed in detail in Chapter 7, the task here is relatively easy. We need only summarize the basic principles involved and then extend these to the valuation of position goods in general.

As we saw in Chapter 7, a positive value for an Old Master derives from the pool of savings which forms the claims side of the pool of fluid capital. In principle, there is no difference in this regard between an Old Master and any other asset, the only essential difference being that Old Masters do not in general yield a prospective stream of quasi-rents. The willingness-to-pay for an Old Master (as an investment), accordingly, will be determined by the amount (appropriately discounted) that a prospective purchaser expects that someone else will be willing to pay at some time in the future, or (if investment *per se* is not the motivation) by the maximum amount that a prospective purchaser is willing to pay simply for sake of ownership.

Extension of these considerations to position consumption goods is in general straightforward. As with any asset, two necessary conditions must be in place for a position good to come into existence with a non-zero value. The first condition is that the good must satisfy some want, either as an end in itself or as a potential investment, while the second condition is that there must exist a non-empty pool of fluid capital. The former provides the motivation for owning, while the second provides the wherewithal for actually doing so.[4]

As the concern in this section is not with the how and why position goods exist, but only in their existence as such, we can, without loss of anything essential, extend our concept of Old Masters to cover position goods in general. With this extension, it is clear from the discussion in Chapter 7 that the aggregate valuation of position goods is subject to the usual constraints imposed by the pool of fluid capital. At any point in time, position goods compete with all other assets for the pool of unexercised claim tickets defining the claims side of the pool of fluid capital. The sum total of all asset values (which will include the aggregate value of all position goods) will accordingly be bounded by the aggregate value of the pool of fluid capital.[5]

QUESTIONS RELATED TO ENGEL CURVES AND INCOME ELASTICITIES

As was noted in the introduction to this chapter, the economic drivers in an economy have been seen in this book in terms of the owners/operators of existing productive capacity deciding how much of that capacity to utilize in current production, entrepreneurs deciding how much to invest in new capacity, and households deciding how much of their incomes to consume. Of the three, the last (as recognized by Keynes in the *General Theory*) is the ultimate mover of economic activity. If operators of existing productive capacity do not believe that current production can be sold remuneratively, and if those looking to invest in new capacity do not believe that future production can be sold remuneratively, then current capacity will not be utilized and future capacity will not be added to. In both cases, propensities to consume are of paramount importance. For reasons emphasized by Keynes, the propensity to consume out of current income

---

[4] A problem at the micro level in analyzing position goods is an interdependency of tastes and preferences. Collectibles, which are obvious instances of position goods, provide an excellent general example. For many collectibles, a (potential) collectible will have value for a particular 'collector' only if it is thought that there is at least one other 'collector' who wants the good as well. In short, unavailability for others who want is what drives the desire to have!

[5] A van Gogh can bring $82 million in today's world, not because it is intrinsically worth (whatever that might mean) this amount, but because the world pool of fluid capital is sufficiently large to support such a value. Let there be a worldwide famine (or earthquakes which completely level Japan, the U.S., and Western Europe), and the price of the van Gogh would plummet. On the other hand, let there be strong economic growth in the world for the next 20 years, and a painting (though not necessarily the van Gogh) 20 years from now could easily bring upwards of a billion of today's dollars!

is a prime determinant of the current level of economic activity, while the expected propensity to consume out of future income is a critical determinant of investment in new capacity.

A point that is generally not well understood is that economic growth *requires* the existence of goods with income elasticities of demand in excess of one. If this were not the case -- i.e., if all income elasticities were less than one -- the aggregate average propensity to consume would be falling, and growth would stagnate as there would be nothing to stir the 'animal spirits' which drive investment. A constant emergence of 'luxury' goods accordingly provides the *sine qua non* for sustained economic growth, as ever increasing investment is needed in order to provision their production. An obvious question is whether such a continuing appearance of 'luxury' goods can, in fact, be expected to occur. In my opinion, the answer is clearly in the affirmative, and the argument, briefly, is as follows.[6] In contrast to traditional demand theory, my view is that an individual's main preoccupation is how to spend time rather than income. Unlike income, for which most people have to work, time appears each day as a gift. The amount is fixed and its receipt cannot be escaped. The physiology and psychology of the human organism is such that unless a certain number of neurons are firing at any time, the individual is uncomfortable. In psychological terms, arousal is at too low a level. In general, stimulation in some form is required in order to maintain arousal, and much of this occurs through the consumption of market goods and services. Since goods and services are scarce, some of an individual's time must be spent in acquiring the income needed for their purchase. When not asleep or at work, however, the basic question facing the individual is how to allocate time amongst consumption activities in order to maintain an acceptable level of arousal.

In general, an acceptable level of arousal will involve combining novelty with redundancy, where redundancy in this context refers to the amount of familiarity in a consumption activity and can be identified with what Stigler and Becker (1977) define as consumption capital. Too much redundancy leads to boredom because everything has an aura of *deja vu* (or 'familiarity breeds contempt'), while too much novelty leads to confusion and immobility because one does not know what to expect. Some surprise is highly desirable, but too much causes discomfort because of limited capacity to process new information. Redundancy is created through exposure, and arises through the internal dynamics of a consumption activity.

---

[6] See Taylor (1987, 1988, and 1992). Cf., also Scitovsky (1976).

The quest for novelty, in contrast, is seen as inhering in the psyche. It functions independently of exposure (although exposure to a new activity can remind one how pleasant novelty can be), and provides the motivation for seeking new activities. It is the *raison d'etre* for wants being endless, and continually incites the appearance of new goods. Unboundedness of wants in conjunction with an unceasing desire for new activities and goods, in turn, is what underlies a continuing emergence of goods with income elasticities in excess of one. And it is the recognition of this on the part of entrepreneurs that draws new investment into the production of these goods.[7]

THE HIERARCHICAL NATURE OF THE POOL OF FLUID CAPITAL

In Chapter 2, it was noted that the first fluid capital to come into existence as an economy emerges from an economic state will consist of basic necessities like food and shelter. As a primitive economy progresses, however, inventories of storable consumables come to be included in the pool of fluid capital as well. For the island economy described in the Prologue, the fluid capital in existence at the end of the tales consisted of bread, any paintings that Georgia may have had in inventory, and gold. From this, it is clear that the goods represented in fluid capital reflect a hierarchy of consumption wants, with goods that are basic to physical survival at one end of the hierarchy and goods that (for some) may be important to psychological survival at the other end. Bread is needed for physical survival, but paintings and gold are not. The upshot is that the goods in the pool of fluid capital will be much more heavily weighted toward goods needed for basic survival in a poor economy than in a wealthy economy.

This consumption hierarchy is a straightforward reflection of the factors just described, namely, unbounded wants in conjunction with an unceasing appearance of new goods. An obvious implication of the consumption dynamics generated by these factors is that, as an economy progresses, goods satisfying higher-order wants become increasingly important in the pool of fluid capital. Stores of food grains (or equivalently access to the same through imports) will

---

[7] An important implication of this section is that necessities (income elasticities less than one) in a high-income economy can be luxuries (income elasticities greater than one) in a low-income economy. A television set is a necessity for a household in the U.S., but not in Indonesia. Consequently, what are mature markets in rich countries can be important growth markets in poor countries. Recognition of this disparateness in income elasticities has been a major factor in many of the "Asian miracles" in the 1980s and 1990s. For an entertaining account of such income elasticity 'arbitrage', see Thurow (1999, Chapter 3).

figure much more prominently in the pool of fluid capital in a poor economy than in a wealthy one.

The consumption hierarchy is also manifested in the valuations of assets, especially for those assets which are in the form of position goods. Old Masters provide a good example. As has been noted at several points in these pages, high valuations for Old Masters are in general possible only in economies that have substantial pools of fluid capital, and are underwritten by a similar (if indeed not the same) hierarchy of wants which fuels the continual demand for new goods. Real properties in places with great natural amenities are yet another example. Properties in areas such as Aspen and Jackson Hole could have been acquired for the payment of delinquent taxes during the 1930s, but became expensive position goods after World War II as economic growth increased incomes to the point where wants associated with the ownership of grand second homes could be satisfied.

CHAPTER 13

QUESTIONS RELATED TO ECONOMIC GROWTH

In this chapter, we shall turn our attention to economic growth.[1] There are obviously a variety of ways that economic growth can be defined, but the definition that shall be used in this chapter is an increase in income per capita.

THE GENERAL MECHANICS OF ECONOMIC GROWTH

Assuming that an increase in income does not occur simply by people working longer hours or (if paid by piece-rate) by working harder, the *only* way (in a closed system) that economic development can occur is through investment in additional produced means of production. An increase in the produced means of production increases an economy's capacity to produce and, therefore, the *potential* for generating increased income, not only in total but per capita as well. However, investment in produced means of production only leads to the *possibility* for economic growth. Whether or not this possibility will be realized will depend upon whether the additional capacity to produce is actually utilized, for income is generated only when there is production. On the other hand, for production to take place, owners of productive capacity have to be convinced that the output can be sold, or at least have expectations that it can be sold.[2] If the output is sold at a compensatory price, then economic growth can be said to have occurred. Continued growth, though, obviously requires that what has just

---

[1] Throughout this chapter, economic growth and economic development will be used interchangeably.

[2] The expectations at issue here are not the same ones that drove the decision to invest in new capacity in the first place. The latter expectations were in place yesterday, and there is no guarantee that they have survived intact till today.

been described takes place continually.[3]

Economic growth clearly leads to increases in the pool of fluid capital. Indeed, one can equivalently describe economic growth in terms of an increase in the pool of per capita fluid capital.[4] This is similar to, but not the same thing as, an increase in the capital/labor ratio in conventional growth theory. The phenomena are similar in that both require investment in produced means of production, but are different in that capital in conventional growth theory refers to physical capital as an input into an aggregate production function, whereas capital here refers to fluid capital. The stock of produced means of production is clearly enlarged by investment -- indeed, this as noted is a necessary condition for growth to occur -- but growth in the present context is not seen just in terms of an increase in the amount of physical capital per unit of labor.

Because of diminishing returns, economic growth in conventional growth theory as a result of capital-deepening is taken as being limited, so that the bulk of economic growth is viewed as arising from upward shifts in the aggregate production function -- that is to say from technological change. In the present context, technological change is, indeed, a prime force in growth, for technological change makes newly produced means of production more productive than existing produced means of production and can also (through upgrading and retrofitting) make existing productive capacity more efficient as well. In fact, technological change can lead to economic growth even in the case where all investment is strictly for replacement of existing productive capacity. To see this is straightforward. Assume a constant price level, so that in the absence of technological change a current dollar will buy the same amount of produced means of production as an 'old' dollar at the time it was invested. Assume that the 'old' dollar is returned to the pool of fluid capital through a myros recovery charge, and is now available to fund new investment. Assume that the old produced means of production in question are now replaced dollar-for-dollar by new investment. However, with technological change, the newly produced means of production are more efficient than those replaced. Hence, the current capacity to produce will be increased even though, in terms of dollars, the amount of fluid capital sunk in investment is unchanged.

---

[3] Cf. the discussion in Chapter 12 concerning the importance of a continuing appearance of goods with income elasticities of demand that are greater than one.

[4] Alternatively (and almost equivalently) economic growth can be defined in terms of the increase in real output per unit of labor input -- i.e., increases in labor productivity. Accordingly, to explain income and output differences across countries in terms of productivity differences essentially entails a tautology and is, therefore, not very informative. Hall and Jones (1999) offer a recent example.

One of the beautiful things about investment that increases the capacity to produce, is that utilization of the new capacity generates an additional amount of income just equal, in current prices, to the value of the increased output. Obviously, if the increased output is shoes (say), the shoes are all not going to be sold to those who received the additional income from their production. But this is not the issue. The important consideration is that production from enlarged capacities to produce necessarily, and always, generates just the right amount of income *in principle* to take that production, measured in current prices, from the market. Whether this income is actually spent is, of course, another matter.

To summarize the foregoing:

1. Economic growth requires investment in produced means of production.

2. Investment requires fluid capital for finance, which in turn requires saving, either out of current income or out of income at some point in the past.

3. Increased produced means of production provides the *potential* for economic growth. For the growth to be realized, the increased capacity to produce must be utilized and the increased output resulting therefrom must be purchased at compensatory prices.

4. Continued growth requires that this process be continually repeated.

SOME BASIC TRUTHS CONCERNING ECONOMIC DEVELOPMENT

A few fundamental 'truths' would seem to be apparent at this point concerning economic development. The first truth is that investment cannot take place in the absence of a pool of fluid capital. Saving must occur before there can be an escape from an economic state of nature. However, once a pool of fluid capital exists, investment -- and therefore economic development -- can occur in the absence of current saving. A second truth is that economic development can occur only through investment in produced means of production that is funded out of the pool of fluid capital. Related to this fact -- but also a third truth -- is that, not only investment, but current production as well, must be funded out of the pool of fluid capital.

A fourth fundamental truth is that the first three truths are independent of the institutional structure that an economy might have. For an economy to grow, a pool of fluid capital must be formed and there must be investment from this pool in produced means of production. This must be the case no matter how the economy is organized -- whether market or command -- or what form property rights take -- capitalist, socialist, etc. Different names might be used, but the fundamentals of growth are the same no matter what 'ism' constitutes the organizing structure. Obviously, however, it does not follow from this that economic development in terms of speed and type (or composition) is independent of how economic activity is organized or how property rights are structured.

KEYNES AND ECONOMIC BLISS

Of all Keynes's assumptions about real-world behavior in the *General Theory*, the one I find most indefensible is his belief that two or three generations of stable economic growth would drive the marginal efficiency of capital to zero, at which point capital would cease to be scarce. For this to occur, it has to be assumed that individual wants are bounded, but this assumption is clearly unwarranted in my opinion.[5] Although it may be true for some individuals, it is not universal, and it certainly does not apply across generations.[6] What might be a luxurious level of living for one generation may be scarcely tolerable for a subsequent one.[7] As a consequence, I think Keynes was far too pessimistic in the *General Theory* concerning long-run accumulation. Given proper incentives to save and invest, I see no reason why accumulation should weaken for generations to come. In my opinion, this part of Keynes's analysis reflected, perhaps more than anything else in the *General Theory*, his Cambridge and Bloomsbury attitudes of 'what ought to be'.

Clearly related to this point is Keynes's view on the need to socialize

---

[5] Cf. the discussion in Chapter 12. For discussions of the unboundedness of wants, see (among others) Georgescu-Roegen (1954) and Ironmonger (1967). See also Hawtrey (1925).

[6] Moreover, even the assumption of a decreasing marginal utility of income for individuals is questionable in my view, at least for large changes in income.

[7] A minimum standard of living has, on occasion, been cast in terms of what an individual needs in order to appear in public without shame. When I was in early elementary school in rural Iowa, it was not unusual for me or my classmates to wear to school clothes that had been mended or patched. However, by late grade school incomes had advanced to the point where this was considered socially unacceptable.

investment. Certainly, it is true that there are great needs for certain forms of public investment, but this is an entirely different matter than concluding that all investment should be governmentally directed. In my view, the role of government in relation to private investment should be to foster incentives and provide appropriate rules of the game. Private investment will then be in a position to respond to the unboundedness of wants. And I see no reason why, if appropriate incentives are in place, expectations -- and therefore investment -- will not respond.

THE ENDOGENOUS NATURE OF ECONOMIC GROWTH

The present time is one of considerable reassessment in the study of economic growth. The conventional neoclassical models of the Solow-Swan type in which the prime driver of growth -- technological change -- is exogenous are giving way to models in which the main driving forces are taken to be endogenous.[8] Although I think that the research coming out of this reassessment is extremely useful and beneficial, the models that are emerging are still burdened, in my opinion, with aggregate production functions, a substance theory of capital, and a continuing predilection that an economy can be modeled as though it were a nineteenth-century energy system.

The basic drivers of economic growth, in my view, are two: (1) the unboundedness of human wants in conjunction with a quest for novelty in consumption and (2) those with access to fluid capital who see the opportunity to profit from satisfying these expanded wants. Keynes, as just discussed, overlooked the first driver and as a consequence had to put a heavy burden on the operation of 'animal spirits' in motivating investment. In normal circumstances, the two drivers of economic growth operate in tandem: Entrepreneurs see profit opportunities in expanding capacity, and the increased income generated by operation of the new capacity provides the wherewithal for the new wants to be satisfied. This is not to imply, as Keynes put it, that there are no ". . . slips betwixt the cup and the lip," as crystal balls are never perfect and some expectations will obviously not pan out. But failures of expectations aside, the important thing is that there is a near-mechanical relationship between wants spurring new investment and the income that ultimately satisfies those wants.[9]

---

[8] See Lucas (1985), Romer (1986), and Arthur (1989).

[9] It might be thought that this is simply a restatement of Say's Law, but I do not see the point in these terms, as it is the expectation of demand that drives supply, rather than supply which creates demand. The only sense in which demand can be said to be created is in terms of the income that new production generates, which in current prices is just equal to the value of the new production.

The interaction of these tandem drivers clearly imparts an endogeneity to economic growth: Quests for novelty fuel the expectations that drive investment, investment expands the capacity to produce, operation of the expanded capacity to produce generates additional income, which in turn allows the original 'quests' to be satisfied. The stage is then set for a new set of quests for novelty to come into play, and the process begins anew. The resulting path of economic growth may be higgledy-piggledy, but it is nevertheless largely endogenous.

THE ROLE OF TECHNOLOGICAL CHANGE

Earlier in this chapter, it was noted how technological change embodied in newly produced means of production can lead to economic growth through a simple recycling of the pool of fluid capital. Technological change can thus enable economic growth to occur even in the presence of zero net saving. The real essence of technological change, therefore, is that it increases the productivity of the pool of fluid capital. In traditional growth theory, the productivity-enhancing effects of technological change are usually cast in terms of whether or not technological change is embodied or disembodied. Embodied technological change is described in terms of shifts in the entire production function, while disembodied technological change is seen in terms of factor augmentation. In my view, all technological change is embodied in new investment, and whether the embodiment takes place in physical or human capital is of no great consequence to the theory, for in most cases the investment will involve elements of both.

Neoclassical growth theorists, as well as Schumpeter before them, are clearly correct in focusing on technological change as a prime factor in economic growth. In my view, however, it is better to see technological change as an *enabler* of growth, rather than a *driver*, in the sense that unbounded wants and 'animal spirits' are drivers. By making fluid capital more productive, technological change allows (*a la* Schumpeter) for existing goods to be produced more cheaply and for new goods (in response to incessant quests for novelty) to be produced in the first place.

INVESTMENT IN RESEARCH AND DEVELOPMENT

In a paper given at an OCED Conference on Information Technology in Toronto in late June, 1995, Charles Hulten made the point that investment in

---

Whether or not the new income is spent is another matter. Expectations can fail, and at times massively so. This, of course, was one of the great insights of Keynes in the *General Theory*.

R&D has to be paid for in the sense that consumption or other investment is reduced. This fact puts R&D investment on the same footing as any other form of investment in terms of the conditions that have to be met in order for the investment to take place. As investment in R&D requires consumption of fluid capital, the question emerges of how the fluid capital that is sunk in R&D is eventually to be repatriated. Clearly, this has to occur through charges against current earnings, but it is not always clear which earnings are to be charged. For R&D that results in patents, the quasi-rents associated with the patents can be charged, but for R&D that does not give rise to patents, the investment expenditures involved can be repatriated only via overhead charges.

In general, the new endogenous-growth literature makes economic growth endogenous by endogenizing investment in education and investment in R&D. Since investment in education and R&D leads to technological change, the 'manna-from-heaven' aspect of technological change in the Solow-Swan growth models is thereby eliminated. Growth is made endogenous by the fact that investments in education and R&D have to compete with all other forms of investment. The equilibrium rate of growth will therefore be determined by the condition that rates of return are equalized. However, the problem with this approach to endogenous economic growth is that the analysis continues to be conducted within the framework of an aggregate neoclassical production function. Capital, whether human or nonhuman, remains something that can be objectively measured, and the standard type of time invariances are assumed to exist.[10]

ECONOMIC GROWTH IN REVERSE: LARGE-SCALE DISASTERS IN LOW-INCOME ECONOMIES[11]

In this section, I want to turn to an analysis, using the constraints imposed by the pool of fluid capital, in which a low-income economy is devastated by a large-scale natural disaster. While a crop failure will provide the frame of reference, the principles involved are general, and can be applied equally to phenomena such as earthquakes, floods, or war. As always, when contemplating the impact of a macro event on an economy, the appropriate analytical procedure is to trace out the effects of the event on the pool of fluid capital. For concreteness in the discussion to follow, let us suppose that the economy in question is low-income but above subsistence, primarily agricultural, that the economy is

---

[10] See Appendix 1.

[11] The analysis in this section is due to numerous discussions with Barbara N. Sands.

monetized, and that all money is bank money created initially for the purpose of financing production. Assume that there are two agricultural regions in the country with trade between them, that some farmers own their land while others rent, that existing stores of grain are owned by both farmers and merchant middlemen, that besides land and grain the only other assets owned by farmers are draft animals and Old Masters.[12] Finally, assume that there is a complete crop failure in one of the regions, but a normal harvest in the other.

Under the conditions postulated, the following effects will take place:

1.   There will be a reduction of goods in the pool of fluid capital by the amount of the failed crop.

2.   Initially, aggregate demand will exceed aggregate supply by the amount of the failed crop measured in current prices.

3.   Initially, there will be a 'monetary overhang' by the same amount.

4.   The price of grain will go up by an amount sufficient to eliminate the monetary overhang.

5.   There will be a transfer of wealth from the farmers in the region experiencing the crop failure to the farmers in the other region and to those owning existing stores of grain.

6.   The price of draft animals and Old Masters will fall.

First -- and foremost -- the pool of fluid capital will be reduced by the amount of the crop failure, and it is from this that everything else follows. The destruction of goods by the crop failure implies a like reduction in aggregate supply, but there is no offsetting reduction in aggregate demand. This is because the purchasing power created in anticipation of normal harvests continues to exist. While bank money is always dated in the sense that the loans that created it are expected to be repaid out of revenues generated by the production they financed, this cannot happen in the case of a crop failure, because with no grain there are no revenues. As a consequence, the loans are not repaid and the money they created continues to exist as a monetary overhang. Aggregate demand is, therefore, not destructed in line with the reduction in aggregate supply, so there

---

[12] Obviously, most farmers in a low-income economy do not possess Old Masters. Old Master in this context is intended to refer to any non-income generating asset that can be exchanged for money.

will be excess aggregate demand equal to the value of the failed crop measured in current (i.e., pre-crop failure) prices.

With diminished stocks of grain because of the crop failure, but an undiminished pool of purchasing power, the grain that escaped destruction must go up in price. What really takes place, however, is that the rising price of grain reduces the real value of the pool of purchasing power to a level commensurate with the (now) reduced stock of goods in the pool of fluid capital. The increase in the price of grain is initiated by those experiencing the crop failure, who must purchase grain in order to subsist. To finance their purchases, the farmers in question have to acquire money, either by tapping into their money reserves (should they have some) or by selling draft animals or Old Masters. The prices of these assets must accordingly fall. However, in keeping with the 'consumption hierarchy' that implicitly underlies asset valuations,[13] the price of Old Masters will almost certainly fall more than the price of draft animals.

The grain price increase and the asset price decreases triggered by the crop failure are manifestations of the dual conservation laws imposed by the pool of fluid capital. The former reflects the bound that the pool imposes on the real stock of money, while the latter reflect the bound that the pool imposes on the sum total of asset values. Since fluid capital is destroyed by the crop failure, the monetary overhang that is temporarily created has to be destructed through inflation in the price of grain, while the sum total of asset values has to adjust downward through decreases in asset prices.

From the foregoing, it should be clear that, after the crop failure occurs, there is some transfer of wealth from those who do not have grain to those who do. However, one thing that has to be remembered in all this is that, when something like a crop failure occurs that reduces the pool of fluid capital, the rich get richer and the poor get poorer only in a relative sense, not in an absolute sense. Certainly the poor get poorer in an absolute sense and some individuals may be made absolutely better off as well, but since the economy as a whole is impoverished, both the rich and the poor, as groups, are made worse off. Finally, although the analysis in this section has been about a crop failure, the principles involved are perfectly general, and can be applied to any event that causes a destruction of fluid capital -- earthquakes, floods, wars, etc.

---

[13] See Chapter 12.

ECONOMIC GROWTH AND DIFFERENT STAGES OF DEVELOPMENT

One of the major conclusions that emerges from the analysis of this book is that the conservation laws imposed by the pool of fluid capital are independent of the stage of an economy's development. Economic growth requires an increase in the pool of fluid capital, and for this to occur there must be saving and investment. There is, therefore, no 'secret' or 'holy grail' of economic development, no secret formula of growth that is applicable to a poor economy but not to a rich economy. The only secret is an open one: For growth to occur, there must be in place policies that foster the formation of fluid capital and its subsequent investment in produced means of production.[14]

Of course, this is not to say that either the relevant policies or the forms that investment should take are invariant to the stage of development. A low-income country with a poorly educated population and a limited and primitive communications system (say) obviously requires different forms of investment than a rich country with a highly educated labor force and a ubiquitous communications system that is at the cutting edge of technology. However, the basic principle is the same: Economic growth requires saving and investment.[15]

---

[14] I have always been perplexed by the implication of neoclassical growth models of the Solow-Swan type that the equilibrium rate of growth is independent of the rate of saving. As a statement about the real world, this has to be nonsense. In the framework of this book, the growth rate depends on both saving and investment. If both are high, then growth will be high. To me, at least, this is merely common sense.

[15] The search for a "chemistry of growth" nevertheless remains an *ignis fatuus*, a deceptive hope. In a review of the recent book by Ashish Arora, Ralph Landau, and Nathan Rosenberg (*Chemicals and Long-term Economic Growth*, Wiley Interscience, 1999), in *The Economist* (March 6-12, 1999), the author of the review states: "Despite the effort expended over many years on understanding it, economic growth remains a mystery. And the harder you look, the more complicated it becomes." How to put policies in place that foster saving and investment may be difficult, but the mechanics of growth are not themselves a mystery.

CHAPTER 14

THEMES AND COUNTERTHEMES: FLUID CAPITAL IN RETROSPECT

In general, this book has involved exploration of themes related to fluid capital. More explicitly, it has examined the implications of three definitions, one relating to a concept of capital and the other two relating to two macroeconomic identities. The definition of fluid capital provides a root concept of capital from which virtually all existing notions of capital can be connected and rationalized. The two identities, in contrast, involve equalities between the value of production in current prices and the income the production generates, and between the value of goods in the pool of fluid capital and the corresponding value of claims on the same.

From the two identities, it is possible to deduce a number of constraints that the pool of fluid capital imposes on the macro economy. Included among these constraints are:

1. The pool of fluid capital evaluated in current prices provides an upper bound on the real value of the stock of money;

2. The pool of fluid capital evaluated in current prices also provides an upper bound on the aggregate value of an economy's assets.

From these constraints, one can further deduce that, while real-balance effects can exist for individuals, this cannot be the case for the aggregate. Accordingly, the neoclassical conclusion that an economy (with fiat money in its coffers) will necessarily tend towards equilibrium at full employment because of the operation of a real-balance effect cannot be supported.

As a consequence of the constraints that the pool of fluid capital imposes on an economy, fluid capital is seen as being conservative at a point in time, but not between points over time. This is because an economy is not a closed system, but alters over time because of saving and investment that cause changes in the volume of fluid capital, uncertainty that causes failures in expectations, and changes in tastes and preferences that (among other things) cause changes in asset valuations. The upshot, accordingly, is that an economy cannot be analyzed as though it were a nineteenth-century energy system. The fact that this cannot be the case has been one of the primary themes of the book.

A second primary theme has been that money is a social invention that comes into existence as a means of circumventing the inefficiencies of barter. Not only does money make exchange more efficient, it also provides a device for making fluid capital truly fluid, in the sense that the goods in the pool can 'flow' efficiently into current production or into newly constructed produced means of production. As money represents the liquification of the goods in fluid capital, money is seen as a pool of purchasing power that is constantly being created, extinguished, and created anew. Its creation, moreover, is viewed as being endogenous. Two rates of interest are relevant. The natural (or real) rate of interest represents the price that equates the demand for fluid capital with its supply, and the money rate of interest that represents the price at which the pool of fluid capital is monetized.

Equilibrium in the framework of this book can be characterized in three equivalent forms: (1) in terms of the equality of aggregate demand and aggregate supply, (2) as the equality of inflows and outflows from the pool of fluid capital, or (3) in terms of a stable general price level. However, unlike in conventional macroeconomic theorizing, the determination of equilibria has not been center stage in this book. In general, equilibria have been seen in terms of 'magnets' (or 'attractors') towards which economic activity is drawn. Properties of equilibria, however, have generally been ignored. As with Keynes in the *General Theory* (but unlike in standard neoclassical macroeconomics), the framework of this book allows for equilibria at less than full employment. And since saving and investment are just two of the flows into and out of the pool of fluid capital, it is also possible for equilibria to occur in which saving and investment are unequal.

Aggregate demand and aggregate supply in this book are not seen as schedules in which physical measures of aggregate output are related to a measure of the general price level. Aggregate demand is depicted, instead, in terms of the pool of purchasing power created in anticipation of current production, while aggregate supply is described in terms of the stock of currently available goods evaluated at current prices. The general price level is then seen as being determined through the interaction, per these definitions, of aggregate demand and aggregate supply. If the pool of purchasing power that has been created is greater than the stock of goods currently available at current prices, some prices will increase. On the other hand, if the pool of purchasing power is less than the stock of currently available goods evaluated in current prices, some prices will decrease. The general price level as seen in this book is, accordingly, nothing more than the equilibrium value (i.e., the monetary value) of currently available output.

As was noted in Chapter 3, aggregate demand and aggregate supply can differ because the expectations that drive aggregate demand may be different from those determining aggregate supply. The expectations driving the current availability of goods are always those that are in place roughly one-half of an average production period in advance of the expectations that create the current pool of purchasing power. Because the two sets of expectations will almost never coincide, the result will be a general price level that is constantly in a state of flux.[1]

One of the mainstays of traditional monetary theory is a separation (or 'dichotomy') between the real and monetary sectors. Relative prices are seen as being determined in the real sector, while the general price level is seen as being determined in the monetary sector. A constantly recurring theme in this book has been that money is not exogenous to the level of economic activity, but rather is handmaiden to it. Money created (or alternatively borrowed from existing stocks of money held as an asset) in anticipation of current production forms the pool of purchasing power that fuels aggregate demand, and the general price level emerges from the interplay of this pool of purchasing power with the stock of goods that are currently available. Clearly, if a pool of purchasing is created that differs from the available stock of goods measured in current prices, the price level will change. In view of this, it obviously follows that the general price level is determined by the pool of purchasing power which forms aggregate demand. If too much purchasing power is created, the general price level will rise, and vice versa if too little is created. On the other hand, it does not follow that the neoclassical 'dichotomy' will hold, for there is no reason to assume that excess

---

[1] As should be evident from these paragraphs, it is inappropriate in my view to measure changes in the general price level in terms of standard Laspeyres price indices. Only current-quantity weighted chain indices provide meaningful measures of inflation and deflation.

(or deficient) purchasing power will be distributed proportionately across goods. Consequently, one cannot conclude that relative prices will be formed independently of the amount of money that has been newly created.[2]

A third theme of the book is that the consumption structure in an economy is inherently hierarchical. By this, I mean that as an economy becomes wealthier, goods that have previously been luxuries become necessities, and new goods (or new combinations of existing goods) emerge as luxuries. Among other things, this has important implications for the pool of fluid capital: Fluid capital is such only in relation to the level of income. Food, shelter, and basic clothing will represent a relatively small proportion of fluid capital in a high-income economy, but a high proportion in a low-income one. In view of this, one cannot characterize *a priori* the goods that constitute fluid capital. The goods that define fluid capital are simply whatever producers and consumers in an economy demand at current prices.

Closely related to the third theme is the idea that economic growth, at base, is driven by the demand for goods with income elasticities greater than one. In my view, the constant emergence of such goods is assured by the unboundedness of wants. Once a want is satisfied, another unfulfilled want emerges on the margin, and it is the recognition and anticipation of this that fuels the 'animal spirits' underlying investment in newly constructed produced means of production. As development proceeds, moreover, 'position' goods come to assume an ever greater importance, especially in the composition and structure of an economy's assets. Every economy beyond a subsistence level can have 'Old Masters' in some form or another, but only extraordinarily wealthy ones can support $80m van Goghs and Renoirs.

A fifth theme of the book is the importance, in relation to the pool of fluid capital, of fiducial (or accounting) depreciation, as opposed to economic depreciation. In the framework of this book, fiducial depreciation (rather than economic depreciation) is seen as the vehicle whereby capital invested (i.e., sunk) in produced means of production is ultimately returned to the pool from which it came. Economic depreciation is relevant to a number of important decisions, but these are all essentially of the form: How much to produce today as opposed to how much to produce tomorrow, how much to pay for additional capacity, and

---

[2] This will be true, moreover, even in situations in which the stock of money is changed exogenously, as was the case (for example) when East and West Germany merged in 1990. Because of the pegging of the two marks at close to par, there was, in effect, a once-and-for-all increase in the stock of marks, with no offsetting increase in the pool of fluid capital. Again, there is no reason to assume that the part of the increased stock of marks that sought outlet against goods would be spread proportionately.

when is some (or all) of existing capacity to be scrapped? Moreover, none of these decisions actively entails the creation of fluid capital, for there is no necessary connection between the timing of economic depreciation and the timing of 'capital recovery' charges (i.e., fiducial depreciation) against quasi-rents. In short, fiducial depreciation generates fluid capital, but economic depreciation does not.

A sixth theme of the book is that demands on the pool of fluid capital are multifaceted and include the financing of current production as well as investment in newly produced means of production.[3] Indeed, in ordinary circumstances, the amount of fluid capital demanded by the funding of current production will be much greater than the amount demanded by investment. One of the implications of this is that the relationship between investment and the rate of interest need not be negative -- i.e., investment functions do not necessarily slope downward. This conclusion follows from the necessity for interest to be paid on both uses for fluid capital (i.e., both investment and the finance of current production) in conjunction with the possible tradeoff between the 'capital intensity' of production and the length of the period of production.[4]

In conventional economics discourse, little or no attention is given to the finance of current production as a demand on an economy's stock of capital. This would appear to be because capital in most instances is identified with the stock of physical capital, rather than fluid capital, hence the role that fluid capital plays in sustaining production is usually overlooked. The financing of current production tends to be treated as a monetary phenomenon and its role as an integral part of the operation of the real economy is, therefore, neither appreciated nor understood.

Since the framework of this book revolves around fluid capital and two associated identities, the question always to be asked in applying the framework to macroeconomic issues (whether practical or theoretical) is: *How is the pool of fluid capital affected?* To raise and then answer this question is, in essence, to identify the relevant macroeconomic constraints that are to be taken into account. Once this is done, the analysis can usually be reduced to a straightforward assessment of the implications and conditions imposed by the constraints.

---

[3] That capital has to finance both current production and investment in produced means of production has generally been overlooked in the literature on capital theory. A notable, but partial, exception was R.G. Hawtrey in his two early volumes on the trade cycle, *Good and Bad Trade* (1913) and *Currency and Credit* (1919). Hawtrey's focus, however, was on the general availability of money and credit, rather than the relationship of these to fluid capital.

[4] See Appendix 2.

Every question that has been analyzed in this book -- from inflation, to the evaluation of Old Masters, to the gold standard, to the burden of the National Debt, to economic growth, to transfer problems, to destruction caused by natural disasters, etc., -- has been approached in this framework. And the answers are almost always straightforward and unambiguous.

Throughout this book, monetization has been identified with the process whereby specific claims to the goods in the pool of fluid capital are converted into generalized claims through the creation of universal purchasing power. The aggregate value of the goods in the pool of fluid capital, where the goods are valued in current prices, is then seen as providing an upper bound on the real stock of money that can be created. Although the constraints imposed by the pool of fluid capital apply no matter what the monetary system or the actual form that money takes, the perspective of this book has, except for occasional references to fiat money, been that of a banking system that creates universally transferrable deposits. The 'money-creation principle' of the book is accordingly that of the venerable English Banking School (or Real Bills Doctrine): Loans should be self-liquidating and if prudence reigns -- and expectations are fulfilled! -- just the 'right' amount of money will always be created.[5]

The core of current-day macroeconomics, as it is presented in most intermediate textbooks, can be stated in three propositions:

1. There is a lower limit of unemployment, the Non-Acceleration Rate of Unemployment (NAIRU), below which inflation will pick up;

2. There is an upper limit on the growth that an economy can sustain, the 'potential rate of growth,' that is determined by the growth of the labor force and the pace of technical change;

3. In the long run, the rate of inflation is determined by the rate of growth of the money supply.

Of these three propositions, the only one that is in general agreement with the arguments of this book is the third, that the rate of inflation is determined by the rate of growth of the money supply. Even so, I would prefer to see the proposition reworded to read:

---

[5] 'Right' in this context is taken to mean that the pool of purchasing power that is created is consistent with a stable general price level.

3a. The rate of inflation depends upon the size of the pool of purchasing power that is created in relation to the available stock of goods evaluated in current prices.

With respect to proposition (2), if the 'potential rate of growth' is taken to mean that the potential is a structural characteristic of an economy, then I disagree with the proposition sharply. An economy grows because of enlargement of the capacity to produce through saving and investment. As technical change is embodied in investment, how potent a dollar of new investment will be in expanding the capacity to produce will clearly depend upon the pace of technical change, but technical change (as is being emphasized in the New Growth Theory) is itself dependent upon investment, namely, investment in education and research and development. The key, accordingly, is investment, which in turn depends upon the availability of a pool of savings. One economy grows faster than another because the one saves and invests more. Japan and Germany grew much faster than the United States for much of the post-WWII period because of higher saving and investment than in the United States. The United States has grown faster in the latter part of the 1990s than before that because it has invested more. On the other hand, saving and investment are themselves dependent upon expectations, so it is really expectations that drive economic growth. If entrepreneurs invest prudently (i.e., direct their 'animal spirits' mostly to areas that produce goods with income elasticities greater than one), then (because of the unboundedness of wants) the new capacities to produce will, in fact, be utilized. In short, there is no upper limit to the rate of growth for an economy. High saving and investment can lead to high growth without inflation. There need be no structural NAIRU.

As this book has progressed, some readers may have noticed an evolution in the definition of fluid capital. In the beginning, fluid capital was defined in terms of the unconsumed surplus from current and past production, but with familiarity the term has increasingly been identified with goods in the process of production plus inventories of finished goods. Since, in a high-income economy, the latter will be small in relation to the former, the goods component of the pool of fluid capital in a high-income economy can essentially be identified with goods in process. When this observation is combined with the Banking Principle of money creation, one can then interpret the monetization process as one in which goods are, in essence, transformed into universal purchasing power simultaneous with their production. When cast in this light, money, in conjunction with a well-functioning banking system, has to be hailed an astounding marvel of social invention.

Three final comments are in order in closing. The first is that in the many years that I have thought about the topics discussed in this book, I have come to appreciate tremendously the understanding of both Keynes and Schumpeter as to what makes real-world economies tick. Keynes's focus was almost always on the here and now of economic activity, while Schumpeter's was usually on an economy's longer-term evolution. Their concepts of capital are similar (although Schumpeter's is much better developed), and the same is true of their concepts of money and how money comes into existence. The economics of the two are complementary in my view, and I think it unfortunate that they are often cast as rivals, with strongly conflicting 'visions' of what economics is all about and how real-world economies operate. For the most part, they were simply concerned with different questions.

The second comment concerns Keynes's dictum in the *General Theory* that one must constantly be on guard in macroeconomic theorizing against fallacies of composition. Keynes dispelled a number of such fallacies, and I hope this book has taken care of several more.

Finally, let me finish with how I began this book, by speaking about the venerable word *capital*. One of my intents in the book has been to forge a root concept of capital that can rescue the word capital from what has become a scrapheap of overuse and confusion, and imbue it with the possibility of relating the many existing concepts of capital to one another in a consistent fashion. Fluid capital, in my opinion, provides the appropriate instrument. If the ideas in this book should ever catch on, ultimate success would occur if 'fluid' in 'fluid capital' should become redundant. Capital, without an adjective, could come to refer to fluid capital, as it has been defined in these pages, and all other concepts of capital could then be identified by appropriate adjectives.

ON THE ROLE OF THEORY IN ECONOMIC ANALYSIS

INTRODUCTION

The purpose of this essay is to offer an assessment of the role of theory in the practical applications of economic analysis. More than any other social science, economics has a well-developed body of theory that is *de rigueur* for aspiring young economists to learn, and which informs and guides both empirical research in economics and practical advice on economic policy questions of the day. For more than a generation, economic theorists have stood at the pinnacle of the discipline, and for years economics departments have practiced peer review in terms of the stature of their resident theorists. And in keeping with this, the vast majority of Nobel prizes in economics have been awarded for contributions to economic theory.

Yet, in no discipline is the role of theory a completely settled matter, including physics, the science that economics most aspires to emulate. Despite the fact that modern physical theory is for all intents and purposes formal mathematics, there is still debate amongst physicists whether mathematics is "nature's language" or is simply a tool for discovering her laws. Modern economic theory is almost as mathematized as modern physical theory, though at a lower level of mathematics, as graduate students in economics do not yet have to learn non-Euclidian geometry, complex variables, and non-abelian group theory. And there is wide support within economics for the view that mathematics is also the language of economic behavior.

It is not my intent in this essay to provide yet another polemic against neoclassical economic theory, but rather to assess what neoclassical theory is (and is not) capable of accomplishing in the pursuit of practical economic analysis. To give some flavor of the discussion to follow, it is my view that neoclassical theory is most appropriate when the questions being asked are of the 'what if' type, or, equivalently, when choices between different courses of action are involved. It is in these situations that the strong conservation assumptions underlying neoclassical theory can reasonably be expected to be fulfilled. Neoclassical theory is inappropriate, again in my opinion, in situations that call for assessment of real-time events. Comparative statics/comparative dynamics are appropriate for assessing conceptual contingencies, but are almost never appropriate for modeling the unfolding of real-time dynamics.

The questions addressed in this essay are ones that have troubled or puzzled me for years, but it was not until I read the recent book by Mirowski (1989) on the relationship of neoclassical economic theory to nineteenth-century mechanics that I have been able to identify the root causes of some of my problems. Especially illuminating for me in this regard is Mirowski's discussion of what the conventional neoclassical assumptions of given endowments, tastes, and technology mean in terms of conservative systems, and why conservative systems of the nineteenth-century variety are ill-equipped to analyze real-time economic phenomena.

The points I am interested in discussing can all be conveniently illustrated in the context of the conventional theory of consumer choice. The questions of interest will be identified in the next section.

ECONOMIC THEORY IN ACTION: THE THEORY OF CONSUMER CHOICE

The theory of consumer choice is widely viewed as one of the real triumphs of economic theory, for it yields a conclusion that is not only elegantly derived, but also intuitively satisfying, and felt to be in accordance with real-world behavior. The conventional theory of consumer choice is, in form, a conservative nineteenth-century physics energy system. The utility function is the counterpart to the potential energy function, while the income (or budget) constraint is the counterpart to kinetic energy. Marginal utilities form an invariant vector field of 'forces', and the 'work' function has its counterpart in an expenditure line-integral. The invariants in the choice problem are that marginal utilities are independent of the 'path of motion', while the conservative principle that is counterpart to the conservation of potential and kinetic energy is that the sum of utility and income is conserved. The structure that the vector field of marginal utilities has to satisfy (in vector-field terminology) is that the curl of the vector field must be equal to zero, which is to say that the vector field must be 'irrotational'. In economics terminology, these restrictions represent the well-known integrability conditions.[1]

A number of standard and widely known results have been derived from the neoclassical theory of choice, including a 'law of demand', which states that (income-compensated) demand functions slope downward. The neoclassical framework, in some form or another, lies behind virtually all practical economic analyses of consumer choice and demand, whether qualitative or quantitative, with the apogee almost certainly being the econometric estimation of systems of demand functions that satisfy all of the analytical requirements of a conservative system. Such exercises are usually referred to as the estimation of 'theoretically plausible' demand systems.[2]

What I wish to do now is to discuss several possible applications of the neoclassical theory of consumer behavior as illustrations of both appropriate and inappropriate uses of the theory. As mentioned earlier, neoclassical theory is most appropriately used, in my view, when the questions involved are of the 'what if' variety. Such would the case, for example, if the questions being asked (with reference to a given-choice set of market baskets of goods and services) were of the form:

1. Assuming the vector of prices to be held constant, which market basket would be chosen given income A as opposed to the market basket chosen if income were B?

2. Assuming income to be held constant, which market basket would be chosen if the price vector were x as opposed to the market basket chosen if the price vector were y?

The first question relates to the derivation of what are ordinarily referred to as Engel schedules, while the second question relates to the derivation of demand schedules. In neither case is there any assumption that the behavior at issue is

---

[1] Although economists are well-versed in linear algebra, this is generally not the case with respect to the concepts of vector fields. Mirowski (1989) provides some discussion of the concepts in question, but not in sufficient detail for a full understanding of the relationship between neoclassical theory and nineteenth-century conservative physical systems. The needed concepts, which include gradient, vector cross (or outer) product, curl and divergence, can be found in any standard advanced calculus textbook, such as Apostal (1957).

[2] The literature on the estimation of theoretically plausible demand systems is huge, with many monographs devoted to the subject as well as a large number of papers. See, for instance, Deaton (1975), Deaton and Muellbauer (1980), Houthakker and Taylor (1970, Chapter 5), Phlips (1983), and Pollak and Wales (1992).

actually to be observed. Indeed, the presumption (although usually tacit) is that it is not. Contrast these questions with the following two questions:

1*.   If an individual (with a given level of income A) were repeatedly (i.e., during a sequence of consumption periods) to be faced with the same price vector x, what would be the market basket of goods consumed?

2*.   If in a subsequent sequence of periods, the individual continued to face price vector x, but with income B rather than A, what would be the market basket consumed?

In these two questions, the assumption is that consumption actually occurs within each of the consumption periods. Nevertheless, for neoclassical theory, this should not matter. The market baskets consumed in the sequence of consumption periods in (1*) should be the same market basket as would have been chosen in (1), while the market baskets consumed in the sequence of consumption periods in (2*) should be the same as would have been chosen in (2).

Almost certainly, however, this is not what would be observed. With consumption actually taking place in (1*)and (2*), there would in all likelihood be an interaction between the consumption in one period and the marginal utilities operative during the next period. Because of the intrusion of real-time dynamics, the assumptions for a conservative vector field would accordingly be violated. For the questions in (1) and (2), in contrast, this would not be a problem, for one could reasonably expect that marginal utilities would remain invariant in the face of 'what if' questions, since no consumption actually takes place.

I wish to emphasize that the issue involved here is not, as a practical matter, the ignoring of some factors that impinge upon consumption and that behave randomly from one consumption period to the next. The issue, rather, is one involving real-time irreversible alterations of marginal utilities in a systematic, yet not necessarily predictable, manner. The question of whether the standard paradigm can be modified in a way to accommodate such 'endogenous taste changes' will be addressed below.

Let me now turn to another example that illustrates the problems at issue. Suppose, as frequently happens, there is a question before a regulatory commission regarding the amount of 'repression' on telephone usage that might be expected to occur as a result of a proposed increase in tariffs. In assessing this question, the usual procedure is to use a price elasticity that has been estimated from an econometric model to calculate the expected amount of repression. The expected repression can be calculated either by using the price elasticity directly or (what, in fact, is usually done) by simulating the model first under the status quo, then with the new tariff, and then attributing repression to the difference. The models in question are usually theoretically based, often with considerable dotting of i's and crossing of t's. Question: Is this procedure an appropriate application of the underlying theory?[3]

The answer is clearly yes, in my opinion, provided the question is framed in terms of comparative statics (i.e., of the 'what if' variety) as opposed to real-time dynamics. However, if the question is framed in terms of estimating what the actual impact of the tariff change would be on telephone usage, then the question would involve real-time dynamics and the answer would in general be no, for the invariances required of a conservative system would once again be unlikely to be fulfilled.

The upshot would seem to be that the conventional theory of consumer choice can be used in assessing alternative courses of action at a planning stage, but cannot be used in predicting the result that will materialize from a course of action actually selected. As a general conclusion, this is a correct statement, for conventional theory imposes invariance assumptions that real-time consumption behavior almost certainly invalidates. Yet, this is not to say that conventional theory cannot be modified to accommodate the invalidations that arise. This can be done, but the modifications required have to be embedded in a theoretical structure that allows for an 'arrow of time'. It is to this that I now turn.

MODELING REAL-TIME DYNAMICS

The central point of the preceding section is that real-time consumption behavior invalidates the invariance assumptions which underlie the neoclassical theory of consumer choice. Specifically, the theory requires that the vector field of marginal utilities be invariant to any market basket that is actually consumed. However, this is almost certainly not the case, for acts of consumption give rise to internal dynamic processes that alter tastes and preferences, and hence alter the marginal utilities defining the components of the vector field. The vector field is therefore not conservative with respect to real-time consumption (as opposed to notional consumption).

---

[3] I leave until later the question of whether the parameters estimated in the econometric model can be identified with the parameters of the theoretical model.

Among other things, the absence of a conservative vector field of preferences means that the dynamics of real-time consumption cannot be analyzed as an exercise in nineteenth-century mechanics, which is to say that real-time consumption equations of motion cannot be interpreted in terms of a particle wending its way through a field of forces. That consumption behavior needs to be analyzed taking dynamics explicitly into account has been recognized for years, and has been the subject of much empirical research, including a number of my own efforts. For the most part, however, the dynamics that have been postulated are of a classical form. The notion of 'earlier and later' is center stage, but the laws of motion ply in mechanical time, motion is reversible, and real time is important only for purposes of measurement and empirical application. Heraclitus's dictive that "one cannot step into the same river twice" is not observed by most existing dynamical models. However, as I shall now discuss, it might seem that applied econometricians go to great lengths in attempts to assure that this is the case.

Something generally not recognized, at least in the terms being discussed in this essay, is that the conditions that must be satisfied for the validity of statistical inference in applied econometrics are in a sense isomorphic to the invariance conditions for a conservative vector field.[4] For illustration, consider the estimation of a system of theoretically plausible demand functions that have been derived (say) from the Stone-Geary-Samuelson utility function. Suppose the demand functions are estimated, subject to all of the integrability conditions, from an appropriate body of data.

In this situation, since the demand functions are estimated subject to the integrability conditions, a conservative vector field of preferences is not only assumed, but is, in fact, imposed as part of estimation. Assuming the econometrician is well-schooled in the Haavelmo paradigm, however, this imposition is not as mechanical as it might appear. For a number of problems have to be dealt with before estimation actually occurs, most of them related to the fact that the data set being analyzed arises not out of controlled laboratory conditions, but from a natural experiment generated by history. Be that as it may, the *sine qua non* of the Haavelmo paradigm nevertheless is a presumption that the observations in the data set being analyzed can be viewed as a sample drawn at random from a common underlying population.

---

[4] That this is indeed the case was already implicit in the classic monograph on the probability approach in econometrics of Haavelmo (1944). It is also just below the surface in the reinterpretation and extension of the Haavelmo paradigm by Spanos (1989). My own reinterpretation of the Haavelmo paradigm is given in Chapter 10 of Taylor (1994).

For this presumption to be justified, it becomes a major task of the analysis to model not only the phenomenon of interest (namely, the relationship between consumption, prices, and income), but also the structure of the natural experiment that generated the data to begin with. 'Structural changes' during the period of the sample have to be taken into account, as well as the fact that most of the behavior represented in the data set will reflect disequilibria. I put structural changes in quotation marks because, in the natural experiment that generated the data, there are two different forms of structural change to contend with. The first refers to an autonomous structural change arising from the 'outside' that affects preferences (and therefore consumption), but which is not, itself, consumption caused. The other form of structural change is the endogenous change in the field of marginal utilities caused by real-time consumption.

Of the two types of structural change, the second type is clearly the most problematic to take into account, for it requires an explicit representation of the feedback on preferences of consumption as it occurs. The usual way of accomplishing this empirically is to specify a model in which current consumption depends not only upon current income and prices, but upon past consumption as well.[5] Endogenous preference changes are assumed to be reflected in the coefficient on past consumption.[6] An alternative procedure is to postulate a state-dependent vector field of marginal utilities in which the composition of the field at any point in time depends upon a set of state variables, which themselves evolve in response to real-time consumption together with the passage of mechanical time.[7]

If the econometrician is successful in specifying a model that appropriately takes into account the two types of structural change (and also appropriately reflects the probability structure of the random component of the implicit natural experiment), then the requirements of the Haavelmo paradigm will be satisfied. Moreover, it can also be argued that the invariance conditions for a conservative vector field will be satisfied as well. Estimation of the model can then proceed under the presumption that the parameters estimated in the econometric model are to be identified with the parameters of the underlying theory.

---

[5] Care must be taken at this point to distinguish between mechanical dynamics that occur in mechanical time (and reflect disequilibrium behavior), and real-time dynamics that reflect the feedback of consumption on preferences. With the way that many models are specified, it is unlikely that these two forms of dynamics can be separately identified.

[6] See, among others, Pollak (1978) and Von Weisaeker (1971).

[7] See Houthakker and Taylor (1966,1970).

The argument that the invariance conditions for a conservative vector field are satisfied when the Haavelmo assumptions are met can be stated as follows: If the real-time feedback of consumption on preferences is appropriately modeled, then the sample can be viewed as a sequence of state-dependent conservative vector fields in which the states are determined exogenously.[8] Historical time is no longer reflected in the data, because its effects are held constant through the explicit modeling of how the states, themselves, evolve. Dynamics may still be present, but these would be of the mechanical variety and, therefore, invariant to historical time. Thus, each observation in the data set can be viewed as having arisen in answer to a 'what if' type of question, namely: What quantities would be demanded if income were this and prices were thus and so?

Though the conditions for a conservative vector field may be satisfied for purposes of estimation, it does not follow (as already discussed) that they would be satisfied for purposes of using the estimated model to predict the evolution of real-time consumption in response (say) to a change in prices. As was noted, one could use the model to analyze 'what if' types of questions in which there is no presumption of actual consumption ever occurring. But to predict real-time consumption would require one also being able to predict the real-time evolution of the state-dependent vector fields of preferences.[9]

The problem, clearly, is that predicting human consumption behavior is very different than predicting the motion of an inanimate particle, for the motion of an inanimate particle does not interact with the forces defined in the field. With human behavior, on the other hand, motion does interact with these forces, for what one consumes today alters the marginal utilities that determine what one will consume tomorrow -- perhaps in unpredictable ways.

CONCLUSIONS

The main points of this essay concerning the role of the neoclassical economic theory in practical economic analysis can be summarized as follows:

---

[8] Accomplishing this requires, in my opinion, the formulation of consumption models which have a basis in the functional organization and operation of the brain. My own first effort in this direction is given in Taylor (1992).

[9] This is obviously a very tall order, but I am optimistic that, as we come to better understand how the brain is organized and how it functions, appropriate evolutionary laws (perhaps even of the mechanical variety) can be formulated.

1. Models based upon neoclassical principles can be used in assessing the relative merits of alternative courses of action at a planning stage, but in general should not be used in predicting the outcome of the course of action that is actually selected.

2. The reason for this conclusion is that neoclassical theory postulates a conservative vector field whose components are independent of actual behavior. In the case of the theory of consumer choice, the marginal utilities defining the vector field must accordingly be independent of any market basket the consumer might consume. Invariance of the preference field is a reasonable assumption for questions of the 'what if' type in which consumption is purely notional, but not in situations in which consumption is presumed to actually occur. Actual consumption almost certainly alters marginal utilities, in which case the preference field is not conservative but becomes real-time dependent.

3. With regard to the estimation of econometric models derived from neoclassical theory, it is argued that the conditions that must be satisfied for the validity of statistical inference (*a la* Haavelmo) in an econometric model are isomorphic to the invariance conditions for a conservative vector field, in which case the parameters of the econometric model can be identified with the parameters of the theory. Accomplishing this, however, requires that the real-time dependence of the field of marginal utilities be explicitly accounted for in the econometric model.

4. Although removing the real-time effects of history is, in principle, possible in estimating an econometric model derived from neoclassical theory, it is much more problematic whether real-time effects can be removed in using the model to make a prediction of actual behavior. This is the basis for the negative conclusion concerning prediction in (1).

In my view, conventional economic theory is often called upon to perform tasks in practical economic analysis which is beyond its scope to execute. I have in mind particularly its use in predicting the actual outcome of an action, as opposed to assessing the relative merits of alternative actions. Comparative static or comparative dynamic analyses based upon conservative vector fields are appropriate to the latter, but not to the former. Progress is not going to be made in rectifying the problems involved, in my opinion, until (for the study of consumer behavior) models are formulated that are embedded in the organization and functioning of the brain. Such an approach offers hope that the real-time consumption dynamics that make preference fields real-time dependent can be explicitly modeled, in which case the underlying vector fields can, indeed, be treated as conservative.

INVESTMENT FUNCTIONS DON'T NECESSARILY SLOPE DOWNWARD

INTRODUCTION

One of the longtime centerpieces of economics and economic theory is that investment depends negatively upon the rate of interest. The classical economists embraced it, as did the nineteenth-century neoclassical economists and their twentieth-century descendants. The Austrians accepted it, and so did Keynes in his schedule of the marginal efficiency of capital. The only economists not to accept a negative relationship between investment and the rate of interest appear to be the Cambridge-on-the-Cam (as opposed to Cambridge-on-the-Charles) participants in the Capital Controversy of the 1960s and the 1970s. Their argument would appear to be based upon the possibility of 'reswitching', i.e., the same capital-labor ratio can be associated with two different rates of interest.

The purpose of this appendix is to discuss a circumstance in which an increase in the rate of interest may well lead to an increase in investment, even though reswitching (as ordinarily understood) is not at issue. The critical factor that appears to have been ignored in previous discussions of the determinants of investment is that capital funds not only investment, but current production as well. The well-known tradeoff between labor and capital in the method of production, therefore, means that there will also be a tradeoff between the physical capital intensity of production and the amount of interest that must be paid in order to finance current production. In short, there is also a tradeoff between the amount of capital that is used in constructing the physical plant used in production, and the amount that is required to finance the operation of that plant. A higher rate of interest can, accordingly, lead to an increase in the capital intensity of the method of production, in order to reduce the interest costs of production. The result may be an investment function that slopes upward with the rate of interest rather than downward.

Although the words that describe the reasoning underlying the conclusion of this paper are familiar ones, the analysis is dependent upon the root concept of capital -- fluid capital -- that has been the focus of analysis throughout this book.

THE RELATIONSHIP BETWEEN INVESTMENT AND THE RATE OF INTEREST

The vantage point in the discussion to follow will be that of an individual firm considering whether to invest in additional produced means of production. Let the investment in question be represented by the present value of a stream of prospective quasi-rents:

$$(1) \quad V = \sum_{i=1}^{n} \frac{R_i - C_i(\tau, r)}{[1 + \rho(r)]^i},$$

where:

V = present value of quasi-rents

R_i = revenues expected in period i

C_i = avoidable cost of generating R_i

τ = capital-intensity of the method of production

r = interest rate

ρ = discount rate

n = investment horizon.

Per usual, a necessary condition for the investment to be undertaken is for the present value of the quasi-rents V to be at least as great as the cost of the investment, which will be denoted by C. The net present value of the investment as a function of τ and r can accordingly be written as:

$$(2) \quad N(\tau, r) = V(\tau, r) - C(\tau, r).$$

The key to the analysis is the dependence of both the avoidable costs of production and the cost of the investment on the capital-intensity of the method of production and the interest rate. This dependence allows for the establishment of a tradeoff between the rate of interest and the capital-intensity of the method of production, and it is this tradeoff that, in turn, allows for the possibility of a positive relationship between investment and the rate of interest.

Before going into detail, I should clarify what is intended to be conveyed in the capital-intensity parameter τ. The usual interpretation of this parameter would be that it represents the capital-output ratio. While, strictly speaking, this is not incorrect, it is better in my view to interpret τ as representing the output-labor ratio, where labor is assumed to be measured in efficiency units. Among other things, this captures the tradeoff between labor (measured in efficiency units) and the amount of capital embodied in a production process, and at the same time avoids having to treat capital as a substance once it is embodied in produced means of production. Also, as will be seen below, interpreting τ as the output-labor ratio focuses attention on the interest costs of financing current production, which can be avoided through the use of more capital-intensive methods of production.

Expression (2) is the relationship of interest because it represents the relationship between the willingness-to-pay for investment in produced means of production and the cost of that investment as a function of the output-labor ratio and the rate of interest. As noted earlier, the key to the result about to be obtained is that the pool of fluid capital funds current production as well as investment. As a consequence, the interest costs associated with the avoidable costs of current production have to be taken into account in determining the amount of investment, as well as the interest costs of the capital associated with the investment.

We can make this dependence of avoidable costs of production on the rate of interest explicit by writing $C_i(\tau, r)$ as:

$$(3) \quad C_i(\tau, r) = (1 + (r/2)\hat{C}_i(\tau),$$

where $\hat{C}$ denotes the non-interest component of avoidable cost, and where it is assumed that avoidable costs are incurred evenly throughout the period of production. Expression (2) written out in full accordingly becomes:

(4) $$N(\tau, r) = \sum_{i=i}^{n} \frac{R_i - (1 + \frac{r}{2})\hat{C}_i(\tau)}{[1 + \rho(r)]^i} - C(\tau, r).$$

The relationship of interest is the slope of this expression with respect to r, which will be given by the partial derivative of $N(\tau, r)$ with respect to r, *viz*:

(5) $$\frac{\partial N}{\partial r} = \sum_{i=1}^{n} - \frac{(1 + \rho)^i \left[(1 + \frac{r}{2})\frac{\partial \hat{C}_i}{\partial \tau}\frac{d\tau}{dr} + \frac{1}{2}\hat{C}_i\right] + i\left[R_i - (1 + \frac{r}{2})\hat{C}_i\right](1 + \rho)^{i-1}}{(1 + \rho)^{2i}} - \frac{\partial C}{\partial \tau}\frac{d\tau}{dr} - \frac{\partial C}{\partial r},$$

where it is assumed, without loss of anything essential, that $\partial\rho/\partial r$ is equal to 1. Evaluation of the sign of this expression requires an explicit expression for $d\tau/dr$, which represents the tradeoff, holding output constant, between the interest rate and the labor-intensity of the method of production.

To obtain an expression for this tradeoff, we proceed as follows: Expression (4), as it stands, represents the *net profitability* of the contemplated investment. This will be at a maximum when a dollar of interest cost incurred to finance current production makes the same contribution to net profit as a dollar of capital embodied in investment. To get this tradeoff, we accordingly take the total differential of expression (4), with respect to τ and r:

(6) $$dN = \sum_{i=1}^{n} \frac{-(1 + \rho)^i\left[(1 + \frac{r}{2})\frac{\partial \hat{C}_i}{\partial \tau}d\tau + \frac{1}{2}\frac{\partial \hat{C}_i}{\partial r}dr\right] - i\left[R_i - (1 + \frac{r}{2})\hat{C}_i\right](1 + \rho)^{i-1}dr}{(1 + \rho)^{2i}} - \frac{\partial C}{\partial \tau}d\tau - \frac{\partial C}{\partial r}dr.$$

The relationship desired is then obtained by equating this total differential to 0 and solving for $d\tau/dr$.

(7) $$\frac{d\tau}{dr} = - \frac{\dfrac{\displaystyle\sum_{i=1}^{n}\frac{1}{2}(1 + \rho)^i\,\hat{C}_i + [R_i - (1 + \frac{r}{2})\hat{C}_i](1 + \rho)^{i-1}}{(1 + \rho)^{2i}} + \dfrac{\partial C}{\partial r}}{\dfrac{\displaystyle\sum_{i=1}^{n}(1 + \rho)^i[(1 + \frac{r}{2})\frac{\partial \hat{C}_i}{\partial \tau}]}{(1 + \rho)^{2i}} + \dfrac{\partial C}{\partial \tau}}.$$

The usual presumption would be that $d\tau/dr$ is negative. Inspection of the right-hand side of expression (7), however, shows that the sign of dτ/dr depends upon the sign of the denominator. Since all of the terms in the numerator are positive, the numerator will clearly be positive. In the denominator, on the other hand, we see that the term in the summation contains $\partial \hat{C}/\partial \tau$, which (as has been discussed) can be assumed to be negative. The denominator, accordingly, can be negative, depending upon the size of the term in the summation in relation to $\partial C/\partial \tau$, which can obviously be assumed to be positive. If $\partial \hat{C}/\partial \tau$ is strong enough, the denominator can be negative, which means that dτ/dr can be positive.

Since the sign of dτ/dr is ambiguous, it follows that the sign of $\partial N/\partial r$ in expression (5) is ambiguous as well. In short, investment functions do not necessarily vary inversely with the rate of interest.

FURTHER DISCUSSION AND CONCLUSIONS

An inverse relationship between investment and the rate of interest has been a cornerstone of economic analysis for more than 200 years. While there have been occasional challenges, such as emerged during the capital controversy during the 1960s and 1970s, the possibility of an upward-sloping investment function as a practical matter has never been taken seriously. Theoretically, demand functions can slope upward as well, but the usual place that such a phenomenon is sought is in the study of potato demand in nineteenth-century Ireland. The conclusion of this paper may appear in a similar light.

In my view, however, the novelty of this exercise lies not in the conclusion itself, but in the mechanism whereby the ambiguity of sign arises. Once one takes into account that capital (viewed as a pool of accumulated savings) funds not only investment but current production as well, the relationship between investment and the rate of interest becomes anything but straightforward. Interest is not only a factor in determining the cost of investment, but is also a component of the current cost of production. More capital-intensive methods of production involve lower avoidable costs of production and therefore lead to lower interest costs for 'working capital'. The result, accordingly, can be an inverse relationship between the labor intensity of the method of production and the rate of interest, which is equivalent to a *positive* relationship between investment and the rate of interest.

This result would not appear to be a reflection of reswitching, for the possible positive relationship between investment and the rate of interest depends upon the wage rate for labor. A labor-intensive method of production implies large wage payments that have to be financed during the period of production, thereby implying a high interest cost for 'working capital' when the rate of interest is high. A part of these high-interest carrying costs can be avoided by a more capital-intensive process.

The same phenomenon can obviously arise, indeed, with even greater force, in connection with the length of the period-of-production. A simple example will illustrate the point. Consider an earth-moving contractor whose 'book of blueprints' for moving dirt includes a variety of earthmoving equipment of varying capacities per unit of time. A 20-cubic-yard machine can clearly move considerably more volume in an hour than a five-cubic-yard machine. The larger wagon will obviously embody more capital, but it will also require less labor input because projects will take less time. The period-of-production will be shorter, which means that 'working-capital' interest costs will be smaller. In this situation, it is accordingly possible that a high interest rate combined with a high wage rate will lead to investment in the more capital-intensive machine.

This example assumes that the complete method of production is up for grabs. Most of the time this is not the case, as choice will refer to investment that alters the method of production on the margin. But even so, the phenomenon adheres, for a high wage rate combined with a high interest rate can lead to capital-intensive alterations to the production process in order to economize on 'working-capital' interest costs.

APPENDIX 3

IMPLICATIONS OF THE OIL PRICE
INCREASES OF THE 1970S

INTRODUCTION

In the fall of 1973, the Organization of Petroleum Exporting Countries
(OPEC) succeeded in quadrupling the world price of oil, with a further doubling
in 1979. Economies that were heavy importers of oil almost immediately went
into recession, inflation mounted, and a lengthy period of slow growth (or even
stagnation) was initiated. This was especially the case in the U.S. Not only did
the U.S. economy suffer both recession and inflation, but the stage was set for
a slowdown in labor productivity which continued into the 1990s. Most
macroeconomists see this prolonged slowdown in labor productivity as a major
macroeconomic puzzle. That it seems to date from the 1973 energy crisis is more
commonly viewed as coincidental than causal.

The purpose of this appendix is to argue the contrary, that the OPEC-
induced oil price increases were in fact a principal cause of the productivity
slowdown, specifically as a consequence of a classic 'transfer' problem that
involved the transfer of a massive amount of real wealth from oil consumers to
oil producers. While a number of mechanisms were involved in effecting this
transfer, the end result necessarily and inevitably entailed a decrease in real
income on the part of oil consumers.

In essence, there were two ways that this decrease in real income could come
about: through inflation or through unemployment. With inflation, the cut in real
income would occur through goods prices increasing just a little faster than the
increase in money wages, while with unemployment, the cut in real income
would occur through the loss of income for those who lost their jobs. What
generally is not appreciated is that real output would necessarily be reduced in
either case.

Moreover, the transfer involved was neither a relative price problem (although in time substitution away from energy as an input as a result of changed relative prices both could and did alleviate some of the adverse effects) nor a recycling problem.

INSTANTANEOUS EFFECTS OF THE OIL PRICE INCREASES

It is useful at the outset to separate, at least conceptually, the instantaneous effects of the OPEC-induced oil price increases from the longer-run effects. The immediate effects of a large and instantaneous increase in the price of a commodity such as oil is to transfer wealth from those who consume the commodity to those who produce it. The mechanism by which this occurs is as follows.

In the very short run, production coefficients are essentially fixed, which is to say that the level of final output is essentially proportional to the amount of the (now much higher priced) commodity available for use as an input. Assuming that the price increase was unexpected, the existing pool of purchasing power would have been created in anticipation of the old price. At the new price, production must necessarily be lower (because of fixed production coefficients) than what was anticipated at the old price. Expenditures for inputs will be the same, but a much larger proportion of these expenditures will go to the suppliers of the now much higher priced input. Receipts of other input suppliers will necessarily be lower. The initial effect, accordingly, is a transfer of wealth from these other input suppliers and producers of final goods (since there will be less output to be sold) to the suppliers of the now higher priced input. Since labor, in the short run, cannot be substituted for this input, unemployment must inevitably arise.

In the first production period following the price rise, two cases need to be considered. The first of these, which corresponds to the way Germany and Switzerland dealt with the 1973 oil price increase, is where the input price rise is contained by the monetary authority and is not allowed to affect the general price level. Accomplishing this requires restricting the new pool of purchasing power to be created to be no greater than it would have been in the absence of the price rise. Banks, in this situation, will not be able to increase the size of loans they make to their business customers in order to offset the now higher costs of production. The effect of this policy is to ratify the unemployment that the price rise initially induced. The unemployment will endure, under this policy, until such time as there is substitution away from the higher priced input.

The second case, which corresponds to the way the U.S. dealt with the problem, is where the monetary authority allows the pool of newly created purchasing power to increase in proportion to the higher input price. Such a policy would appear to allow production to return to its former level, but this could never, in fact, be the case. While the enlarged pool of purchasing power would enable non-oil inputs to receive the same money income as before, the higher cost of oil would obviously be translated into higher output prices. With higher output prices, but the same non-oil money incomes, not all of the old output could be purchased. Almost certainly, some unemployment would appear which, in general, would be scattered throughout the economy, rather than being restricted to the large oil-consuming industries. The amount of unemployment, however, would probably be smaller than in the first case. As in the first case, though, real incomes would, once again, necessarily be reduced.

In the first case, containing the price increase of oil through a restrictive monetary policy, the cut in real income would fall primarily on the unemployed. In the second case, in which the decrease in real income comes about through goods prices increasing faster than increases in money wages, the burden of the decrease in real income would be much more widely dispersed amongst the population. Germany and Switzerland used the first method to deal with the 1973 oil price shock by 'inviting' their alien 'guest' workers to quit the country. In this case, the cuts in real incomes fell on non-nationals. Had the same policy been followed in the U.S., millions of aliens would have been forced to leave the country. As such a policy was obviously socially and politically unacceptable, the inflation route was followed instead.

The foregoing conclusions can also be arrived at through consideration of the conservation laws imposed by the pool of fluid capital. As discussed at numerous points in the body of this book, one of these laws is that the real value of the stock of money is bounded by the goods side of the pool of fluid capital valued in current prices.[1] Since an arbitrary increase in the price of oil cannot (instantaneously) increase the number of goods in the pool, the real stock of money is subject to the same bound immediately after the price increase as before. As a result, any increase in the nominal stock of money must necessarily be offset by inflation.

Moreover, not only is the pool of fluid capital not increased by the oil price increase, but the pool is actually reduced in the sense that its productivity is lessened from what it was before the price increase. Suppose that, prior to the

[1] See Chapter 3.

price increase, a dollar of fluid capital (valued in then current prices) would purchase one unit of oil. After the price increase, the number of units of oil that the same dollar of fluid capital can purchase will be less than one. There is, accordingly, no escaping the decrease in productivity that the transfer entails.

SOME REAL-TIME DYNAMICS

The discussion to this point has been in terms of the instantaneous effects of the arbitrary increase in the price of oil. With the passage of time, two forces come into play that will soften the impact of the initial reduction in productivity, namely, substitution away from the now greatly more expensive energy and a return of some of the initial transfer through both increased and higher-priced exports. Let us examine substitution first.

The standard approach that economists and econometricians have followed for dealing with substitution away from energy in production is to include energy alongside capital and labor in industry or aggregate production functions. In some cases, materials are included as a separate argument as well. The problem with this procedure is that it attempts to deal, in a static framework, with matters that are inherently real-time dynamical. In this framework, adjustment to higher energy prices is assumed to occur via a substitution of 'capital' (and possibly other materials) for energy in the context of an *invariant* production function.

The problem with this framework is the assumption that the physical capital that embodies the more efficient use of energy can somehow be divorced from the 'location' and 'shape' of the production function. In my view, this is a completely unwarranted way of going about doing things, as the very nature of substitution involves altering the structure of the production function. Specifically unwarranted, in my opinion, is the assumption that there exists a set of parameters that are invariant to the processes of substitution.[2]

As time passes (and the higher oil prices are incorporated into expectations), substitution away from oil will begin to take place on the margin, as investment in new energy-conserving plant and equipment is undertaken. This investment can take many forms: retrofitting of existing plant, replacement of equipment, use of different fuels, alteration of processes, etc. As this occurs, the capacity of the economy to produce begins to recover some of the productivity that was lost initially as a result of the arbitrary increase in oil prices. However, since much

---

[2] This criticism is obviously much broader than what is just being discussed here. A much more detailed critique of the problems involved is given in Appendix 1 above.

energy-consuming plant and equipment is extremely long-lived, complete adjustment will take years, perhaps even decades. In the household sector, for example, a major energy-consuming appliance is the house itself, and it may take upwards of 50 years for the housing stock to turn over completely.

As time passes, some of the original transfer will be returned as the OPEC countries and other recipients of the transfer increase their imports of goods and services from the oil-importing countries. This, too, will lead to a recouping of some of the productivity that was initially lost. This recouping will take two forms: (1) an increase in the amount of goods and services that are exported and (2) an increase in the nominal prices of exports as the inflation which the oil-price increase initially triggered (as in the U.S.) permeates the prices of all goods (traded as well as non-traded). The faster the capacity to produce can be restructured to produce exports, the smaller will be the transfer.[3] Similarly, the quicker that export prices inflate, the faster will be a partial return of the transfer.[4]

IMPLICATIONS FOR SUBSEQUENT PRODUCTIVITY GROWTH

While it is clear that, in time, a part of the original loss in productivity can be either recovered or made up through substitution, increased exports, and inflation, it is another matter whether permanent damage may have been done to productivity growth. In my view, a strong case can be made that some permanent damage, in the sense of a prolonged period of reduced productivity growth, has in fact occurred. This section develops the argument as to why this may have been the case.

The key to the analysis, obviously, is what happens to the output/labor ratio as substitution and other forces initiated by higher oil prices are set in motion. There are three questions to be considered:

1. The type of substitution that occurs within the framework of *existing* technology;

---

[3] If the capacity to produce could instantaneously be restructured for exports and the oil exporters were instantaneously to spend all of their additional revenues on the affected country's exports, then the transfer would, in principle, be netted out. In reality, of course, this could never happen.

[4] This assumes, of course, that export prices inflate everywhere. If this is not the case, then exports of the countries not inflating will benefit at the cost of those countries that do inflate. Thus, it may have made very good economic sense for Germany and Japan to contain the oil price increases through restrictive monetary policies because of their large export markets.

2.   The type of substitution that occurs with *new* technology;

3.   The output/labor ratio in the export industries in relation to the same in the industries bearing the brunt of higher energy prices.

Substitution that occurs with existing technology

This is the type of substitution that conventional neoclassical analysis focuses on. The production technology is fixed, and higher relative energy prices lead to a substitution of 'capital' and other inputs for energy along given isoquants. In the terminology of the Cambridge Capital Controversy of the 1960s and 1970s, higher relative prices for energy lead to the selection of a different plant from the *same* book of blueprints.

Almost certainly, some substitution of this type occurred. However, if this were the only form of substitution, the original level of productivity could never be reattained. The reason for this is that, if labor is substituted for energy, it must necessarily be done at a lower real wage, while if 'capital' is substituted for energy, one of two things would have to occur: If the substitution is labor-saving as well as energy-saving, the real wage might be higher for the labor employed, but less labor will be employed; if the substitution is both capital- and labor-augmenting, the real wage must once again be reduced.

The operative constraint driving all of these conclusions is the one imposed by the pool of fluid capital on productivity. As was noted in the preceding section, an arbitrary increase in oil prices necessarily reduces the productivity of the existing pool of fluid capital in the sense that the pool can no longer support the same level of production after the price increase as before. In more conventional terminology, what the constraint implies is that even after movements along isoquants have occurred the new levels of production will necessarily lie on lower isoquants.

Substitution that occurs with new technology

We have just seen that because of the constraint imposed by the pool of fluid capital, substitution embodied in existing technology cannot simultaneously save energy and increase output. The only way the existing pool of fluid capital can simultaneously support both a higher level of output and a lower consumption of energy per unit of output is through investment in new technology of a type which both alters the shapes of isoquants and shifts production frontiers outward. It is the latter which allows the pool of fluid capital to recover its former level of productivity.

While investment in new technology will allow the pool of fluid capital to eventually recapture its former level of productivity, the productivity recovered represents only the *static* losses that arose from the initial transfer. There will be *dynamic* productivity losses, however, and these can never be completely recovered. These dynamic losses represent the potential increases in productivity that are foregone as a result of the necessity to divert investment that would otherwise have expanded the frontiers of production into substitution away from energy.

Not only are the productivity gains foregone by these 'pure' substitution investments effectively lost forever, but the way these losses show themselves is through a drag on real-time productivity growth, which may be quite prolonged. As was noted earlier, the stock of energy-consuming plant and equipment is both large and long-lived, and it could be decades before the 'pure' substitution effects are fully worked out. Almost certainly, this was a factor in the poor performance of productivity during the 1970s and 1980s.

The output/labor ratio in the export industries

As noted earlier, a part of the initial transfer should eventually be recouped through increased exports. The implications of this for labor productivity, however, will depend upon the relative labor intensities of production in the export industries and the industries in which production was initially curtailed. In general, the recoupment will be larger the less labor-intensive is production in the export industries, in relation to production in the non-export industries. The maximum recoupment would occur, of course, in a situation in which there is excess capacity in the export industries, all of the initial transfer is recycled as export demand, and all of the labor released by the curtailed production in the non-export industries is absorbed by the export industries at no reduction in the money wage rate.

Recovery of the transfer through the export sector brings one additional extremely positive benefit, for much of the drag on productivity described in the preceding section need not come into play. The drag will be minimized, and possibly avoided altogether, to the extent that:

1. The initial transfer reappears as export demand;

2. There is a smooth reallocation of production from domestic to export industries;

3. The initial transfer is dissipated through higher export prices.

The reason exports are privileged is that they provide the only vehicle for escaping the negative income effect that was induced by the initial transfer. This is because the increased export demand represents, in essence, a return of the transfer. While the static losses associated with the initial transfer cannot be escaped, the real-time dynamic losses associated with 'pure' substitution investment described in the preceding section will be smaller with investment in the export industries than with investment in the domestic industries. This is because investment in the export industries (whether in the form of new or existing technology) is for the purpose of expanding capacity, whereas the investment associated with 'pure' substitution in domestic industries is for the purpose of producing given outputs at lower cost.

FINANCIAL RECYCLING

It was thought by some in the 1970s that the transfer problem could be greatly alleviated, if not overcome entirely, through financial recycling. Funds acquired by OPEC oil producers would be recycled through the international banking system as loans to pay the higher cost of oil imports or, alternatively, to finance third-world economic development. That massive financial recycling occurred is evident; that it did not have the intended effect is also evident. The question I want to address in this section is whether, even in the absence of fiducial imprudence, the intended effect could ever have occurred. That is, could perfect financial recycling have solved the transfer problem?

In general, the answer is no, the reason being that, short of the initial transfer returning dollar-for-dollar to those having to pay the higher oil costs, the transfer involved a massive redistribution of claims to the existing world pool of fluid capital. Initially, these claims were transferred to oil producers from oil consumers. But once the funds were on deposit at large international banks, many of the claims were then loaned to countries either already with balance-of-payment problems or wishing to finance ambitious development projects. The net result was a substantial redistribution of fluid capital from the major industrialized oil-importing countries to the world at large, with a handful of OPEC countries and the international banks functioning as intermediaries. Financial recycling did not solve the transfer problem, it simply altered the mechanisms through which the transfers occurred.

If the fluid capital transferred from oil-importing countries had genuinely added to the world's capacity to produce and generate income, then the overall productivity effect of the transfer would have probably been minor. Slow productivity growth in countries like the U.S. would have been offset by rapid productivity growth in countries like Brazil and Argentina. In the event, however, many of the OPEC funds that were recycled ended up financing consumption, so that much of the fluid capital that was redistributed was, in fact, consumed. The end result of the transfer was accordingly a permanent reduction in the world's pool of fluid capital. Consequently, not only did the donors of the transfer suffer from a drag on productivity, but so too did the world at large.

CONCLUSION

At this point, the sluggish growth in labor productivity that the U.S. experienced between the mid-1970s and the mid-1990s should not be viewed as a puzzling coincidence of the oil price shocks that occurred in 1973 and 1979, but rather as a necessary consequence of those price shocks. The oil price increases involved a massive redistribution of the world's pool of fluid capital away from the major industrialized oil-importing countries, including the United States. The redistribution necessarily reduced the productivity of the U.S. pool of fluid capital, impelling the country into a prolonged period of slowed productivity growth as substantial volumes of investment had to be devoted to reducing the energy-intensity of production. Investment devoted to 'pure' substitution led to real-time productivity losses, as investment that otherwise would have enlarged capacities to produce was diverted to reducing the cost of producing existing levels of output.

ADDITIONAL TALES INVOLVING A PRIMITIVE ECONOMY

This appendix, which was the initial Prologue to the book, presents a much more detailed and pedestrian description of the emergence of a primitive economy from an economic state of nature than is the case with the present Prologue. It is included here at the suggestion of one of my colleagues at the University of Arizona who has used it for a number of years (as have I) as introductory reading in upper division economics courses. While the content is similar to that presented in the current Prologue, it describes a greater variety of transactions -- including the production of widgits! -- so that students (and others) can get a better feel for how transactions, production structures, and goods become more complex as economies grow and develop. At various points in the narrative, tables are provided that tally up the amounts of fluid capital (in the form of bread) and other assets that exist at that point in the economy. These tables provide not only an accounting of the creation and destruction of fluid capital, but also the ingredients for the construction of an elementary set of National Income Accounts. Such an exercise should bring home to students in a simple, yet forceful, way the inherent arbitrariness that underlies any system of National Accounts. Decisions must be made as to what to define as income, what to include in the stock of fluid capital and the stock of produced means of production, what to define as money, what period over which to measure economic activity, the difference between stocks and flows, etc. For the most part, all of these decisions contain elements of arbitrariness. Hence, students should come to understand that there is no necessarily 'right' way to measure income, GDP, etc.

Imagine, as before, that there is a group of people who lived on an isolated island. The climate was mild and benevolent, and everyone lived at a subsistence level and slept under the stars. As before, the only product in the land was 'bread', which was mined by hand. There was no capital equipment. Everyone worked an eight-hour day in the community mine in order to acquire an amount of bread that was just sufficient for survival. Everyone had the same productivity mining bread. People could work more than eight hours, but no one had ever previously seen a reason to accumulate a stock of bread. The island economy, in short, was in a 'thorough-going equilibrium' at a subsistence level. This is where we pick up the story.

Assume, now, that one of the inhabitants of the island, A (say), decides (for whatever reason) that he wants to live under a roof and decides to build a house. Building the house, however, will take 10 eight-hour days of labor, during which time he will not be able to mine his needed daily bread. In view of this, A decides to work 12 hours for 20 days in order to build up a stock of bread to sustain himself during the 10 days that the house is being built. The stock of bread is created, and A proceeds to build his house.

Next, assume that B, who has some artistic talent, decides that she wants to paint a picture and it will require two days of her time to do so. For 'finance', B decides to work four 12-hour days in order to provide sustenance during the two days that will be devoted to the painting.

Usually, people 'die in the harness' on the island, but C fears that this may not be the case for him and thinks that it would be a good idea to build up a 'nest egg' for use during his final days when he may not be able to work. He accordingly decides to work 100 12-hour days, which results in a 'rainy-day' fund that would provide for up to 50 days of 'retirement'.

Once C's retirement stock of bread is completed, however, C sees B's painting and tells B that he would like to buy it in exchange for four days of bread. B accepts C's offer, and accordingly gives up her painting. C's 'assets' now consist of the painting, plus a stock of 46 days of bread, while B's assets consist of four days of bread.

Assume, next, that D, E, and F also become concerned about retirement and work 100 12-hour days to build up retirement funds of 50 days each. Total savings in the economy is now 200 days of bread as follows:

A	0
B	4
C	46
D	50
E	50
F	50.

As it turns out, bread will begin to deteriorate after a while if it is not stored in a 'safe'. G notices this and decides to build such a safe. The safe, however, will take five days to construct, so G decides to work 10 12-hour days in order to accumulate the necessary 'finance'. Once the safe is completed, D, E, and F bring their stocks of bread to G to store in his safe. To each of his clients, G gives a receipt signifying how much bread is on deposit in the safe. From each client, however, G demands (and receives) an up-front charge of one day's bread as a storage fee.

F sees B's painting which C now owns and offers C six days of bread for it. C accepts the offer. F goes to G, collects six days of bread from his stock in G's safe and gives it to C in exchange for the painting. C takes the six days of bread that he has just gotten from F back to G for storage. G, of course, is happy to do so, gives C a receipt, but insists upon one-half day of bread as a storage fee.

There are still 200 days of savings in the economy as follows:

A	0
B	4
C	51.5
D	49
E	49
F	43
G	3.5.

E sees B's painting, which F now has, and offers eight days of bread for it, which F accepts. E writes a note addressed to G instructing G to transfer to F eight days' bread from E's stock in G's safe. F tells G to add the eight days of bread to his stock, which G does after deducting one-half day of bread for the service. The 200 days of savings are now owned as follows:

A	0
B	4
C	51.5
D	49
E	41
F	50.5
G	4.

H, who has just started working, decides that he, too, needs a house and approaches E for a 'loan' of 10 days' bread in order to finance the time it will take to build it. E agrees, but tells H that he must have one day of bread in payment in addition to the repayment of the loan of 10 days' bread. H builds his house, and then works 22 12-hour days in order to satisfy his obligation to E. The 'balance sheet' for the economy now looks as follows:

	Bread	Other Assets
A	0	10 (house)
B	4	
C	51.5	
D	49	
E	42	8 (painting)
F	50.5	
G	4	5 (safe)
H	0	10 (house).

I, also new to the scene, decides that she, too, wants a house, but approaches G for a loan of 10 days of bread. G only has four days of his own bread, but notes that there are nearly 200 days of bread in his safe that is being stored for B, C, D, E, and F. G also notes that there is no prospect that all five claimants will remove their bread from storage for at least 40 days, and decides it is safe to make I the loan from these stocks. He, too, asks for one day of bread for his service fee for providing the loan. I builds her house and then works 22 12-hour days to repay her debt of 11 days of bread to G.

The 'balance sheet' for the economy is now as follows:

	Bread	Other Assets
A	0	10 (house)
B	4	
C	51.5	
D	49	
E	42	8 (painting)
F	50.5	
G	5	5 (safe)
H	0	10 (house)
I	0	10 (house).

J now arrives on the scene and begins working. One day while mining his daily bread, he chances onto a lump of a pretty, lustrous, yellow metal, which he instantly becomes attached to and calls Au. He carries it with him everywhere, and one day D spots it and immediately wants to buy it. He offers J two days of bread for the lump, which J accepts because he thinks he knows where he can find more. D signs a note instructing G to give J two days of bread from holdings in G's safe. J then asks G to store his bread, which G agrees to do for a service fee of one-half day of bread.

The 'balance sheet' for the economy is now as follows:

	Bread	Other Assets
A	0	10 (house)
B	4	
C	51.5	
D	47	2 (Au)
E	42	8 (painting)
F	50.5	
G	5.5	5 (safe)
H	0	10 (house)
I	0	10 (house)
J	1.5.	

F now decides that he is getting too old to continue sleeping under the stars and approaches H with the idea of buying H's house. He offers H 11 days of bread, but H asks for 12, which upon reflection F agrees to pay. F prepares a note for G instructing G to give H 12 days of bread from F's stock in G's safe, which H in turn leaves 'on deposit' with G, following an up-front payment to G of one-half day of bread.

The total unconsumed savings of bread remains at 202 as follows:

	Bread	Other Assets
A	0	10 (house)
B	4	
C	51.5	
D	47	2 (Au)
E	42	8 (painting)
F	38.5	12 (house)
G	6	5 (safe)
H	11.5	
I	0	10 (house)
J	1.5.	

Assume, now, that K, L, and M make appearances, each with a strong desire to prospect for Au, but in order to 'finance' their enterprises they must build up stocks of savings (i.e., bread) first. Working 20 12-hour days, they each accumulate stocks of 10 days of bread. They then search for Au for 10 days, at the end of which each has 10 lumps, making 30 new lumps of Au in all. Comparison of the new lumps of Au with the lump possessed by D revealed that D's was twice as heavy. In total, therefore, there now exist 32 'light' lumps (or 16 'heavy' lumps) of Au in the island economy.

The 'balance sheet' for the economy is now:

	Bread	Other Assets
A	0	10 (house)
B	4	
C	51.5	
D	47	2 (Au)
E	42	8 (painting)
F	38.5	12 (house)
G	6	5 (safe)
H	11.5	
I	0	10 (house)
J	1.5	5 (Au)
K	0	5 (Au)
L	0	5 (Au)
M	0	5 (Au).

Next, N comes into town. N can not only mine bread, but also has a talent for making 'widgets'. She is capable of making two in an eight-hour day. She begins by working six 12-hour days, building up a stock of three days of bread. She then builds widgets for two days, making four in all. When K, L, and M see N's widgets, K and L each want to buy one, while M wants to buy two. They each offer N one 'heavy' lump of Au for a widget. N accepts and gives up her four widgets in exchange for four 'heavy' (or eight 'light') lumps of Au.

The 'balance sheet' for the economy at this point is as follows:

	Bread	Other Assets
A	0	10 (house)
B	4	
C	51.5	

D	47	2 (Au)
E	42	8 (painting)
F	38.5	12 (house)
G	6	5 (safe)
H	11.5	
I	0	10 (house)
J	1.5	
K	0	4 (Au)
		1 (widget)
L	0	4 (Au)
		1 (widget)
M	0	3 (Au)
		2 (widgets)
N	1	4 (Au).

It turns out that the widgets are like bread and are used up in consumption. However, they really catch on, and soon other members of the population are pestering N to provide them with widgets, either at a price of one 'heavy' lump of Au or (for those who do not have any Au) for two days' bread. N actually prefers making widgets to mining bread, and is happy to spend her days making widgets so long as she gets at least one day's bread in return (either directly or the equivalent in Au). Those without stocks of bread begin working overtime in order to 'finance' their purchase of widgets.

Eventually, enough Au is mined that all transactions for widgets are conducted through the medium of 'light' lumps of Au. Two 'light' lumps of Au are equivalent to one widget, and each 'light' lump of Au is equivalent to one day's bread.

Finally, a couple, O and P, arrive on the island. Each of them immediately begins working 12-hour days in order to build up a stock of bread that can be used to finance the construction of a house. When their stock of bread reaches 15 days of consumption for the two of them, they quit going to the mine for five days while they build their house. At the end of the five days, they have their house and an unconsumed stock of five days of bread. They return to working in the mine. Both of them, though, have a taste for leisure, and they feel that they would be better off if O, rather than spending eight hours mining bread, could spend that time keeping their house in order. That way they could spend all of their leisure time in play. P figures that he knows how to make a tool (a shovel) that will allow him to obtain a day's bread in four hours rather than eight, so that in eight hours he will be able to mine not only his bread, but O's as well. Making the shovel takes two days. The shovel works, and O is able to quit going to the mine. At this point, we end our tales.

QUESTIONS AND EXERCISES FOR DISCUSSION AND ANALYSIS

1. At what point does saving first occur in the economy? When does fluid capital first come into existence?

2. At what point does exchange first occur? Could exchange occur if everyone on the island had identical tastes?

3. At what point does investment in produced means of production first occur?

4. Should the painting be treated as produced means of production? Why or why not?

5. Should houses be treated as produced means of production? Why or why not?

6. Suppose that, except for B and C, no one else on the island placed a value on the painting (i.e., were willing to trade bread for it). Could the painting still be treated as an 'asset'?

7. At what point does a store of value emerge in the economy? At the end, how many stores of value are in existence? Are widgets a store of value?

8. At what point does a 'bank' begin to emerge? What functions does this 'bank' subsequently perform?

9. What is the 'unit of account' in the economy?

10. What functions as a 'standard of deferred payment'?

11. Is there a 'medium of exchange' in the economy? How about 'media of exchange'?

12. Which emerges first, a 'store of value' or a 'medium of exchange'? Must one always precede the other?

13. Is there an interest rate (or rates) in the economy? When does the payment of interest first occur? What would have to be present in order for a single interest rate to emerge?

14. Suppose that, rather than taking two days to make the shovel, it took four days to do so, but that P's productivity was tripled rather than just doubled. Suppose, also, that O and P decided to borrow the bread needed for 'finance' from F, rather than 'self-financing' through a prior accumulation of bread. How much interest might O and P have been willing to pay F for the loan? How might the amount that was actually paid have been determined?

15. Are there any myros recovery charges in the economy? Should there be? For whom would they be relevant?

16. Are there prices in the economy? If so, at what point do they first emerge?

17. Construct a table that describes the price structure for the economy at the end of the story.

18. How might a general price level be defined for the economy?

19. Construct a final 'balance sheet' for the economy.

20. Construct a table describing the level and changes in the stock of fluid capital.

21. Devise a simple set of National Income Accounts for this economy.

22. Should G's fee for storing bread be treated as income or a transfer payment?

23. When B sells her painting to C, should the bread received in payment be treated as income? What about when C sells the painting to F? Should the 'capital gain' that C receives in the transaction be treated as income? Why or why not? (In thinking about this question, be sure to take care to distinguish between individuals and the economy as a whole.)

24. How should O's 'work at home' be treated in the Accounts?

25. Note that the Au of K, L, and M is 'valued' at one day of bread per lump, rather than two. Why is this? If it were two, rather than one, what 'theory of value' would thereby be implied?

BIBLIOGRAPHY

Arthur, W.B. (1989), "Competing Technologies, Increasing Returns, and Lock-in by Historical Events," *Economic Journal*, Vol. 99, March 1989, pp. 116-31.

Apostal, T.M. (1957), *Mathematical Analysis*, Addison-Wesley Publishing Co.

Barro, R.J. (1973), "Are Government Bonds Net Wealth?," *Journal of Political Economy*, Vol. 82, No. 6, Nov.-Dec. 1973, pp. 1095-1117.

Baumol, W.J. (1953), "The Transactions Demand for Cash: An Inventory Theoretic Approach," *Quarterly Journal of Economics*, Vol. 61, November 1953, pp. 545-56.

Baumol, W.J. (1971), "Optimal Depreciation Policy: Pricing the Products of Durable Assets," *The Bell Journal of Economics and Management Science*, Vol. 2, No. 2, Autumn 1971, pp. 638-56.

v. Böhm-Bawerk, E. (1959), *Positive Theory of Capital*, translated by G.D. Huncke, Libertarian Press.

Boiteux, N. (1960), "Peak-Load Pricing," *Journal of Business*, Vol. 33, No. 2, pp. 157-79.

Buchanan, J.M. (1969), *Cost and Choice*, University of Chicago Press.

Buchanan, J.M. and Thirlby, G.F. (1981), *L.S.E. Essays on Cost*, New York University Press.

Burton, M. and Lombra, R. (2000), *The Financial System & the Economy* (second edition), Southwestern College Publishing.

Cassell, G. (1903), *The Nature and Necessity of Interest*; reprinted by Kelley Millman, 1957.

Clark, J.B. (1899), *The Distribution of Wealth: A Theory of Wages, Interest, and Profits*, Macmillan; reprinted by Augustus M. Kelley, 1965.

Clarke, P. (1988), *The Keynesian Revolution in the Making 1924-1936*, Oxford University Press.

Clower, R.W. (1967), "A Reconsideration of the Microfoundations of Monetary Theory," *Western Economic Journal*, Vol. 6, No. 1, December 1967, pp. 1-8; reprinted in *Money and Markets: Essays by Robert W. Clower*, ed. by D.A. Walker, Cambridge University Press, 1984.

Davidson, P. (1978), *Money and the Real World* (second edition), John Wiley and Sons.

Deaton A. (1975), *Models and Projections of Demand in Post-War Britain*, John Wiley and Sons.

Deaton, A. and Muellbauer, J. (1980), *Economics and Consumer Behavior*, Cambridge University Press.

Emmerson, R.D. (1991), "Theoretical Foundation of Network Costs," in *Marginal Cost Techniques for Telephone Services: Symposium Proceedings*, ed. by W. Pollard, National Regulatory Research Institute, Columbus, OH, January 1991.

Fisher, I. (1911), *The Purchasing Power of Money*, reprinted by Augustus M. Kelley, 1963.

Fisher, I. (1906), *The Nature of Capital and Income*, Macmillan; reprinted by Augustus M. Kelley, 1965.

Fisher, I. (1930), *The Theory of Interest*, reprinted by Augustus M.Kelley, 1961.

Frank, R.H. (1985), *Choosing the Right Pond*, Oxford University Press.

Friedman, M. (1956), "The Quantity Theory of Money -- A Restatement," in *Studies in the Quantity Theory of Money*, ed. by M. Friedman, University of Chicago Press.

Friedman, M. (1957), *A Theory of the Consumption Function*, Princeton University Press.

Friedman, M. (1974), "A Theoretical Framework for Monetary Analysis," in *Milton Friedman's Monetary Framework*, ed. by R.J. Gordon, University of Chicago Press.

Garegnani, P. (1983), "Notes on Consumption, Investment, and Effective Demand," in *Keynes's Economics and the Theory of Value and Distribution*, ed. by J. Eatwell and M. Milgate, Duckworth.

George, H. (1929), *Progress and Poverty*, Vanguard Press.

Georgescu-Roegen, N. (1954), "Choice, Expectations, and Measurability," *Quarterly Journal of Economics*, Vol. 68, No. 4, November 1954, pp. 503-34.

Gurley, J. and Shaw, E.S. (1965), *Money in a Theory of Finance*, The Brookings Institute, Washington, D.C.

Haavelmo, T. (1944), "The Probability Approach in Econometrics," *Econometrica*, Vol. 12 (Supplement), pp. 1-115.

Haberler, G. (1937), *Prosperity and Depression* (fourth edition, 1958), George Allen and Unwin.

Hahn, F. (1975), "Money and General Equilibrium," *Indian Economic Journal*, Vol. 23, Oct.-Dec. 1975, pp. 109-22. (Reprinted in *Money, Growth and Stability* by F. Hahn, MIT Press, 1985.)

Hall, R.E. and Jones, C.I. (1999), "Why Do Some Countries Produce so Much More Output per Worker than Others?," *Quarterly Journal of Economics*, Vol. 114, No. 1, February 1999, pp. 83-116.

Hall, R.J. and Hitch, C.J. (1939), "Price Theory and Business Behavior," *Oxford Economic Papers*, May 1939.

Harcourt, G.C. (1972), *Some Cambridge Controversies in the Theory of Capital*, Cambridge University Press.

Hasse, R. (1993), "German-German Monetary Union: Main Options, Costs, and Repercussions," in *The Economics of German Unification*, ed. by A.G. Ghaussy and W. Schäfer, London and New York, Routledge.

Hawtrey, R.G. (1913), *Good and Bad Trade: An Inquiry into the Causes of Trade Fluctuations*, Longmans and Green; reprinted by Augustus M. Kelley, 1962.

Hawtrey, R.G. (1919), *Currency and Credit* (second edition, 1923), Longmans and Green.

Hawtrey, R.G. (1925), *The Economic Problem*, Longmans and Green.

Hayek, F.A. (1941), *The Pure Theory of Capital*, University of Chicago Press; reprinted 1975.

Hicks, J.R. (1946), *Value and Capital* (second edition), Oxford University Press.

Hirsch, F. (1976), *Social Limits to Growth*, Twentieth Century Fund, Harvard University Press.

Hirshleifer, J. (1970), *Investment, Interest, and Capital*, Prentice Hall.

Hlusek, M. (1999), "Why Expectation Theory Does Not Hold," CERGE-EI, Charles University, Prague, The Czech Republic.

Houthakker, H.S. and Taylor, L.D. (1970), *Consumer Demand in the United States* (second edition), Harvard University Press.

Ironmonger, D.S. (1972), *New Commodities and Consumer Behaviour*, Cambridge University Press.

Jevons, W.S. (1871), *Theory of Political Economy* (fourth edition, 1911; reprinted 1924, 1931), Macmillan.

Keynes, J.M. (1923), *A Tract on Monetary Reform*, Macmillan.

Keynes, J.M. (1930), *A Treatise on Money, Volume 1: The Pure Theory of Money*, Macmillan.

Keynes, J.M. (1936), *The General Theory of Employment, Interest, and Money*, Macmillan.

Keynes, J.M. (1937a), "The General Theory of Unemployment," *Quarterly Journal of Economics*, February 1937.

Keynes, J.M. (1937b), "Alternative Theories of the Rate of Interest," *Economic Journal*, June 1937, pp. 241-52.

Keynes, J.M. (1937c), "'Ex Ante' Theory of the Rate of Interest," *Economic Journal*, December 1937, pp. 663-69.

Keynes, J.M. and Henderson, H.D. (1929), "Can Lloyd George Do It?: An Examination of the Liberal Pledge," reprinted in *The Collected Writings of John Maynard Keynes*, ed. by D.E. Moggridge, 1973, Vol. XIX, St. Martin's Press, pp. 808-16.

Kiyotaki, N. and Wright, R. (1989), "On Money as a Medium of Exchange," *Journal of Political Economy*, Vol. 97, August 1989, pp. 927-54.

Kiyotaki, N. and Wright, R. (1991), "A Contribution to the Pure Theory of Money," *Journal of Economic Theory*, Vol. 53, pp. 215-35.

Kiyotaki, N. and Wright, R. (1993), "A Search-Theoretic Approach to Monetary Economics," *American Economic Review*, Vol. 83, March 1993, pp. 63-77.

Lewin, R. (1992), *Complexity: Life at the Edge of Chaos*, New York, Macmillan Publishing Co.

Lucas, R.E. (1985), "On the Mechanics of Economic Development," *Journal of Monetary Economics*, Vol. 22, No. 1, pp. 3-42.

McKinnon, R.I. (1991), *The Order of Economic Liberalization: Financial Costs in the Transition to a Market Economy*, Johns Hopkins University Press.

Meltzer, A.H. (1988), *Keynes's Monetary Theory: A Different Interpretation*, Cambridge University Press.

Metzler, L.A. (1951), "Wealth, Saving, and the Rate of Interest," *Journal of Political Economy*, Vol. 59, April 1951, pp. 93-116.

Minsky, H.P. (1975), *John Maynard Keynes*, Columbia University Press.

Mirowski, P. (1989), *More Heat than Light: Economics as Social Physics, Physics as Nature's Economics*, Cambridge University Press.

v. Mises, L. (1934), *The Theory of Money and Credit*, translated from the German by H.E. Batson, Jonathan Cape Ltd., London; Yale University Press, 1953; Liberty Classics, 1981.

Modigliani, F. (1961), "Long-Run Implications of Alternative Fiscal Policies and the Burden of the National Debt," *Economic Journal*, Vol. 71, December 1961, pp. 730-55.

Ohlin, B. (1937), "Some Notes on the Stockholm Theory of Saving and Investment," *Economic Journal*, Vol. 37, March and June 1937, pp. 53-69, 221-40.

Patinkin, D. (1948), "Price Flexibility and Full Employment," *American Economic Review*, Vol. 38, No. 3, September 1948, pp. 543-64.

Patinkin, D. (1965), *Money, Interest, and Prices*, Row Peterson.

Phlips. L. (1983), *Applied Consumption Analysis, Revised and Enlarged Edition*, North Holland Publishing Co.

Pigou, A.C. (1941), *Employment and Equilibrium*, Macmillan.

Pigou, A.C. (1943), "The Classical Stationary State," *Economic Journal*, Vol. 53, December 1943, pp. 342-52.

Pigou, A.C. (1947), "Economic Progress in a Stable Environment," *Economic Journal*, Vol. 57, August 1947, pp. 180-88.

Pollak, R.A. (1978), "Endogenous Tastes in Demand and Welfare Analysis," *American Economic Review, Papers and Proceedings*, Vol. 68, No. 2, May 1978, pp. 374 -379.

Pollak, R.A. and Wales, T.J. (1992), *Demand System Specification & Estimation*, Oxford University Press.

Reclam, M. (1984), *J.A. Schumpeter's 'Credit' Theory of Money*, University Microfilms, Ann Arbor, MI (Ph.D. dissertation, Department of Economics, University of California, Riverside, 1984).

Robertson, D.H. (1926), *Banking Policy and the Price Level: An Essay in the Theory of the Trade Cycle*, P.S. King and Co.; reprinted by Augustus M. Kelley, 1949.

Robertson, D.H. (1937), "Alternative Theories of the Rate of Interest," *Economic Journal*, Vol. 47, September 1937, pp. 428-36.

Robinson, J. (1953), "The Production Function and the Theory of Capital," *Review of Economic Studies*, Vol. XXI, No. 2, pp. 81-106.

Robinson, J. (1956), *The Accumulation of Capital*, Macmillan.

Robinson, J. (1975), "The Unimportance of Reswitching," *Quarterly Journal of Economics*, Vol. 89, February 1975, pp. 32-39.

Romer, P.M. (1986), "Increasing Returns and Long-Run Growth," *Journal of Political Economy*, Vol. 94, No. 5, October 1986, pp. 1002-37.

Samuelson, P.A. (1962), "Parable and Realism in Capital Theory: The Surrogate Production Function," *Review of Economic Studies*, Vol. XXIX, June 1962, pp. 193-206.

Samuelson, P.A. (1966), "A Summing Up," *Quarterly Journal of Economics*, Vol. 80, November 1980, pp. 568-83.

Samuelson, P.A. (1975), "Steady-State and Transient Relations: A Reply on Reswitching." *Quarterly Journal of Economics*, Vol. 89, February 1975, pp. 40-47.

Samuelson, P.A. (1976), "Interest Rate Determinations and Oversimplifying Parables: A Summing Up," in *Essays in Modern Capital Theory*, ed. by M. Brown, K. Sato, and P. Zarembka, North Holland Publishing Co.

Schumpeter, J.A. (1934), *The Theory of Economic Development*, Harvard University Press.

Schumpeter, J.A. (1954), "The Crisis of the Tax State," translated by W.F. Stolper and R.A. Musgrave, *International Economic Papers*, Vol. 4, ed. by A. Peacock *et al.*, Macmillan, pp. 5-38; reprinted in *Joseph A. Schumpeter, The Economics and Sociology of Capitalism*, ed. by R. Swedberg, Princeton University Press, 1991.

Schumpeter, J.A. (1970), *Das Wesen des Geldes*, Göttingen, Vandenhoeck & Ruprecht, 1970.

Schwartz, A.J. (1987),"Banking School, Currency School, Free Banking School," in *The New Palgrave: A Dictionary of Economics*, ed. by J. Eatwell, M. Milgate and P. Newman, Macmillan.

Scitovsky, T. (1976), *The Joyless Economy*, Oxford University Press.

Shackle, G.L.S. (1967), *The High Years of Theory*, Cambridge University Press.

Sinn, G.S. and Sinn, H.W. (1992), *Jumpstart*, translated by J. Irving-Lessmann, Cambridge, MA, MIT Press.

Solow, R.M. (1956), "A Contribution to the Theory of Economic Growth," *Quarterly Journal of Economics*, Vol.70, No. 1, February 1956, pp. 65-94.

Solow, R.M. (1967), "The Interest-Rate and Transition Between Techniques," in *Socialism, Capitalism and Economic Growth*, Essays presented to Maurice Dobb, ed. by C.H. Feinstein, Cambridge University Press.

Solow, R.M. (1965), *Capital Theory and the Rate of Return*, Rand McNally & Co.

Spanos, A. (1989), "On Rereading Haavelmo: A Retrospective View of Econometric Modeling," *Journal of Econometric Theory*, Vol. 5, No. 3, December 1989, pp. 405-29.

Steiner, P.O. (1957), "Peak Loads and Efficient Pricing," *Quarterly Journal of Economics*, November 1957.

Stigler, G.J. and Becker, G.S. (1978), "De Gustibus Non Est Disputandum," *American Economic Review*, Vol. 67, No. 2, March 1977, pp. 76-90.

Swedberg, R. (1991), ed., *Joseph A. Schumpeter: The Economics and Sociology of Capitalism*, Princeton University Press.

Taylor, L.D. (1987), "Opponent Processes and the Dynamics of Consumption," in *Economic Psychology: Intersections in Theory and Application*, ed. by A.J. MacFadyen and H.W. MacFadyen, North Holland Publishing Co.

Taylor, L.D. (1988), "A Model of Consumption Based on Psychological Opponent Processes," in *Psychological Foundations of Economic Behavior*, ed. by Paul Albanese, Praeger.

Taylor, L.D. (1991), "Calculating Short-Run Avoidable Cost as a Floor to Price in the Telephone Industry," in *Marginal Cost Techniques for Telephone Services: Symposium Proceedings*, ed. by W. Pollard, National Regulatory Research Institute, Columbus, OH, January 1991.

Taylor, L.D. (1992), "Brain Structure and Consumption Dynamics," in *Aggregation, Consumption and Trade: Essays in Honor of Hendrik S. Houthakker*, ed. by Louis Phlips and Lester D. Taylor, Kluwer Academic Publishers.

Taylor, L.D. (1994), *Telecommunications Demand in Theory and Practice*, Kluwer Academic Publishers.

Taylor, L.D., (1998), "On Depletion of an Exhausting Natural Resource," *Non-Renewable Resources*, Vol. 7, No. 3, September 1998, pp. 225-32.

Thurow, L.C. (1999), *Building Wealth: The New Rules for Individuals, Companies, and Nations in a Knowledge-Based Economy*, Harper-Collins.

Tobin, J. (1956), "The Interest Elasticity of Transactions Demand for Cash," *Review of Economics and Statistics*, Vol. 38, No. 3, August 1956, pp. 241-47.

Tobin, J. (1958), "Liquidity Preference as Behavior Toward Risk," *Review of Economic Studies*, Vol. 25, No. 67, February 1958, pp. 65-86.

Tobin, J. (1969), "A General Equilibrium Approach to Monetary Theory," *Journal of Money, Credit, and Banking*, Vol. 1, No. 1, February 1969, pp. 15-29.

Tobin, J. (1980), *Asset Accumulation and Economic Activity*, University of Chicago Press.

Tobin, J. and Buiter, W. (1980), "Fiscal and Monetary Policies, Capital Formation, and Economic Activity," in *The Government and Capital Formation*, ed. by G.M. von Furstenberg, Vol. II in the Series on Capital Investment sponsored by the American Council of Life Insurance, Ballinger Publishing Co.

Turvey, R. (1968), *Optimal Investment and Pricing in Electricity Supply*, MIT Press.

Turvey, R. (1969), "Marginal Cost," *Economic Journal*, Vol. 79, June 1969, pp. 282-99.

v. Weizsacker, C.C. (1971), "Notes on Endogenous Change of Tastes," *Journal of Economic Theory*, Vol. 3, December 1971.

Wicksell, K. (1936), *Interest and Prices* (translated by R.F. Kahn), reprinted by Augustus M. Kelley, 1965.

Woodruff, D.M. (1999), *Money Unmade: Barter and the Fate of Russian Capitalism*, Cornell University Press.

INDEX